THE VOGUE/BUTTERICK

Step-by-Step Guide to Sewing Techniques

BY THE EDITORS OF VOGUE AND BUTTERICK PATTERNS

THE VOGUE/BUTTERICK

Step-by-Step Guide to Sewing Techniques

Prentice Hall Press

NEW YORK · LONDON · TORONTO · SYDNEY · TOKYO

Prentice Hall Press
Gulf + Western Building
One Gulf + Western Plaza
New York, New York 10023

Copyright © 1989 by Butterick® Company, Inc.

All rights reserved including the right of reproduction in whole or in part in any form.

PRENTICE HALL PRESS and colophon are registered trademarks of Simon & Schuster Inc.

Library of Congress Card Catalog Number: 89-60522

ISBN 0-13-944125-5

Designed by Karen Salsgiver Design
Manufactured in the United States of America

10 9 8 7 6 5 4 3 2 1

First Edition

EDITOR-IN-CHIEF
Janet DuBane

CONTRIBUTING EDITOR
Jane Glanzer

MANAGING EDITOR
Carol Sharma

COPY EDITOR
Janet L. Offerjost

TECHNICAL ADVISORS
Barbara Geibar
Crystal McDougald
Helen Vanterpool

ILLUSTRATIONS
Cynthia Ngai

EDITORIAL STAFF
Celie Fitzgerald
Beverly Matthews
Norma Rosa
Renee Ullman

ART STAFF
Janet Lombardo
Carol Young-Hall

PROJECT DIRECTOR
Martha K. Moran

ART DIRECTOR
Karen Salsgiver

SENIOR DESIGNER
Susan Carabetta

PRESIDENT, BUTTERICK COMPANY, INC.
John Lehmann

EXECUTIVE EDITOR
Patricia Perry

DIRECTOR, BUTTERICK PUBLICATIONS
Art Joinnides

How to Use This Book

The Vogue/Butterick Step-By-Step Guide To Sewing Techniques provides quick access to the most frequently used and popular sewing procedures found in Vogue and Butterick Patterns. We have selected more than 500 of the most essential dressmaking methods and techniques out of more than 2,000 standard dressmaking and tailoring procedures used in Vogue and Butterick Patterns.

The Table of Contents lists 47 broad sewing procedure categories, or "sections" alphabetically from Appliqué to Zippers and the essential techniques therein. Under the "Pockets" listing, for example, you'll find Mock Flap, Mock Welt, Patch, Side Seam, Side Slant, and Welt pockets. Since we give you several different variations for most procedures, the index provides a much more detailed listing. If you look under "Patch Pockets", you'll find these variations: lined, self-faced, self-faced *and* topstitched, self-lined, slanted edge and self-flap.

Each technique is presented in a detailed, illustrated step-by-step format, from the beginning of the procedure to its completion. When fundamental preparatory steps are common to several techniques, these steps have been organized into an introductory "Basics" section.

The step-by-step illustrations have the right side of the fabric shaded for easy identification. In some cases, part of an illustration is enlarged and circled so that fine details can be seen clearly. When garment sections are machine-stitched, the stitching is shown in the direction it would be stitched on your machine; thread ends are always shown at the end of the stitching, not at the beginning.

Vogue/Butterick Sewing Vocabulary Terms recur throughout this book. These terms refer to very basic sewing procedures every sewer needs to know to follow and execute sewing instructions. Each one of these terms is defined and illustrated in the book, and the Quick-Reference Sewing Vocabulary List, in the back of this book, provides quick access to them.

Vocabulary terms always appear in all caps, and are not defined each time they appear in an instruction. For instance, the Flat Collar instructions say: "INTERFACE wrong side of one collar section". While the accompanying illustration may show this procedure in one step, if you don't know how to interface, you'll find the complete step-by-step instructions by looking for INTERFACE in the Quick-Reference Vocabulary List or the index. Every set of instructions focuses on a specific garment area or technique. To avoid unnecessary repetition, clear referrals are made to other sections of the book for recurring preliminary or ending steps. For instance, since there are several options for finishing a sleeve lower edge, you would be referred to "Casings", "Cuffs" or "Hems". In some cases, such as the finishing variations of Edgestitching, Topstitching or Edgestitching *and* Topstitching, references may direct you to another technique within the same section. For example, there are two separate techniques for making a Flat Collar, but the edge finishes are the same in each technique. The second Flat Collar technique refers you to the first Flat Collar for the illustrated edge finish.

The Vogue/Butterick Step-By-Step Guide To Sewing Techniques will be useful any time you sew: when using patterns, altering or repairing garments, or even creating your own designs.

Table of Contents

Table of Contents

Table of Contents

Table of Contents

THE VOGUE/BUTTERICK

Step-by-Step Guide to Sewing Techniques

Hand-sewn Appliqués

TRANSFERRING DESIGNS

Dressmaker's Carbon Paper

Using dressmaker's carbon paper and a pencil or tracing wheel, trace design onto right side of appliqué fabric. Design can be reused.

If using white or very light-colored threads and/or fabrics, transfer design using *white* dressmaker's carbon paper.

Heat Transfers

Heat transfers are included in some patterns. Use an iron to transfer design lines from heat transfer directly to appliqué fabric. Usually, heat transfers can be used only once. Follow transfer instructions that come with the pattern.

CUTTING AND POSITIONING APPLIQUÉS

1
Cut appliqué allowing ¼" (6mm) seam allowance.

2
If appliqué will be padded with fleece or batting, pin appliqué fabric right side up over padding. Cut appliqué and padding together along appliqué design lines.

3
Trim padding ¼" (6mm) smaller than appliqué fabric.

4
Baste to appliqué.

Whenever possible, work with a flat garment section. Attach appliqué and then complete garment.

Hand-sewn Appliqués

SEWING APPLIQUÉS

1

Straight-stitch ¼″ (6mm) from outside edges.
Turn and press raw edges to wrong side along
stitching, clipping as necessary. Baste to
garment; SLIPSTITCH invisibly.

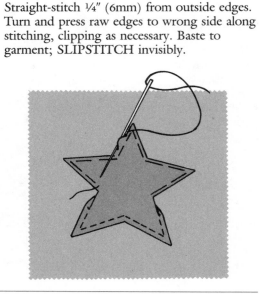

3

For manufactured appliqués, pin or baste
appliqué to garment section. Hand-sew
securely in place.

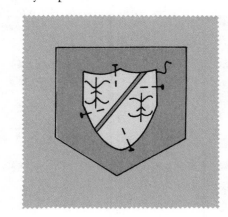

2

If fabric does not ravel (e.g., felt), eliminate
stitching and cut directly on design outline.
Baste, then sew with BLANKET STITCHES.

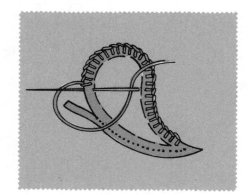

Machine-stitched Appliqués

TRANSFERRING DESIGNS

Dressmaker's Carbon Paper

Using dressmaker's carbon paper and a pencil or tracing wheel, trace design onto right side of appliqué fabric. Transfer can be reused.

If using white or very light-colored threads and/or fabrics, transfer design using *white* dressmaker's carbon paper.

Paper-backed Fusible Web

To make fusible appliqués, use products with fusible web on a see-through release paper (Stacy TRANSFUSE™ II or Pellon® WONDER-UNDER™ Transfer Web).

Trace design directly onto paper backing (smooth side). Trace asymmetrical shapes (i.e. different right and left sides, such as letters) *in reverse*.

Heat Transfers

Heat transfers are included in some patterns. Use an iron to transfer design lines from heat transfer directly to appliqué fabric. Usually, heat transfers can be used only once. Follow transfer instructions that come with the pattern.

Appliqués

3

Machine-stitched Appliqués

MAKING FUSIBLE APPLIQUÉS: REGULAR FABRIC

Bonding Fusible Web to Fabric

Place fusible web over wrong side of appliqué fabric. Place Norlon® or Teflon® release sheet (available at fabric or craft stores) over web. Fuse, following manufacturer's instructions, OR

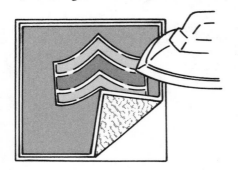

Place rough side of paper-backed fusible web against wrong side of appliqué fabric. Fuse, following manufacturer's instructions. Peel paper backing away.

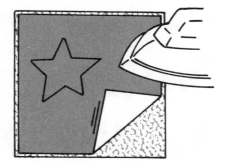

Cutting Fusible Web With Fabric

Place wrong side of appliqué fabric over fusible web. Pin in place from right side as shown. Cut appliqué and web together.

Machine-stitched Appliqués

CUTTING APPLIQUÉS

1
Cut appliqué along design lines.

2
If appliqué will be padded with fleece or batting, pin appliqué fabric right side up over padding. Cut appliqué and padding together along appliqué design lines.

3
Trim padding or fusible web slightly smaller than appliqué fabric.

4
Baste to appliqué.

POSITIONING APPLIQUÉS

Whenever possible, work with a flat garment section. Attach appliqué and then complete garment.

1
With fusible web between appliqué and garment, pin appliqué in position on garment.

Fuse appliqué in position, following manufacturer's instructions.

2
If not using fusible web, pin or baste appliqué securely to fabric.

Machine-stitched Appliqués

Note: If appliqué pieces overlap, do not stitch the underneath portion of the appliqué(s) in areas that will be covered by other appliqués.

STITCHING APPLIQUÉS: STRAIGHT STITCHING

1

If using a straight stitch, fuse appliqué before stitching to prevent ravelling (see Making Fusible Appliqués: Regular Fabric).

2

Set machine for a medium length, straight stitch. Stitch close to all edges of appliqué.

Machine Stitched Appliqués

STITCHING APPLIQUÉS: ZIGZAG SATIN STITCHING

1

Set machine for a narrow-to-medium width zigzag stitch, and a short stitch length to produce a smooth, even satin stitch. The smaller and more curved the appliqué shapes, the narrower the zigzag stitch should be. Test settings on fabric scraps to get the desired stitch.

2

To help control stitching, hold fabric taut with left hand behind needle. Use right hand to guide appliqué under needle. Position appliqué to left of needle. When needle swings to the right, it should enter background fabric just outside edge of appliqué shape; stitching should cover edges almost completely.

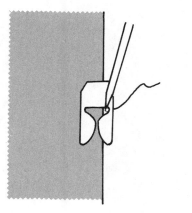

3

Holding needle thread at back of needle, take a few stitches. Keeping needle in position just described, stitch slowly around appliqué. Overlap stitching at beginning, very slightly. Change stitch width to straight stitch and take a few stitches to secure thread ends.

Corners

1

To stitch an *outside* corner, stitch to corner of appliqué, stopping with needle in fabric to the right of and aligned with appliqué at (A). Pivot fabric; continue stitching.

2

To stitch an *inside* corner, stitch past corner onto appliqué for a distance equal to width of zigzag stitch; stop with needle to left and in fabric at (B). Pivot fabric; continue stitching.

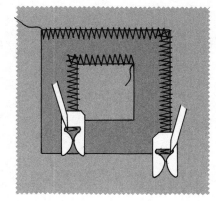

Machine-stitched Appliqués

Stitching Appliqués: Zigzag Satin Stitching, Continued

Curves	Points

Curves

1

On an *outside* curve, as needle swings right, pivot fabric slightly to keep needle from going too far off to the right (A).

2

On an *inside* curve, pivot as needed when needle swings left, to keep needle from going too far away from the curve (B).

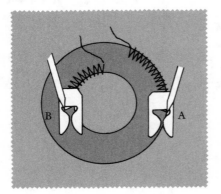

Points

1

Stitch until needle is in left-hand position and just off left-hand edge near point at (A). Pivot fabric slightly to center point under presser foot.

2

Begin decreasing stitch width; continue stitching with needle entering background fabric on each side of point. Stitch slowly, decreasing stitch width until almost zero at point. Pivot fabric; stitch back over first stitching, increasing stitch width gradually until it is the original width. Continue stitching along next edge.

Front Bands

KNIT BAND: SELF FABRIC

1

Hem garment before applying band.

2

Stitch band sections together at center back.

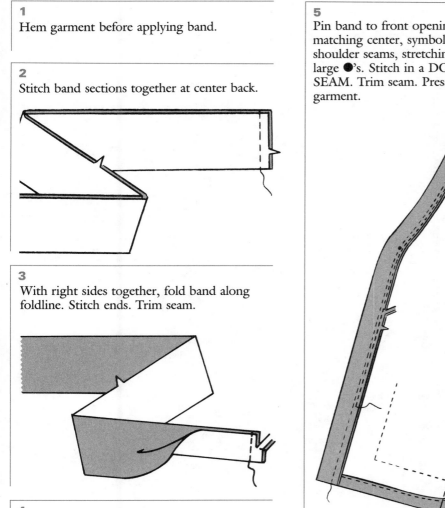

3

With right sides together, fold band along foldline. Stitch ends. Trim seam.

4

Turn. Press. Pin or HAND-BASTE raw edges together.

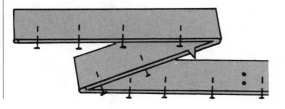

5

Pin band to front opening and neck edges, matching center, symbols and small ••'s to shoulder seams, stretching band to fit between large ●'s. Stitch in a DOUBLE-STITCHED SEAM. Trim seam. Press seam toward garment.

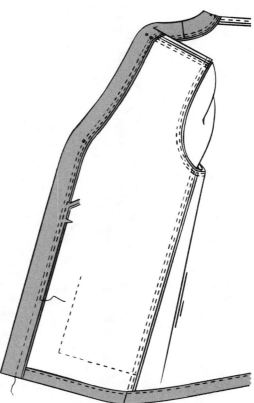

Front Bands

MOCK FRONT BAND

1

Turn right front self facing to inside along foldline. Press. Baste across upper, lower and long raw edges.

2

TOPSTITCH front opening edge.

3

To make tuck, turn band to inside, bringing lines of small •'s together; stitch, encasing raw edge.

4

Press band away from garment and tuck toward side. Baste across upper and lower edges.

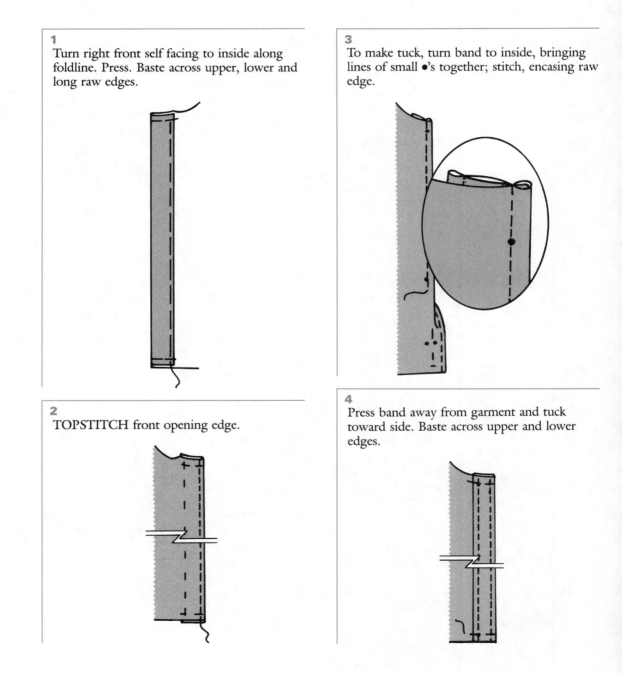

Front Bands

ONE-PIECE BAND: MADE FROM THE RIGHT SIDE

1

INTERFACE wrong side of front band.

2

Turn in ⅜″ (10mm) on long edges of front band; press.

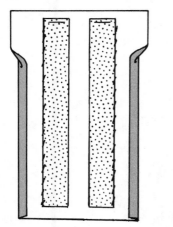

3

With right sides together, pin front band to front, matching stitching lines. Stitch along stitching lines, pivoting at small ●'s.

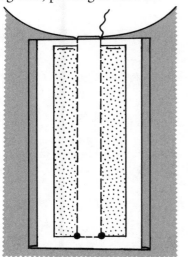

4

Slash between stitching, clipping diagonally to small ●'s. Trim long seam allowances.

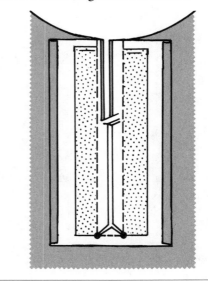

5

Press seams toward front band.

6

For a finished neck edge, with right sides together, fold upper edges of front band along foldlines. Stitch, pivoting across seam allowance at large ●'s. Clip diagonally to large ●'s.

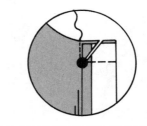

7

TRIM seam.

11

Front Bands

One-piece Band: Made from the Right Side, Continued

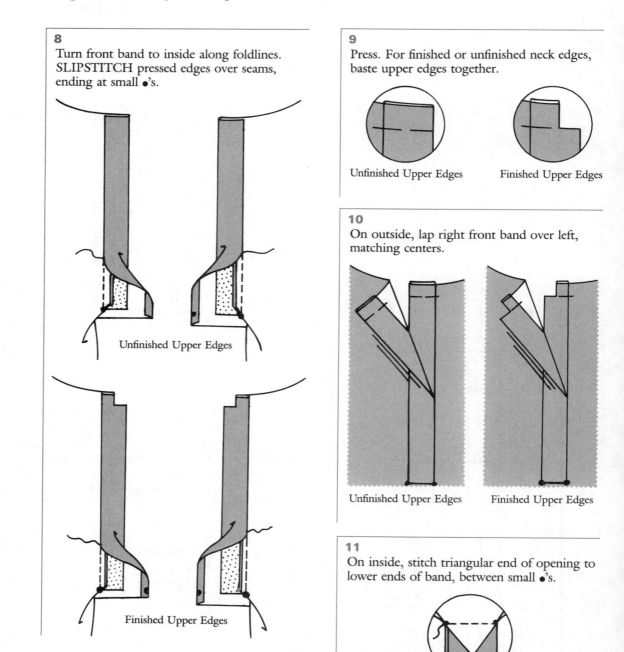

8

Turn front band to inside along foldlines.
SLIPSTITCH pressed edges over seams,
ending at small •'s.

Unfinished Upper Edges

Finished Upper Edges

9

Press. For finished or unfinished neck edges,
baste upper edges together.

Unfinished Upper Edges   Finished Upper Edges

10

On outside, lap right front band over left,
matching centers.

Unfinished Upper Edges   Finished Upper Edges

11

On inside, stitch triangular end of opening to
lower ends of band, between small •'s.

Both

Front Bands

ONE-PIECE BAND: MADE FROM THE WRONG SIDE

1

Cut front band interfacing along cut line.

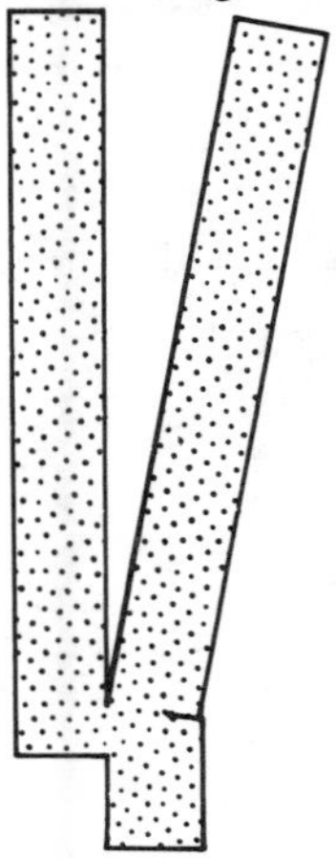

2

INTERFACE wrong side of front band between seamlines and foldlines; baste across upper edge.

3

Turn in ⅜″ (10mm) on sides and lower edge of front band, diagonally folding and trimming corner. Press.

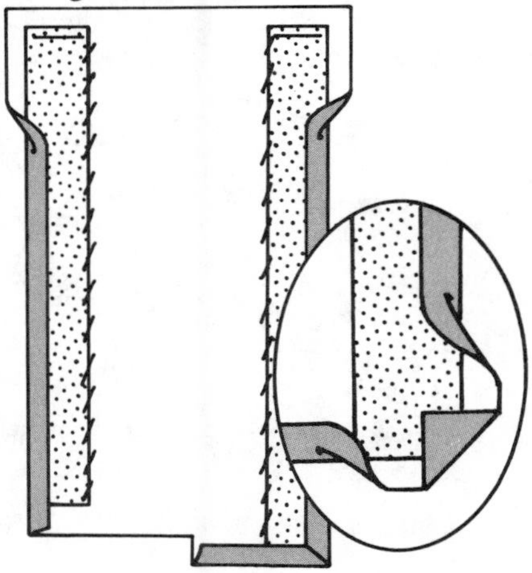

4

Pin right side of front band to wrong side of front, matching stitching lines. Stitch along stitching lines, pivoting at small ●'s.

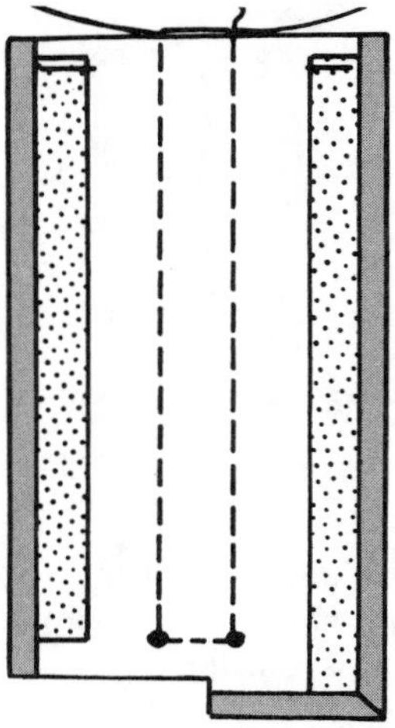

5

Slash between stitching, clipping diagonally to small ●'s. Trim long seam allowances.

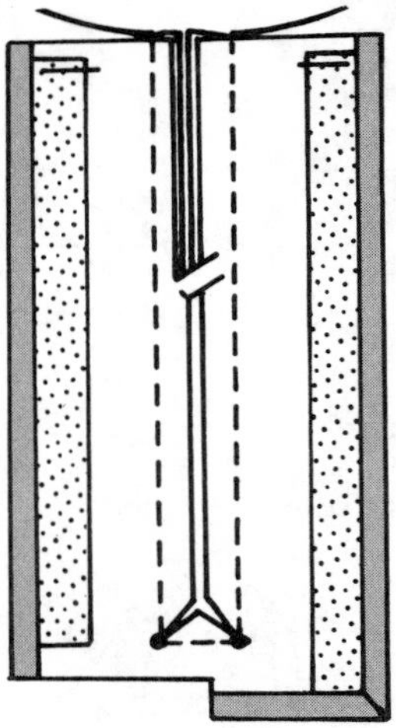

6

Press seam toward front band.

13

Front Bands

One-piece Band: Made from the Wrong Side, Continued

7

For finished neck edge, with right sides together, fold upper edges of front band along foldlines. Stitch, pivoting across seam allowances at large ●'s. Clip diagonally to large ●'s.

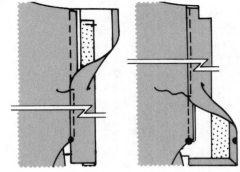

8

TRIM seam. Turn.

9

Fold shorter side of front band along foldline, placing pressed edge over seam. Stitch close to edge, ending at small ●'s.

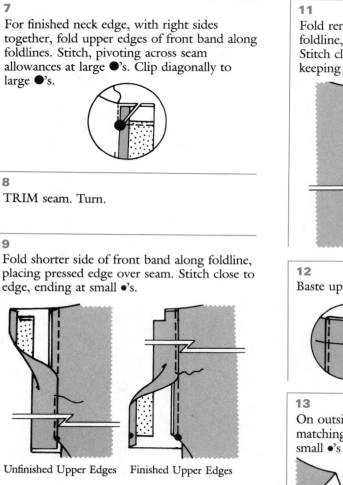

Unfinished Upper Edges   Finished Upper Edges

10

Baste lower edges together.

11

Fold remaining side of front band along foldline, placing pressed edge over seam. Stitch close to edge, ending at small ●, keeping shorter side of front band free.

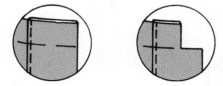

12

Baste upper edges together.

13

On outside, lap right front band over left, matching centers. Stitch close to edges below small ●'s and along stitching line(s).

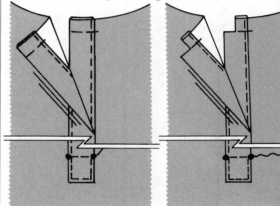

14

Front Bands

TWO-PIECE BAND: WITH FINISHED LOWER EDGES

1

Hem lower edge of garment. Baste front edges together.

Both

2

INTERFACE wrong side of front band.

3

Turn in seam allowance on long unnotched edge of front band. Press. Trim pressed seam allowance to ⅜ (10mm).

4

Pin front band to garment, placing large ● at hemline. Stitch.

5

Trim seam. Press seam toward front band.

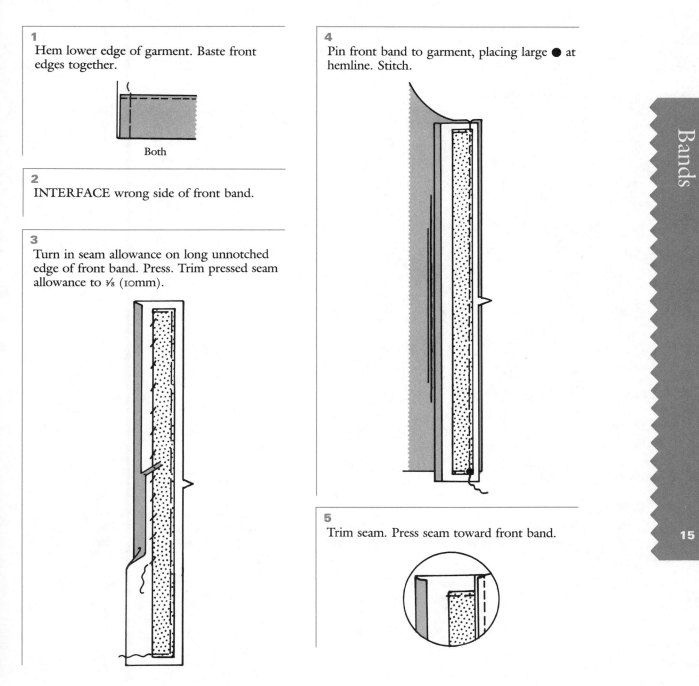

15

Front Bands

Two-piece Band: With Finished Lower Edges, Continued

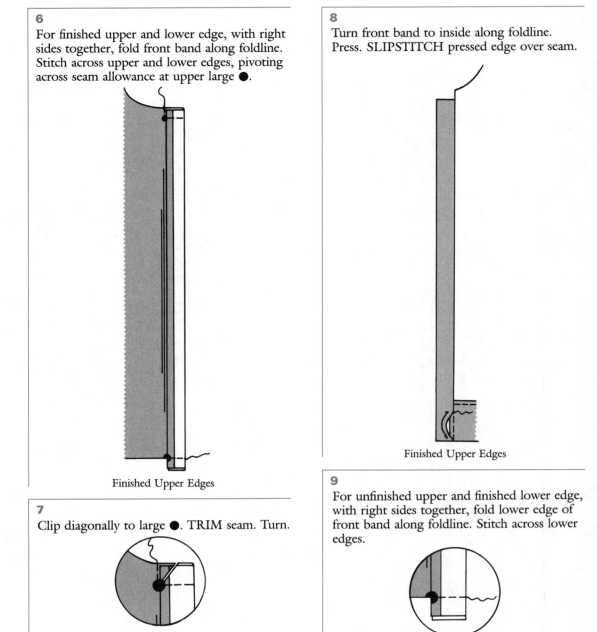

6

For finished upper and lower edge, with right sides together, fold front band along foldline. Stitch across upper and lower edges, pivoting across seam allowance at upper large ●.

Finished Upper Edges

7

Clip diagonally to large ●. TRIM seam. Turn.

Finished Upper Edges

8

Turn front band to inside along foldline. Press. SLIPSTITCH pressed edge over seam.

Finished Upper Edges

9

For unfinished upper and finished lower edge, with right sides together, fold lower edge of front band along foldline. Stitch across lower edges.

Unfinished Upper Edges

Front Bands

Two-piece Band: With Finished Lower Edges, Continued

10
TRIM seam.

11
Turn front band to inside along foldline.
Press. SLIPSTITCH pressed edge over seam.
Baste across upper edges.

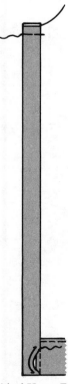

Unfinished Upper Edges

Front Bands

TWO-PIECE BAND: WITH UNFINISHED LOWER EDGES

1

INTERFACE wrong side of front band.

2

Turn in seam allowance on long unnotched edge of front band. Press. Trim pressed seam allowance to ⅜" (10mm).

3

Pin front band to garment, matching symbols. Stitch.

4

Trim seam. Press seam toward front band.

5

For finished upper edges, with right sides together, fold upper edge of front band along foldline. Stitch, pivoting across seam allowance at large ●. Clip diagonally to large ●.

Finished Upper Edges

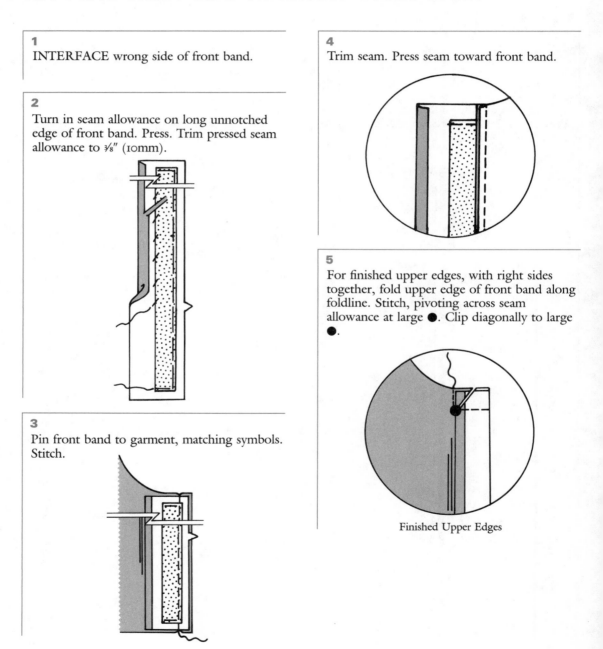

Front Bands

Two-piece Band: with Unfinished Lower Edges, Continued

6

TRIM seam. Turn.

7

Turn front band to inside along foldline.
Press. SLIPSTITCH pressed edge over seam.

8

For unfinished upper edges, baste across
upper edges.

Unfinished Upper Edges

9

Baste across raw lower edges.

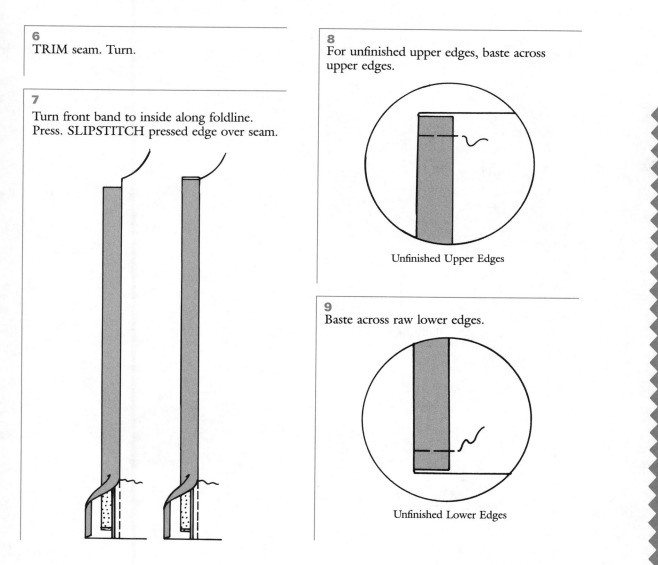

Unfinished Lower Edges

Bands

19

Neck Band

RIB KNIT BAND

1

For woven fabrics, STAYSTITCH bodice neck edge.

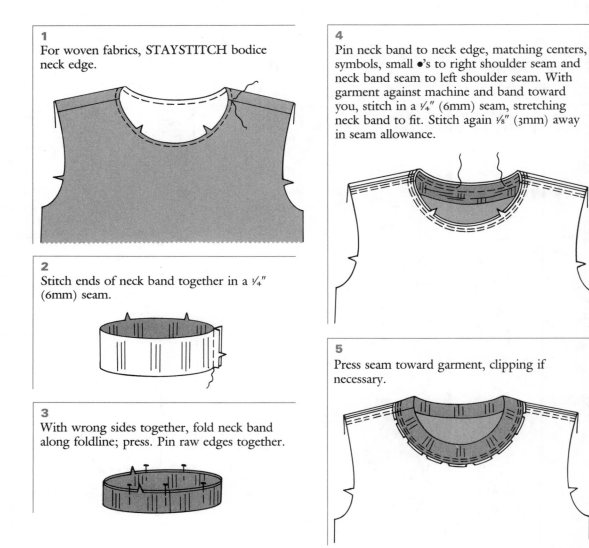

2

Stitch ends of neck band together in a ¼" (6mm) seam.

3

With wrong sides together, fold neck band along foldline; press. Pin raw edges together.

4

Pin neck band to neck edge, matching centers, symbols, small ●'s to right shoulder seam and neck band seam to left shoulder seam. With garment against machine and band toward you, stitch in a ¼" (6mm) seam, stretching neck band to fit. Stitch again ⅛" (3mm) away in seam allowance.

5

Press seam toward garment, clipping if necessary.

Neck Bands

1

STAYSTITCH neck edge of garment.

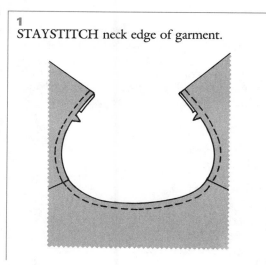

2

INTERFACE wrong side of one set of front and back neck band sections.

Note: Remaining section(s) will be used as facing(s).

3

Stitch interfaced front neck band(s) to interfaced back neck band(s) sections at shoulders. On wrong side, STAY lower edge of neck band with seam binding.

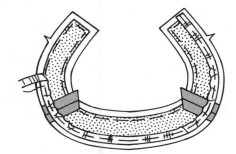

4

Stitch front neck band facing(s) to back neck band facing(s) at shoulders. Turn in seam allowance on notched edge of neck band facing. Press, easing in fullness. Trim pressed seam allowance to ⅜″ (10mm).

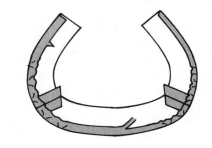

5

Pin neck band facing to neck band. Stitch ends and neck edge.

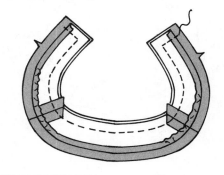

6

Trim seam, clipping if necessary.

Neck Bands

Round band: With Finished Opening Edges, Continued

7

UNDERSTITCH facing.

Note: If edgestitching or topstitching neck band, understitching is not necessary.

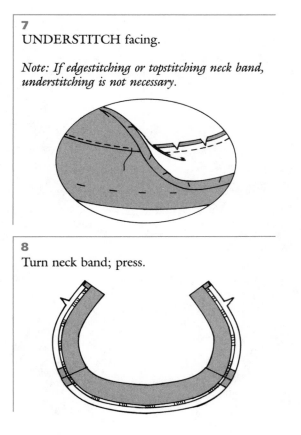

8

Turn neck band; press.

9

Pin neck band to neck edge of garment, matching centers and symbols. Clip garment where necessary; baste. Stitch, keeping pressed edge free. Trim seam, being careful not to cut seam binding. Press seam toward neck band. SLIPSTITCH pressed edge over seam.

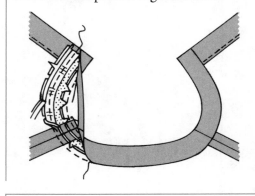

10

Leave neck band plain or use one of the following methods to finished neck band: EDGESTITCHING or TOPSTITCHING (see Neck Bands, Round Band: Without Opening).

Neck Bands

ROUND BAND: WITHOUT OPENING

1
STAYSTITCH upper edge of garment.

2
INTERFACE wrong side of one front neck band section and one back neck band section.

Note: Remaining section(s) will be used as facing(s). Stitch interfaced front neck band to interfaced back neck band at shoulders. On wrong side, STAY lower edge of neck band with seam binding.

3
Stitch front neck band facing to back neck band facing at shoulders.

4
Turn in seam allowance on notched edge of neck band facing. Press, easing in fullness. Trim pressed seam allowance to ⅜″ (10mm).

5
Pin neck band facing to neck band. Stitch neck edge.

6
Trim seam, clipping if necessary.

7
UNDERSTITCH facing.

Note: If edgestitching or topstitching neck band, understitching is not necessary.

8
Turn neck band; press.

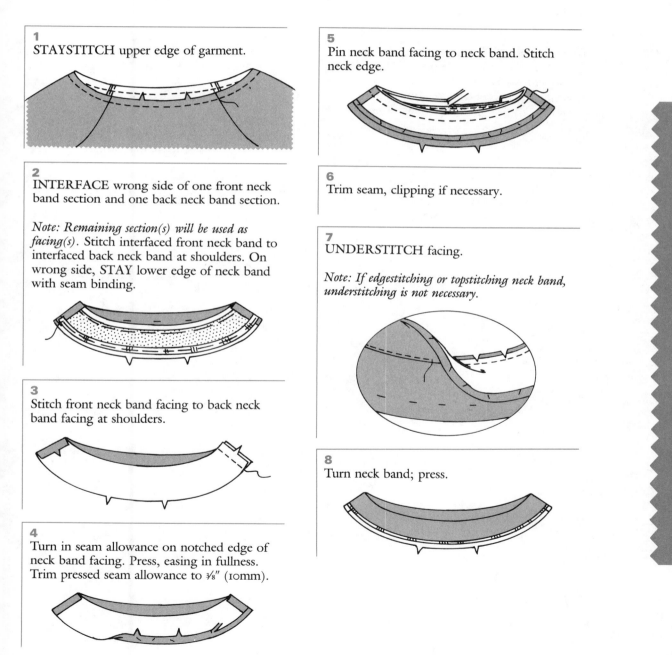

Neck Bands

Round Band: Without Opening, Continued

9

Pin interfaced neck band to upper edge of garment, matching centers and symbols. Clip garment where necessary; baste. Stitch, keeping pressed edge free. Trim seam, being careful not to cut seam binding. Press seam toward neck band.

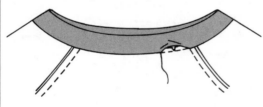

10

SLIPSTITCH pressed edge over seam.

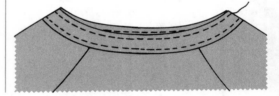

11

Leave neck band plain or use one of the following methods to finish neck band:

EDGESTITCH,

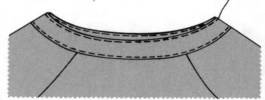

TOPSTITCH,

Neck Bands

SQUARE BAND: WITH FINISHED OPENING EDGES

1

REINFORCE inner corners of neck edge, pivoting at small •'s.

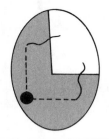

2

INTERFACE wrong side of one set of front and back neck band sections.

Note: Remaining section(s) will be used as facing(s).

3

Stitch interfaced front neck band to back neck band at shoulders.

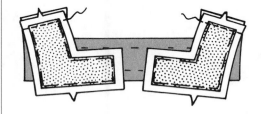

4

Stitch front neck band facing(s) to back neck band facing(s) at shoulders. Turn in seam allowances on outer edges of neck band facing, diagonally folding and trimming corners. Press. Trim pressed seam allowances to ⅜" (10mm).

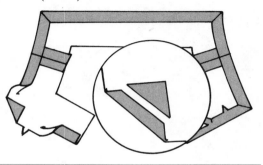

5

Pin neck band facing to neck band. Stitch ends and neck edge, pivoting at small •'s. Clip to small •'s.

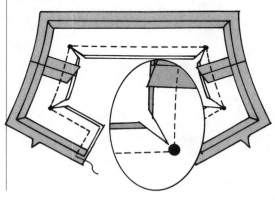

6

Trim seam.

Neck Bands

Square Band: With Finished Opening Edges, Continued

7

UNDERSTITCH facing.

Note: If edgestitching or topstitching neck band, understitching is not necessary.

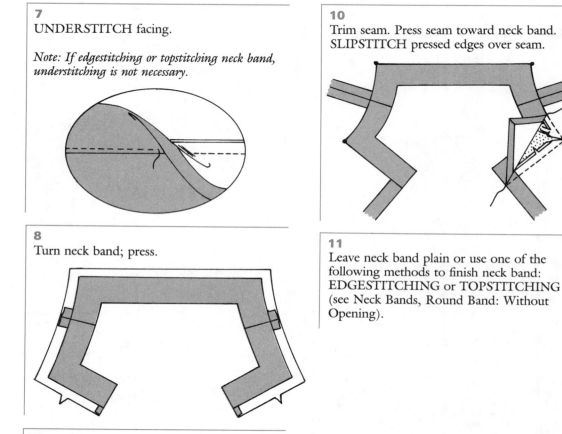

8

Turn neck band; press.

9

Clip garment neck edge to small •'s. Pin neck edge to neck band edge, matching centers and symbols. Baste. Stitch, pivoting at small •'s and keeping pressed edges free.

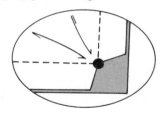

10

Trim seam. Press seam toward neck band. SLIPSTITCH pressed edges over seam.

11

Leave neck band plain or use one of the following methods to finish neck band: EDGESTITCHING or TOPSTITCHING (see Neck Bands, Round Band: Without Opening).

Neck Bands

SQUARE BAND: WITHOUT OPENING

1

REINFORCE inner corners of neck edge, pivoting at small •'s.

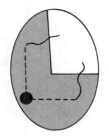

2

INTERFACE wrong side of one front neck band section and one back neck band section.

Note: Remaining section(s) will be used as facing(s).

3

Stitch interfaced front neck band to interfaced back neck band at shoulders.

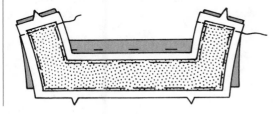

4

Stitch front neck band facing to back neck band facing at shoulders. Turn in seam allowances on outer edges of neck band facing, diagonally folding and trimming corners. Press. Trim pressed seam allowances to ⅜″ (10mm).

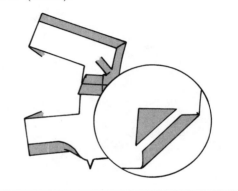

5

Pin neck band facing to neck band. Stitch neck edge, pivoting at small •'s. Clip to small •'s.

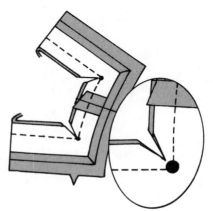

Neck Bands

Square Band: Without Opening, Continued

6

Trim seam.

7

UNDERSTITCH facing.

Note: If edgestitching or topstitching neck band, understitching is not necessary.

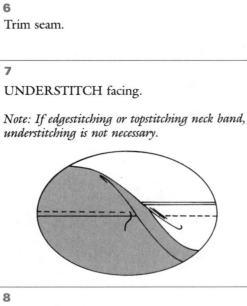

8

Turn neck band; press.

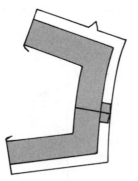

9

Clip garment neck edge to small •'s. Pin neck edge to neck band, matching centers and symbols. Baste. Stitch, pivoting at small •'s, keeping pressed edges free.

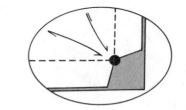

10

Trim seam. Press seam toward neck band. SLIPSTITCH pressed edges over seam.

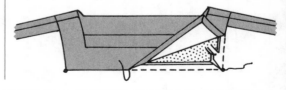

11

Leave neck band plain or use one of the following methods to finish neck band: EDGESTITCHING or TOPSTITCHING (see Neck Bands, Round Band: Without Opening).

Basting Preparation

- Work on a flat, smooth surface.

- Pin pieces together.

- Baste alongside seamline for easy removal.

- Remove basting before pressing permanent stitching.

- Silk thread is recommended for fine fabrics or when hand basting will not be removed before pressing, as is the case with pleats or hems.

- When machine basting. use contrasting color thread in the needle *and* bobbin.

- When hand basting, begin and end with a BACKSTITCH.

- Also, see Hand Sewing Basics.

Basting

Hand Basting Stitches

EVEN BASTING

Use even basting, when basted seams will be subjected to strain and when one layer of fabric is to be eased to the other.

Take even RUNNING STITCHES ¼" (6mm) long and ¼" (6mm) apart.

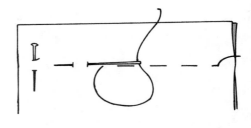

SLIP BASTING

Use slip basting, which is very secure, when matching stripes, plaids and prints, or intricate curved sections and in fitting adjustments from the right side.

Crease and turn under seam allowance on one edge. With right sides up, lay folded edge in position on corresponding piece, matching fabric design and/or symbols at seamline; pin. Slip needle through upper fold, then through underneath section, using ¼" (6mm) stitch length. This will make a plain seam with basting on the wrong side.

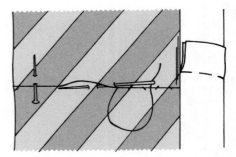

UNEVEN BASTING

Use uneven basting when marking, attaching underlining and interfacing, and holding seams and edges that will not be subjected to strain.

Take a short RUNNING STITCH through the fabric, leaving a long stitch in between.

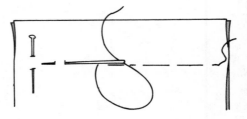

Machine Basting

Set machine on longest stitch length [6–8 stitches per inch (2–3 per cm)]. Clip stitches approximately every 1″ (25 mm) to make removal easier.

Refer to sewing machine manual for other sewing machine basting methods.

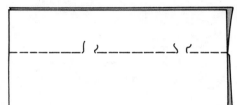

Basting

31

Other Basting Methods

BASTING TAPE

Use basting tape for hard-to-handle fabrics that are slippery or pucker, and for other general basting purposes.

Place tape ¼" (6mm) from seamline in seam allowance so it won't be caught in stitching.

Remove basting tape as soon as machine stitching is finished.

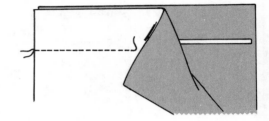

DISAPPEARING BASTING TAPE

Use disappearing basting tape as a substitute for regular basting tape.

Place disappearing basting tape ¹⁄₁₆" (2mm) from seamline in seam allowance. Remove backing and press second layer in place with fingers.

Do not press over tape until after item has been washed to make sure all adhesive is removed.

Other Basting Methods

GLUE STICK BASTING

Use glue stick like basting tape to hold trims, pockets, facings and zippers in place. Glue stick basting works best on firmly woven fabrics and knits.

Test fabric before using glue stick to be sure glue completely washes out.

Roll stick along sections to be basted.

Press in place with fingers.

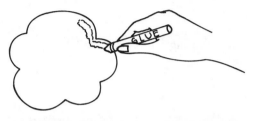

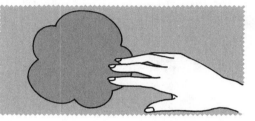

PIN BASTING

Use pin basting when no fitting is required.

Pin corresponding pieces together, inserting pins 1″–4″ (15mm–10cm) apart with heads in seam allowance so pins are easy to remove during sewing.

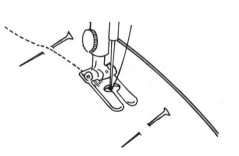

WASH-AWAY BASTING THREAD

Use wash-away basting thread in place of regular thread to hand-baste or machine-baste on any fabric that is not harmed by water or steam. It does not dissolve in dry cleaning fluid.

Follow manufacturer's instructions for specific information.

Belt Buckles

WITH PRONG

1
Make a ⅝" (15mm) long slit where the prong will go through the belt, 1" (25mm) from the end.

2
Work BLANKET STITCHES around the slit.

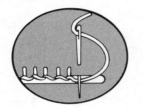

3
Insert prong and follow directions below to attach buckle to belt.

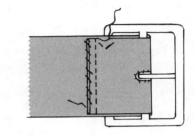

4
Make eyelet for the prong at opposite end of belt (see Eyelets).

WITHOUT PRONG

1
Slip straight end of right belt through bar of buckle, turning back along foldline.

WHIPSTITCH end securely in place. SLIPSTITCH side edges.

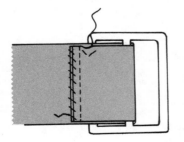

Belt Carriers

FABRIC CARRIER STRIPS: FOLDED AND STITCHED

1

Turn in ¼" (6mm) on long edges of carrier strip; press.

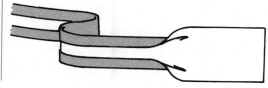

2

With wrong sides together, fold carrier strip in half lengthwise, having edges even; press. EDGESTITCH both long edges.

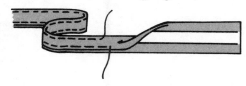

3

Cut carrier strip into number of sections needed. Each carrier should be the same length and long enough to go around the belt with ¼" - ½" (6mm - 13mm) for ease.

4

Apply carriers by hand or by machine (see Fabric Carrier Applications).

For a quick method, also see Overlock, Fabric Belt Carriers.

Belt Carriers

FABRIC CARRIER STRIPS: STITCHED AND TURNED

1

With right sides together, fold carrier strip in half lengthwise. Stitch a ¼" seam, leaving ends open.

2

Turn, bringing seam to center; press.

3

EDGESTITCH both long edges.

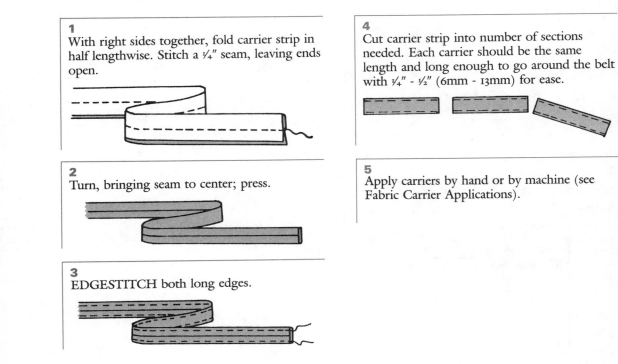

4

Cut carrier strip into number of sections needed. Each carrier should be the same length and long enough to go around the belt with ¼" - ½" (6mm - 13mm) for ease.

5

Apply carriers by hand or by machine (see Fabric Carrier Applications).

Belt Carriers

FABRIC CARRIER APPLICATIONS: HAND-SEWN

1

Overlap ends ¼″ (6mm) and WHIPSTITCH together.

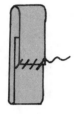

2

Apply carriers to completed garment.

3

On outside, center carrier seam over symbols. WHIPSTITCH securely in place.

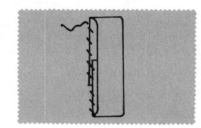

FABRIC CARRIER APPLICATIONS: MACHINE-STITCHED

Caught in Seam and Edgestitched

1

Construct garment up to the waistband application step. Turn in ⅝″ (15mm) on one end of each carrier; press. Trim pressed seam allowance to ¼″ (6mm). Pin remaining end of each carrier to lower edge of waistband, centering over symbol; baste.

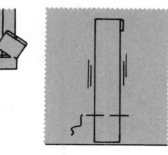

2

Apply waistband.

3

Turn carriers up. EDGESTITCH in place.

Belt Carriers

Fabric Carrier Applications: Machine-stitched, Continued

Caught in Seam And Whipstitched

1

Construct garment up to the waistband application step. Stitch ¼" (6mm) from one end of each carrier.

2

Position remaining end of each carrier on upper edge of garment, centering over symbol.

3

Baste.

4

Apply waistband.

5

Turn carriers up over waistband, turning ends ⅝" (15mm) to inside. WHIPSTITCH in place.

Edgestitched

1

Apply waistband. Turn in ¼" (6mm) on ends of each carrier; press.

2

Pin carriers to waistband, centering between symbols; baste. Stitch close to pressed edges through all thicknesses.

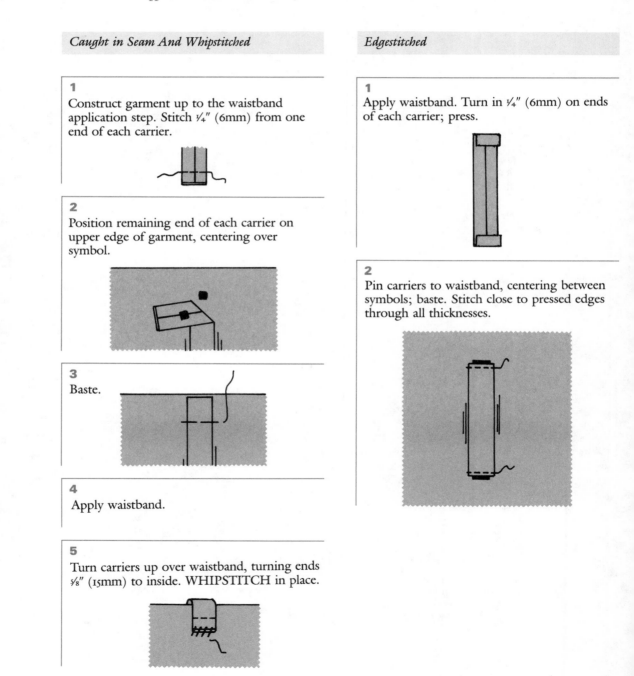

Belt Carriers

To add carriers to a garment without placement symbols, first establish belt position at side seams and waistline of garment. Make two placement marks, one on each side seam. Make thread loops long enough for belt to pass through easily.

THREAD CARRIER APPLICATIONS: HAND-SEWN

1

Working with a double thread, make a thread chain by hand.

2

On outside of garment at placement mark, BACKSTITCH TACK at beginning point of chain. Take another small stitch and form a loop.

3

Hold loop open with thumb and index finger of one hand (a). With middle finger of same hand, reach through loop and pull long end of thread through to form new loop (b). Hold new loop; slide first loop off fingers (c).

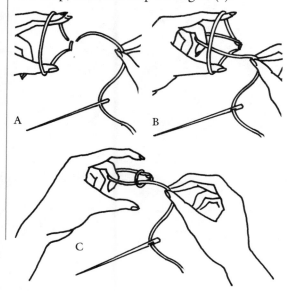

4

Gently pull both new loop and thread until first loop forms a knot at the base.

5

Continue to form new loops until chain makes a carrier long enough for belt to fit through easily. To end, insert needle through last loop.

6

Then, pass needle to inside of garment at placement mark. Knot securely on inside.

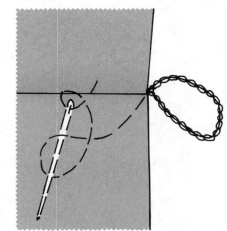

Belt Carriers

THREAD CARRIER APPLICATIONS: MACHINE-STITCHED

1

For loops, make a thread chain (see Overlock Thread Chain Belt Carriers) OR twist several strands of thread together. Hold taut; SATIN-STITCH over threads.

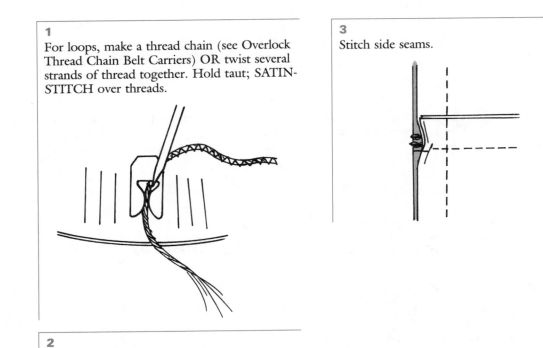

2

Pin each carrier over placement symbol at waistline.

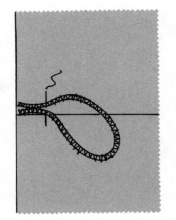

3

Stitch side seams.

Narrow–hemmed Straight Belt or Sash

1

Stitch belt or sash sections together along notched edge. Stitch again ¼" (6mm) away in seam allowance. Trim close to stitching.

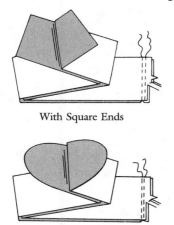

With Square Ends

With Round Ends

2

Press seam toward one side.

3

Make ⅝" (15mm) or ⅜" (10mm) NARROW HEM along all edges. For square ends, diagonally fold and trim corners. For round ends, ease in fullness at curves.

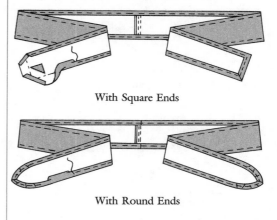

With Square Ends

With Round Ends

Stitched and Turned Belts

CUMMERBUND WITH SOFT TIES

1

INTERFACE wrong side of one belt section.
Note: For self-faced belt, remaining section will be used as facing.

2

Stitch a tie end to each end of belt.

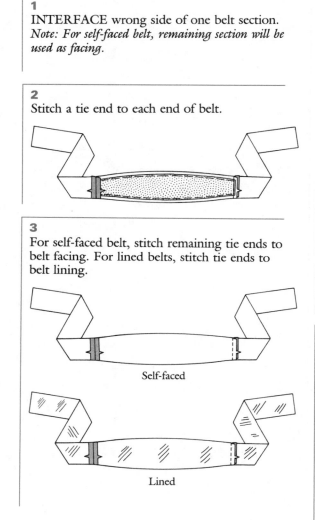

3

For self-faced belt, stitch remaining tie ends to belt facing. For lined belts, stitch tie ends to belt lining.

Self-faced

Lined

4

With right sides together, pin facing or lining to belt. Stitch, leaving an opening. (If small ●'s are indicated, leave opening between symbols).

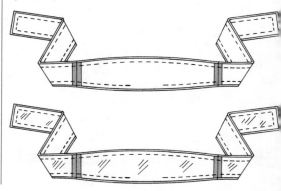

5

TRIM and CLIP seam.

6

Turn. Press. SLIPSTITCH opening.

7

To finish belt, use one of the following methods: EDGESTITCHING, TOPSTITCHING, or EDGESTITCHING and TOPSTITCHING (see Stitched and Turned Belts, Straight Belt or Sash).

Stitched and Turned Belts

1

Stitch belt or sash sections together along notched edge.

2

With right sides together, fold belt or sash along foldline. Stitch, leaving an opening. (If small •'s are indicated, leave opening between symbols).

3

TRIM.

4

Turn. Press. SLIPSTITCH opening.

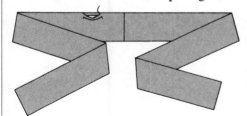

5

To finish belt, use one of the following methods:

EDGESTITCH,

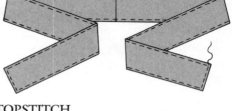

TOPSTITCH,

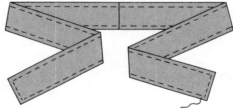

EDGESTITCH and TOPSTITCH.

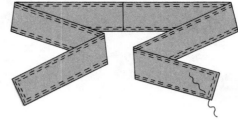

Belts and Sashes

43

Stitched and Turned Belts

1

INTERFACE wrong side of one belt section.

2

Stitch belt sections together, leaving an opening. (If small •'s are indicated, leave opening between symbols).

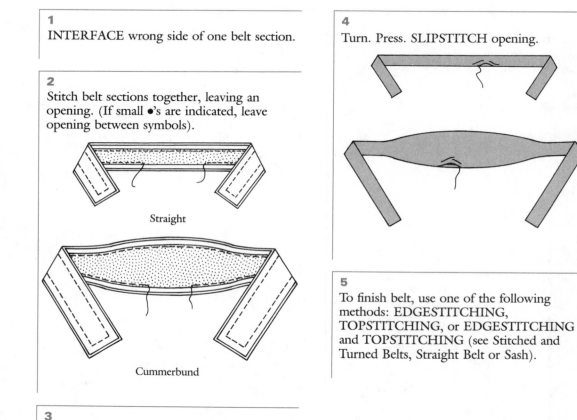

Straight

Cummerbund

3

TRIM. CLIP seam if necessary.

4

Turn. Press. SLIPSTITCH opening.

5

To finish belt, use one of the following methods: EDGESTITCHING, TOPSTITCHING, or EDGESTITCHING and TOPSTITCHING (see Stitched and Turned Belts, Straight Belt or Sash).

Belts and Sashes

Bias Strip Preparation

CUTTING BIAS STRIPS

1

Use a rectangular piece of fabric cut on straight grain. Fold diagonally at one end to find true bias. Using bias fold as a guide, mark fabric with parallel lines the desired width of bias strips, marking as many strips as needed. At top and bottom edges, on straight grain, allow for ¼″ (6mm) seams.

2

Make a diagonal fold along first and last line of markings and cut along both folds, discarding triangular ends. Mark ¼″ (6mm) seamline on both ends.

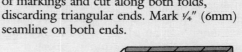
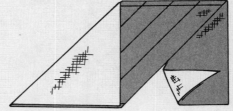

PIECING CONTINUOUS BIAS STRIPS

1

On marked fabric, join straight grain edges right sides together, matching markings and making one strip width extend beyond the edge at each side. Stitch in ¼″ (6mm) seam; press open.

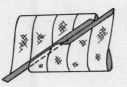

2

Begin cutting on marked line at one end; continue in circular fashion.

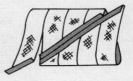

Binding

45

Bias Strip Preparation

PIECING INDIVIDUAL BIAS STRIPS

1

Cut along markings for bias strips. The short ends, previously cut on grain, will appear diagonal. With right sides together, match seamlines (not cut edges) so strips are at right angles; pin. Stitch in ¼" (6mm) seam.

2

Press seam open; trim triangular ends.

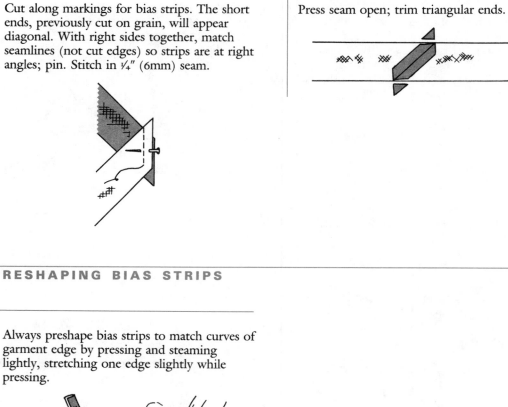

PRESHAPING BIAS STRIPS

Always preshape bias strips to match curves of garment edge by pressing and steaming lightly, stretching one edge slightly while pressing.

Double or French Binding—Hand-finished

FOLDING AND SHAPING BINDING

1

Cut bias strips six times the desired finished width plus ¼" (6mm). Fold strip in half, wrong sides together. Press, stretching bias evenly and gently to remove any slack.

2

Preshape binding to match curves of garment edge.

APPLYING BINDING

1

Place piecing seamlines at inconspicuous locations whenever possible. Leave 1" (25mm) of binding free beyond beginning and ending of any application (for finishing).

2

Trim entire seam allowance from garment edges which will be bound.

3

With raw edges even, pin binding to right side of garment. Baste binding at a distance from the edge slightly less than width of finished binding. Stitch next to (not on) basting.

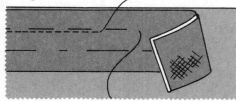

4

Turn binding over seam allowances. Pin; SLIPSTITCH.

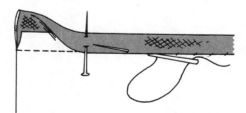

Double or French Binding—Hand-finished

STITCHING CORNERS: INSIDE CORNERS

1

Using small machine stitches, REINFORCE garment corner along seamline. Clip corner almost to stitching.

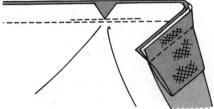

2

Pin binding to right side of garment, opening out corner so raw edges are in a straight line, not at a right angle. Stitch on wrong side.

3

Press binding away from garment, forming a miter on right side. Pull miter through clip to wrong side.

4

Turn binding over raw edges; form a miter in opposite direction from miter on the right side. SLIPSTITCH binding and corner miters in place.

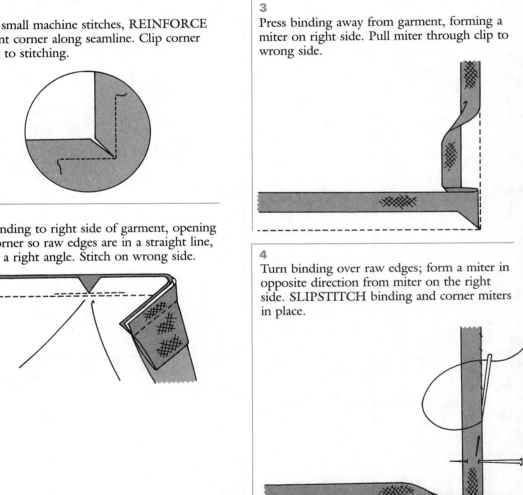

Double or French Binding—Hand-finished

STITCHING CORNERS: OUTSIDE CORNERS

1

Stitch binding to the point where seamlines on each side of corner meet; backstitch. Remove garment from machine.

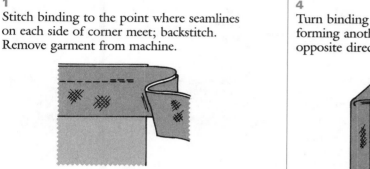

2

Turn binding around corner so edges of binding and fabric match on unstitched side of corner, making a diagonal fold, or miter, at the point. Resume stitching, starting at upper edges.

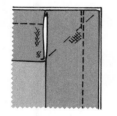

3

On right side, fold to form a miter at corner.

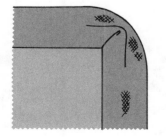

4

Turn binding to wrong side over raw edges, forming another miter on wrong side in opposite direction from miter on right side.

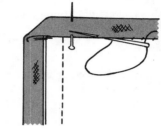

5

SLIPSTITCH binding and corner miters in place.

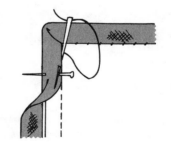

Double or French Binding—Hand-finished

JOINING BINDING

Try to locate joining at an inconspicuous place.

1

Stop stitching slightly before reaching area of joining. Open out binding; fold garment so binding ends are at right angles.

2

Stitch binding ends together very close to garment, but keep garment free. Trim seam allowances to ¼" (6mm).

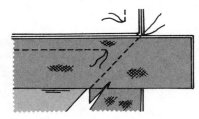

3

Press open. Trim triangular ends. Continue stitching binding to garment across the joining.

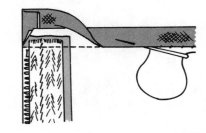

ENDING BINDING

Complete facings and turn seam allowances under or insert zipper before applying binding.

1

Pin, baste, and stitch binding to garment. Trim binding ends to ¼" (6mm) beyond garment edge. Trim seam allowance on a diagonal at corner.

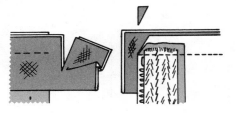

2

Turn extending binding ends to wrong side, even with garment edge. Turn binding over seam allowance, matching folded edge to line of machine stitching. Pin and SLIPSTITCH folded edge to garment.

3

SLIPSTITCH open ends.

Single Binding—Hand-finished

FOLDING AND SHAPING BINDING

If using commercial binding, eliminate the next two steps.

1

Cut bias strips four times the desired finished width plus ¼" (6mm). Fold strip in half, wrong sides together; press lightly. Open the fold; turn both raw edges in toward center fold; press.

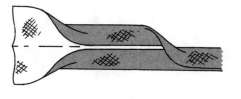

2

Re-fold along center; press, stretching bias evenly and gently to remove any slack.

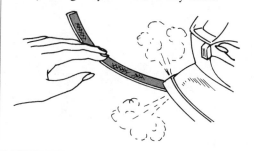

3

Preshape binding to match curves of garment edge.

APPLYING BINDING

1

Place piecing seamlines at inconspicuous locations whenever possible. Leave 1" (25mm) of binding free beyond beginning and ending of any application (for finishing).

2

Trim entire seam allowance from garment edges which will be bound.

3

If using commercial binding, position wider side of binding so it will be on the underneath side of garment when stitching.

4

Open out one folded edge of binding strip. With raw edges even, pin binding to garment, right sides together. Baste binding at a distance from the edge slightly less than width of finished binding. Stitch next to (not on) basting.

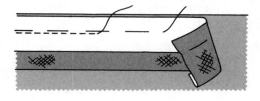

5

Turn binding over seam allowance. Pin; SLIPSTITCH.

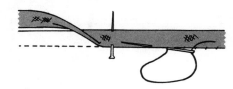

Single Binding—Hand-finished

STITCHING CORNERS: INSIDE CORNERS

1

Using small machine stitches, REINFORCE corner along seamline. Clip corner almost to stitching.

2

Pin binding to right side of garment, opening out corner so raw edges are in a straight line, not at a right angle. Stitch on wrong side.

3

Press binding away from garment, forming a miter on right side. Pull miter through clip to wrong side.

4

Turn binding over raw edges; form a miter in opposite direction from miter on the right side. SLIPSTITCH binding and corner miters in place.

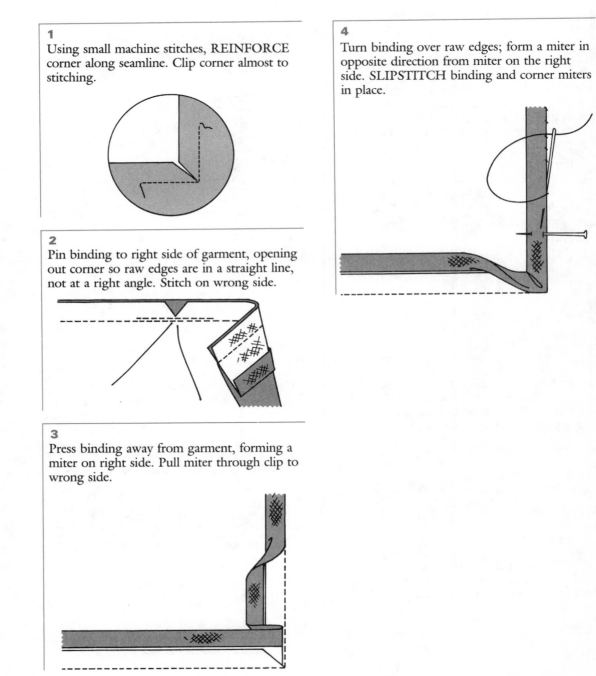

Single Binding—Hand-finished

STITCHING CORNERS: OUTSIDE CORNERS

1

Stitch binding to the point where seamlines on each side of corner meet; backstitch. Remove garment from machine.

2

Turn binding around corner so edges of binding and fabric match on unstitched side of corner, making a diagonal fold, or miter, at the point. Resume stitching, starting at upper edges.

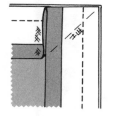

3

On right side, fold to form a miter at corner.

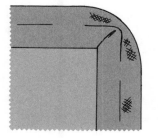

4

Turn binding to wrong side over raw edges, forming another miter on wrong side in opposite direction from miter on right side.

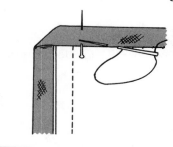

5

SLIPSTITCH binding and corner miters in place.

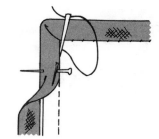

Single Binding—Hand-finished

JOINING BINDING

1

Try to locate joining at an inconspicuous place.

2

Stop stitching slightly before reaching area of joining. Open out binding; fold garment so binding ends are at right angles.

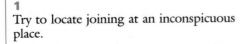

3

Stitch binding ends together very close to garment, but keep garment free. Trim seam allowances to ¼" (6mm).

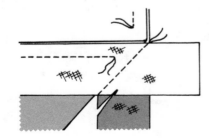

4

Press open. Trim triangular ends. Continue stitching binding to garment across the joining.

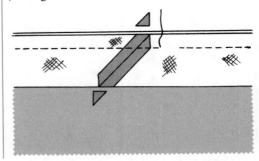

54

Single Binding—Hand-finished

ENDING BINDING

1

Complete facings and turn seam allowances under or insert zipper before applying binding.

2

Pin, baste, and stitch binding to garment. Trim binding ends to ¼" (6mm) beyond garment edge.

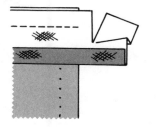

3

Trim garment seam allowance on a diagonal at corner.

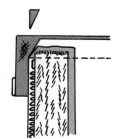

4

Turn extending binding ends to wrong side, even with garment edge. Turn binding over seam allowance, matching folded edge to line of machine stitching. Pin and SLIPSTITCH folded edge to garment.

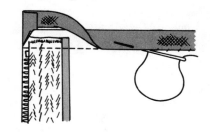

5

SLIPSTITCH open ends.

Single Binding—Machine-finished

FOLDING AND SHAPING BINDING

1

If using commercial binding, eliminate the next two steps.

2

Cut bias strips four times the desired finished width plus ¼" (6mm).

3

Fold strip in half, wrong sides together; press lightly. Open the fold; turn in one raw edge to meet center fold; press. Turn in remaining edge slightly away from center fold; press. Refold along center; press.

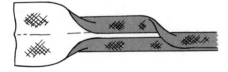

4

Press, stretching binding evenly and gently to remove any slack. Preshape binding to match curves of garment edge.

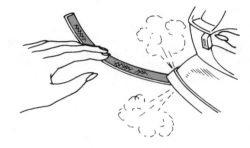

APPLYING BINDING

1

Place piecing seamlines at inconspicuous locations whenever possible. Leave 1" (15mm) of binding free beyond beginning and ending of any application (for finishing).

2

Trim entire seam allowance from garment edges which will be bound.

3

With wider edge on wrong side of garment, encase trimmed edge with binding. Pin; stitch.

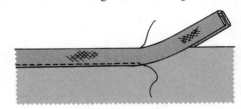

Single Binding—Machine-finished

STITCHING CORNERS: INSIDE CORNERS

1

Using small machine stitches, REINFORCE corner along seamline. Clip corner almost to stitching.

2

Encase raw edge with binding, pin in place. Begin stitching and stop at inner point of corner, keeping needle in fabric. Raise presser foot and open out corner so edges are in a straight line, not a right angle. Continue to stitch on binding.

3

When finished, fold binding at corner to create a miter on right side.

4

On the wrong side, fold the binding as shown and press flat. Machine-stitch the miter; then SLIPSTITCH corner.

STITCHING CORNERS: OUTSIDE CORNERS

1

Stitch binding to edge of corner.

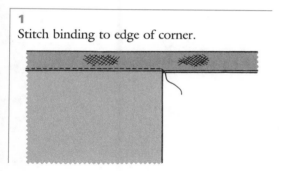

2

Remove garment from machine. Turn binding around corner, forming a miter by making a diagonal fold at corner on both sides. Resume stitching.

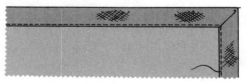

Single Binding—Machine-finished

JOINING BINDING

1

Try to locate joining at an inconspicuous place. Cut any ends to be joined on the straight grain. Turn in overlapping end ½" (13mm); lap over raw end.

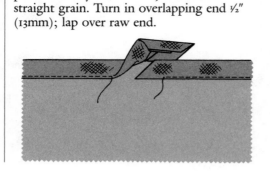

2

Continue stitching binding to garment across the joining. SLIPSTITCH overlapped edges, if necessary.

ENDING BINDING

1

Complete facings and turn seam allowances under or insert zipper before applying binding.

2

For an end at a finished edge, turn under raw end of binding so folded edge of binding matches finished edge of garment. On right side, stitch close to folded edge of binding, catching in both edges of binding.

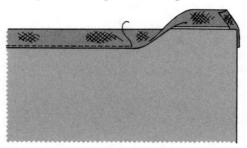

3

SLIPSTITCH ends.

Buttonhole Preparation

PLACEMENT

- Horizontal buttonholes begin ⅛″ (3mm) beyond the button marking toward the closing edge. This distance allows for the natural tendency of the garment to "pull" away from the closing and for the thickness of thread holding button in place. This is the most secure type of button closing.

- The buttonhole markings on patterns have allowed for this placement, which is usually ⅛″ (3mm) beyond the center front or center back line toward the garment edge. Use the markings to position buttonholes accurately.

- Vertical buttonholes begin ⅛″ (3mm) above the button marking, directly on the lengthwise placement line. The "pull" is downward for this type of button placement. These buttonholes are generally used on narrow plackets, such as those found on a man- tailored shirt, or in non-functioning positions.

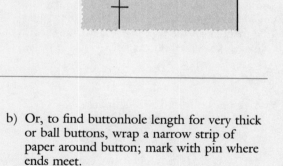

BUTTONHOLE SIZE

- Most patterns include markings on the tissue for the buttonhole size that corresponds to the button size recommended on the pattern envelope. For buttons that are a different size than pattern envelope recommends, measure button as follows to determine length of buttonhole:

a) Minimum buttonhole length is equal to button diameter plus thickness plus ⅛″ (3mm).

b) Or, to find buttonhole length for very thick or ball buttons, wrap a narrow strip of paper around button; mark with pin where ends meet.

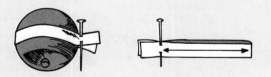

Fold paper strip in half; measure between pin and fold and add ⅛″ (3mm) to determine correct buttonhole size. In general, make buttonholes about ¼″ (6mm) wide, with each lip ⅛″ (3mm) wide. The lip width may vary slightly with the fabric weight.

Buttonholes

Buttonhole Preparation

INTERFACING

- Make most buttonholes through three layers: outer fabric, interfacing and facing fabric. This gives the best support for buttonholes.

- Choose interfacing to complement fabric weight; then apply to garment.

MARKING

- Use tracing wheel and dressmaker's carbon, pins, tailor's chalk, removable marking pen, hand or machine basting, or thread tracing for marking.

- It is easiest to mark bound buttonhole placement on the wrong side of the fabric or interfacing, at the same time other construction symbols are marked. Then use basting, pins or thread tracing to transfer markings to the right side. However, after garment is complete, the position of machine-worked buttonholes may be marked on the right side of the fabric with any marking method that is removable.

Mark center line first.

Mark one end of horizontal buttonholes ⅛" (3mm) from center, toward outside edge of garment.

Mark vertical buttonholes, starting at center, ⅛" (6mm) above button marking.

Mark other end of buttonhole.

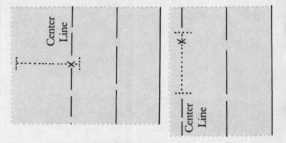

If pattern is altered, reposition buttonhole markings. To find new position, divide new length of pattern between top and bottom buttonhole by the number of *spaces* between buttonholes. Re-mark buttonholes an equal distance from each other.

BUTTONHOLE TYPES

- There are three types of buttonholes: bound, hand-worked and machine-worked. Always test the method desired on scraps of the same fabric as garment. Prepare fabric test sample using interfacing and the same number of fabric layers that will be used on garment. Buttonholes may be corded for additional body, strength and durability.

Bound Buttonholes

1

Accurately mark buttonhole placement, transferring markings to the right side with thread tracing.

2

Complete garment up to applying facing.

3

Cut a strip of self-fabric 1" (25mm) wide and long enough for all the buttonholes, making sure strip is cut exactly along straight grain of fabric. For the length of this strip, multiply the length of each buttonhole plus 1" (25mm) by twice the number of buttonholes.

4

Wrong sides together, fold strip in half lengthwise and press lightly. MACHINE-BASTE ⅛" (3mm) from folded edge exactly along straight grain of fabric. Trim the cut edge to a scant ⅛" (3mm) from the stitching.

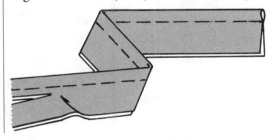

5

Strip can easily be corded as you baste, if desired. Fold strip, wrong sides together, around cable cord or twine before you begin to construct the buttonhole. Using a zipper foot, machine-baste close to the cord.

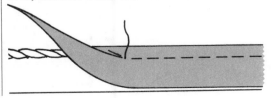

6

Cut the strip into sections the length of the buttonhole plus 1" (25mm).

7

Baste one strip to the right side, placing the cut edge along the thread-traced position line. Using small stitches, stitch the length of the buttonhole through all thicknesses directly over the stitching on the strip. Leave the thread ends long enough to tie. Repeat for the second strip on the opposite side of the marked line so the cut edges meet.

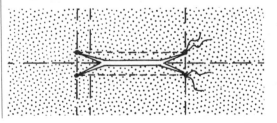

8

Pull the thread ends through to the wrong side and tie. On wrong side of garment, slash along center line and diagonally into corners, being careful not to cut stitching or strips.

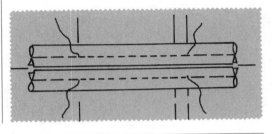

9

Turn strips through slash to wrong side of garment; press.

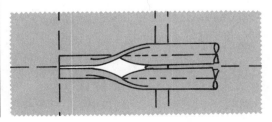

Bound Buttonholes

10

From right side, loosely WHIPSTITCH buttonhole lips together. Fold back garment at each end of buttonhole to reveal ends with fabric triangle on top. Using a short stitch length, stitch across ends, being careful to stitch straight from one corner to the other. Stitch back and forth across the base of each triangle a few times to square corners and straighten ends.

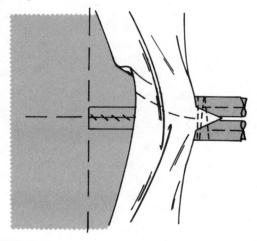

11

Trim ends to ¼" (6mm) and CATCHSTITCH to interfacing.

12

Attach garment facing. Pin or baste facing around buttonholes. With facing in position, place pins through all four corners of each buttonhole. Carefully mark corners of buttonholes on the right side of facing.

13

Remove pins. Using a short stitch length and pivoting at each corner marking, stitch a rectangle the size of the buttonhole between markings. Cut through facing between the pins and carefully clip diagonally to corners.

14

Turn in the raw facing edges along stitching; press.

15

Sew facing to buttonhole around each buttonhole.

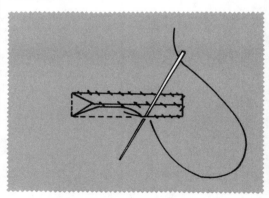

Hand-worked Buttonholes

BUTTONHOLE STITCH

1

Accurately mark buttonhole placement.

2

Using a short stitch length, machine-stitch a scant ⅛″ (3mm) away from either side of the buttonhole marking and across both ends.

3

Carefully slash along buttonhole marking.

4

Use an 18″ (13cm) length of buttonhole twist or topstitching thread. On wrong side of one end of buttonhole, anchor thread with BACKSTITCHES. Work buttonhole stitch by inserting needle through slash from right side of fabric and bringing it out on the outside of the stitching line through loop formed when inserting the needle.

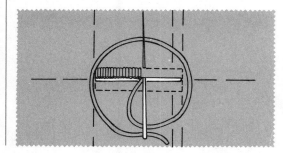

5

Draw up the needle so a purl (knot) is formed at buttonhole edge.

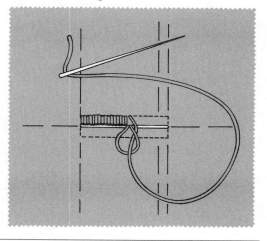

6

Repeat, keeping stitches even and each purl exactly on edge of slash. If corded effect is desired, see Cording. Add a Bar Tack to finish both ends, or work a Keyhole around the end nearest the garment edge for a custom-tailored effect (see Bar Tack below and Keyhole, next page).

BAR TACK BUTTONHOLE

To finish both ends of buttonhole with a bar tack, take 3 or 4 stitches across width of buttonhole at each end. Work BLANKET STITCHES over threads through all thicknesses.

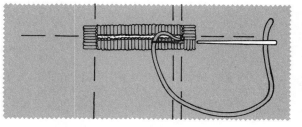

Hand-worked Buttonholes

CORDED BUTTONHOLE

To cord buttonhole, work BUTTONHOLE STITCH over a strand of buttonhole twist or topstitching thread secured at one end with a pin. Clip cord ends after completing buttonhole.

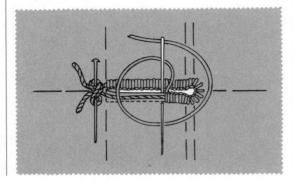

KEYHOLE BUTTONHOLE

1
Accurately mark buttonhole placement.

2
Complete garment.

3
Using a short stitch length, machine-stitch a scant ⅛" (3mm) on either side and at both ends of the buttonhole marking.

4
With an awl, make a hole at end nearest opening edge; then carefully slash along remaining buttonhole marking.

5
Work BUTTONHOLE STITCH around the hole and slash. Finish end with a Bar Tack.

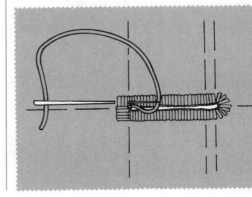

Machine-worked Buttonholes

1

Accurately mark buttonhole placement.

2

Attach facing or complete section of garment before making buttonholes.

3

Make buttonholes with built-in buttonhole stitch setting, zigzag machine or buttonhole attachment. See sewing machine manual for specific information. To cord buttonhole, use a special buttonhole foot or guide cord by hand while stitching.

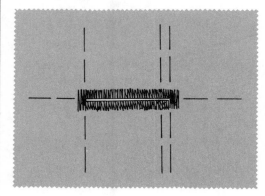

Button Size and Placement Guidelines

- Choose buttons according to size and type recommended on pattern envelope.

- Make sure there are buttons located at all points of stress, such as fullest part of bustline.

- If using a belt or sash, place buttons sufficiently above or below belt so they won't interfere.

- Generally, position buttons on the center front or center back line, unless the pattern instruction and tissue direct otherwise.

- After buttonhole is completed, lap garment edges the necessary amount and poke a pin through buttonhole to mark button position at center front or back. Make sure center lines of both garment edges are aligned, as well as top and bottom garment edges.

- Horizontal buttonholes are designed to extend past the button ⅛″ (3mm) toward the finished garment edge.

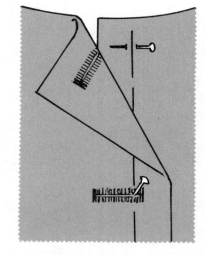

- Vertical buttonholes should start ⅛″ (3mm) above button marking at center front or back.

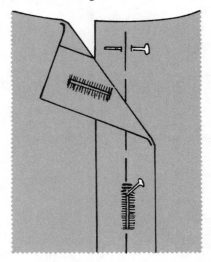

- Sew center of button at the marked position.

Attaching Buttons

SEW-THROUGH BUTTONS

Sew-through buttons should have a thread shank equal to thickness of garment at buttonhole plus ⅛" (3mm) for movement.

1

Take a couple of BACKSTITCHES at button marking on right side of fabric.

2

When sewing on button by hand, place pin, matchstick, toothpick or other object above button and sew over object.

3

Remove object; raise button to top of stitches. To form thread shank under button, wind thread tightly around shank a few times under button. BACKSTITCH several times into the shank for a secure finish.

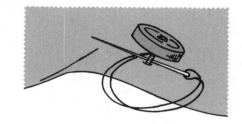

4

Sew-through buttons can also be sewn on by zigzag or specialty stitch machines. See sewing machine manual for specific information.

SHANK BUTTONS

1

Take a couple of BACKSTITCHES at button marking on right side of fabric.

2

Attach button with small stitches sewn through shank.

3

If fabric is very thick and bulky, also make a thread shank the same size as for a Sew-through Button.

67

Reinforcing Buttons

HEAVYWEIGHT FABRICS OR GARMENTS

1

Place a small flat button on back of garment under large button.

2

Sew directly from one button to the other, allowing for a shank.

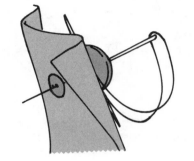

3

Complete shank same as for Sew-through Button.

LIGHTWEIGHT FABRICS OR GARMENTS

1

Place a small folded square of seam binding or self fabric on back of garment under the button. Sew from button through folded square, allowing for a shank.

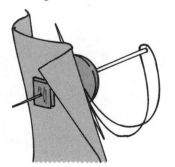

2

Complete shank same as for Sew-through Button.

Drawstring Openings

BUTTONHOLE

1

Note: Make drawstring openings before forming casing. Do not use with casing in seam allowance.

REINFORCE garment section(s). Cut appropriate number of self- fabric pieces, each a little larger than buttonhole. Baste to wrong side, centering over buttonhole markings.

2

Make machine-worked or hand-worked buttonholes at markings.

3

Trim fabric piece close to stitching.

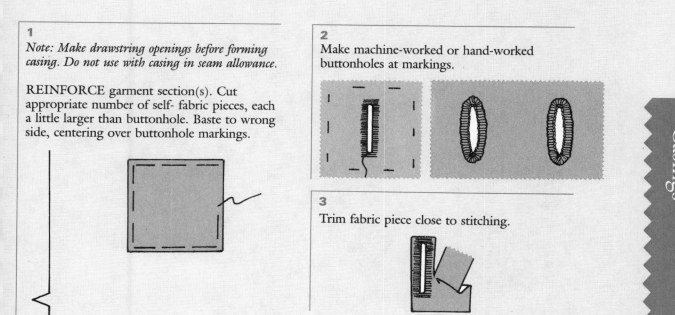

IN SEAM

1

Note: Make drawstring openings before forming casing. Do not use with casing in seam allowance.

Stitch seam, leaving an opening the width of drawstring.

2

REINFORCE each end with BACKSTITCHING.

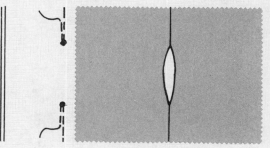

Applied Casings

BIAS TAPE CASING: APPLIED OVER PLACEMENT LINE

1

To form casing on inside, center bias tape over placement line, turning in ends to meet at one seam. Stitch close to both long edges.

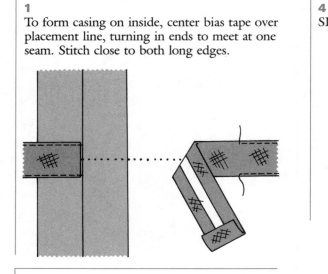

2

Cut elastic the measurement of body area plus 1″ (25mm), or follow elastic chart on pattern instruction sheet.

3

Insert elastic through opening in casing, lapping ends; hold with safety pin. Try on and adjust, if necessary. Stitch ends of elastic securely.

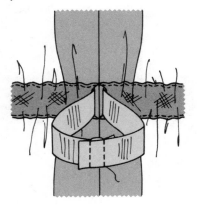

4

SLIPSTITCH opening in casing.

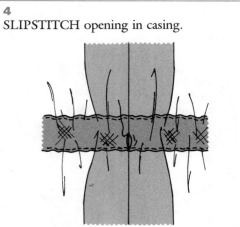

Applied Casings

1

Open out one folded edge of bias tape; press.

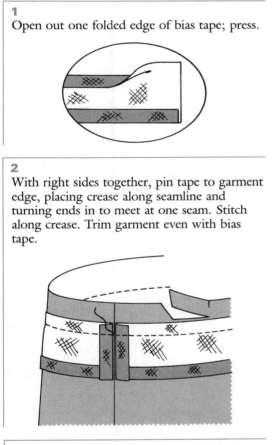

2

With right sides together, pin tape to garment edge, placing crease along seamline and turning ends in to meet at one seam. Stitch along crease. Trim garment even with bias tape.

3

Turn bias tape to inside along seam; press. To form casing, stitch close to both long edges.

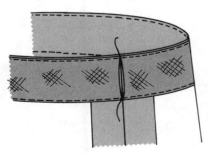

4

Cut elastic the measurement of body area plus 1" (25mm), or follow elastic chart on pattern instruction sheet.

5

Insert elastic through opening in casing, lapping ends; hold with safety pin. Try on and adjust, if necessary. Stitch ends of elastic securely.

6

SLIPSTITCH opening in casing.

Casings

71

Casing In Seam Allowance

1

Trim seam allowance that will be against garment to a scant ¼″ (6mm).

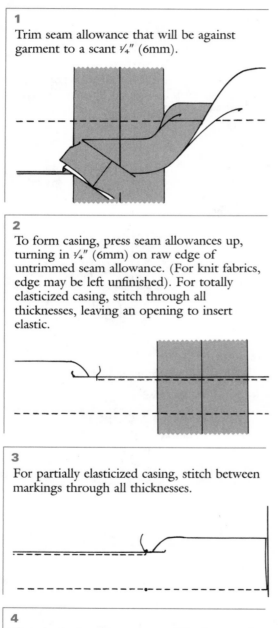

2

To form casing, press seam allowances up, turning in ¼″ (6mm) on raw edge of untrimmed seam allowance. (For knit fabrics, edge may be left unfinished). For totally elasticized casing, stitch through all thicknesses, leaving an opening to insert elastic.

3

For partially elasticized casing, stitch between markings through all thicknesses.

4

Cut elastic the measurement of body area plus 1″ (25mm), or follow elastic chart on pattern instruction sheet.

5

For totally elasticized casing, insert elastic through opening in casing, lapping ends; hold with safety pin. Try on and adjust, if necessary. Stitch ends of elastic securely.

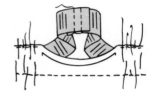

6

Stitch opening, stretching elastic, so garment is flat while stitching.

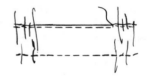

7

For partially elasticized casing, insert elastic through opening in casing, extending ends ½″ (13mm) beyond markings. Baste ends securely.

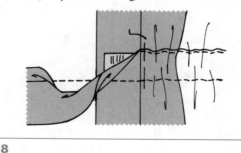

8

Try on and adjust, if necessary. STITCH-IN-THE-DITCH across casing along seam. If casing does not end at a seam, stitch along stitching line to small ●.

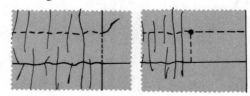

Turned-in Casing

1

To form casing, turn garment edge to inside along foldline, turning in ¼" (6mm) on raw edge. (For knit fabrics, edge may be left unfinished). Press. Stitch close to garment edge.

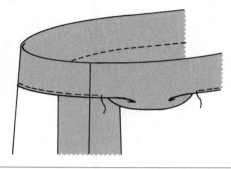

2

Cut elastic the measurement of body area plus 1" (25mm), or follow elastic chart on pattern instruction sheet.

3

Insert elastic through opening, lapping ends; hold with safety pin. Try on and adjust, if necessary. Stitch ends of elastic securely.

4

Stitch opening, stretching elastic, so garment is flat while stitching.

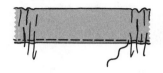

Collar With Band

CUT IN ONE

1

Turn self facing to inside along foldline; press. Baste raw edges together. STAYSTITCH neck edge.

2

INTERFACE wrong side of one collar section. Turn in seam allowance on notched edge of interfaced collar section. Press, easing in fullness. Trim pressed seam allowance to ⅜″ (10mm).

3

Stitch collar sections together, pivoting at small ●'s and leaving notched edges open. Clip to small ●'s.

4

TRIM and CLIP seam.

5

Turn; press.

6

Pin collar to neck edge, matching small ● ●'s to shoulder seams and clipping garment neck edge where necessary. Stitch, keeping pressed edge free.

7

Trim and clip seam. Press seam toward collar. SLIPSTITCH pressed edge over seam.

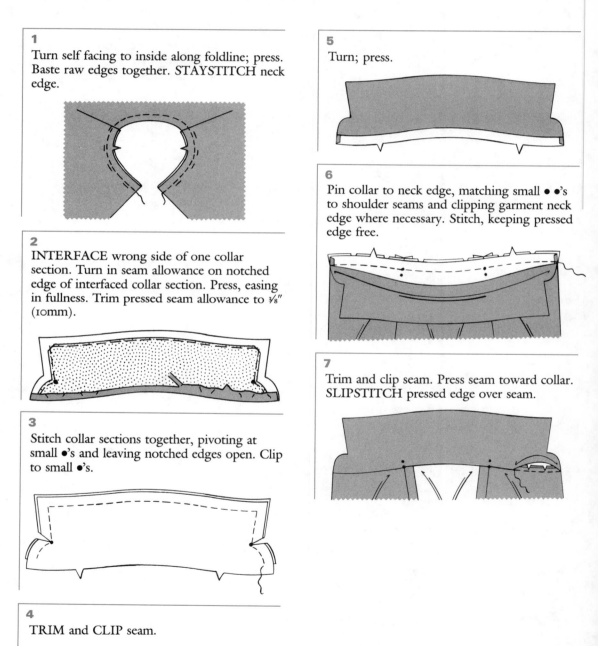

Collar With Band

8

Leave collar plain or use one of the following methods to finish collar and band:

EDGESTITCH,

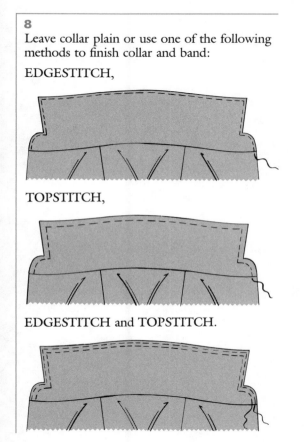

TOPSTITCH,

EDGESTITCH and TOPSTITCH.

Collar With Band

CUT SEPARATELY

1

Turn self facing to inside along foldline; press. Baste raw edges together. STAYSTITCH neck edge.

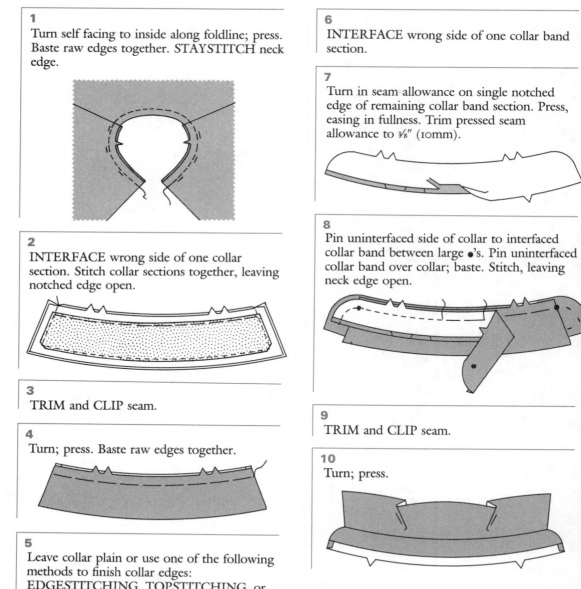

2

INTERFACE wrong side of one collar section. Stitch collar sections together, leaving notched edge open.

3

TRIM and CLIP seam.

4

Turn; press. Baste raw edges together.

5

Leave collar plain or use one of the following methods to finish collar edges:
EDGESTITCHING, TOPSTITCHING, or EDGESTITCHING and TOPSTITCHING (see Collar With Band, Cut In One, and Stand-up Collar, Without Neckline Facing).

6

INTERFACE wrong side of one collar band section.

7

Turn in seam allowance on single notched edge of remaining collar band section. Press, easing in fullness. Trim pressed seam allowance to ⅜" (10mm).

8

Pin uninterfaced side of collar to interfaced collar band between large ●'s. Pin uninterfaced collar band over collar; baste. Stitch, leaving neck edge open.

9

TRIM and CLIP seam.

10

Turn; press.

Collar With Band

Cut Separately, Continued

11

Pin interfaced collar band to neck edge, matching small ●●'s to shoulder seams and clipping garment neck edge where necessary. Stitch, keeping pressed edge free.

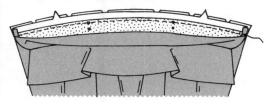

12

Trim and clip seam. Press seam toward collar band. SLIPSTITCH pressed edge over seam.

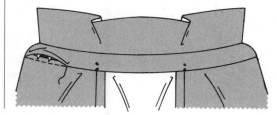

13

If desired, EDGESTITCH collar band.

Collars

Collar With Tie

1

Turn self facing to inside along foldline; press. Baste raw edges together. STAYSTITCH neck edge.

2

Stitch collar sections together at center back.

3

REINFORCE neck edge of collar through symbols.

4

With right sides together, fold collar and tie ends along foldline. Stitch tie ends, leaving open between symbols.

5

Clip to symbols.

6

TRIM seam.

7

Turn; press.

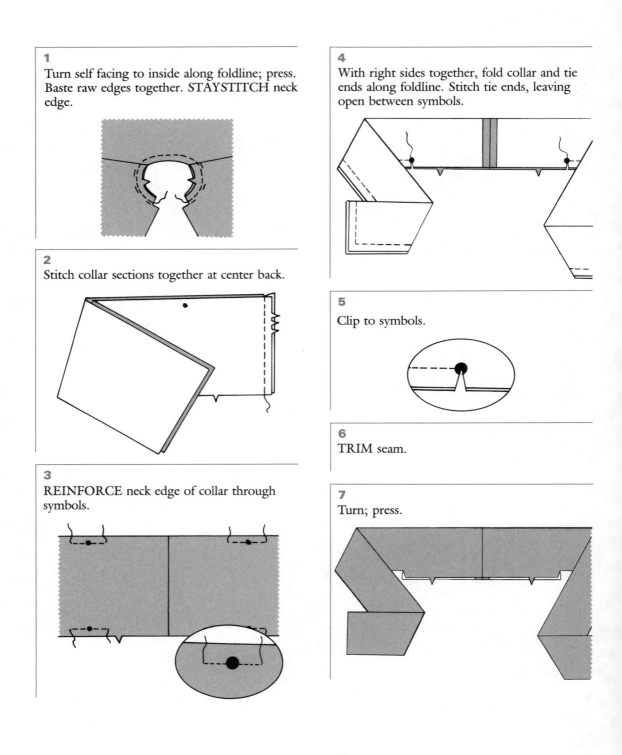

Collar With Tie

Continued

8

Turn in seam allowance on unnotched edge of collar; press. Trim pressed seam allowance to ⅜" (10mm).

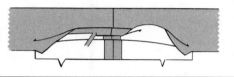

9

Pin collar to neck edge, matching small ●●'s to shoulder seams and clipping garment neck edge where necessary. Stitch, keeping pressed edge of collar free.

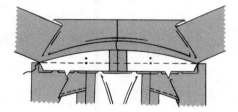

10

Trim and clip seam. Press seam toward collar. SLIPSTITCH pressed edge over seam.

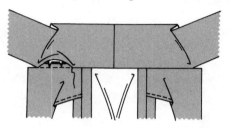

Flat Collar

WITH FOLDED FRONT OPENING EDGES

1

STAYSTITCH neck edge.

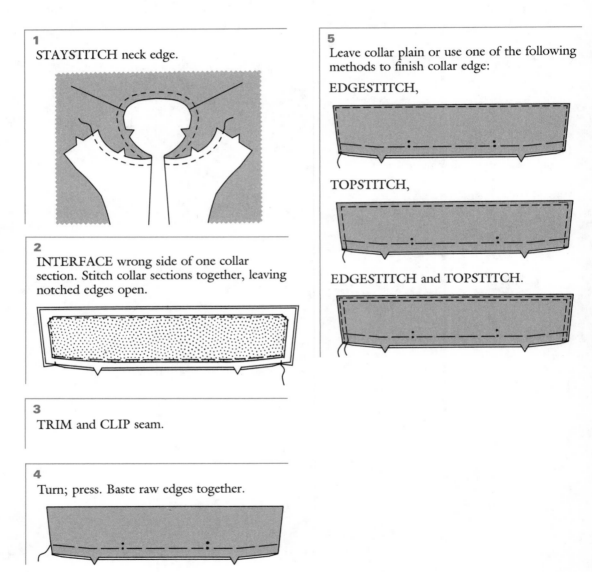

2

INTERFACE wrong side of one collar section. Stitch collar sections together, leaving notched edges open.

3

TRIM and CLIP seam.

4

Turn; press. Baste raw edges together.

5

Leave collar plain or use one of the following methods to finish collar edge:

EDGESTITCH,

TOPSTITCH,

EDGESTITCH and TOPSTITCH.

Flat Collar

With Folded Front Opening Edges, Continued

6

Pin collar to neck edge between large ●'s, interfaced side up, matching small ●●'s to shoulder seams and clipping garment neck edge where necessary; baste.

7

STAYSTITCH neck edge of back neck facing.

8

Stitch back neck facing to front self facings at shoulders. FINISH outer edge.

9

Turn self facings to outside along foldlines. Pin facing to neck edge over collar, clipping facing where necessary. Stitch.

10

TRIM and CLIP seam.

11

Turn facing to inside; press. TACK at shoulder seams.

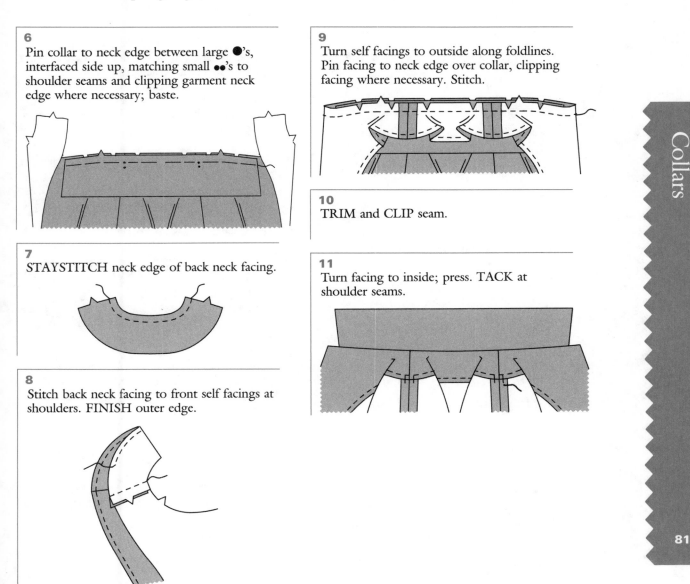

Collars

Flat Collar

WITH SEAMED FRONT OPENING EDGES

1

STAYSTITCH neck edge between large ●'s.

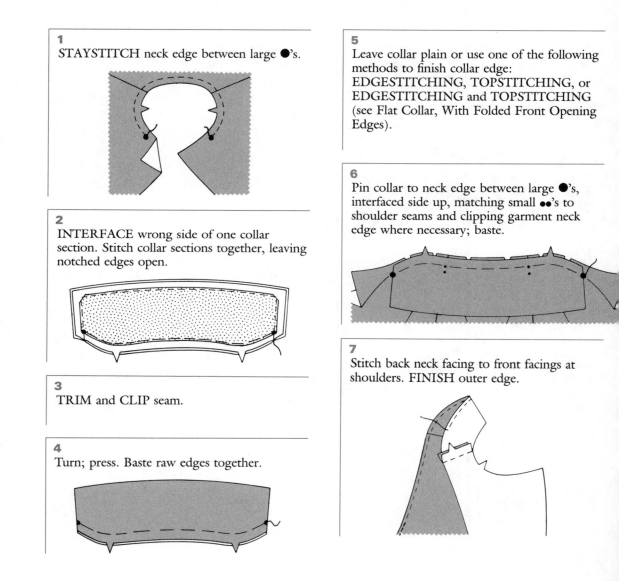

2

INTERFACE wrong side of one collar section. Stitch collar sections together, leaving notched edges open.

3

TRIM and CLIP seam.

4

Turn; press. Baste raw edges together.

5

Leave collar plain or use one of the following methods to finish collar edge: EDGESTITCHING, TOPSTITCHING, or EDGESTITCHING and TOPSTITCHING (see Flat Collar, With Folded Front Opening Edges).

6

Pin collar to neck edge between large ●'s, interfaced side up, matching small ●●'s to shoulder seams and clipping garment neck edge where necessary; baste.

7

Stitch back neck facing to front facings at shoulders. FINISH outer edge.

Flat Collar

With Seamed Front Opening Edges, Continued

8

STAYSTITCH facing neck edge between large ●'s.

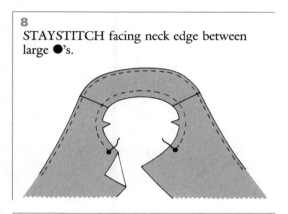

9

Pin facing to front and neck edge, matching seams and symbols and clipping facing where necessary. Stitch.

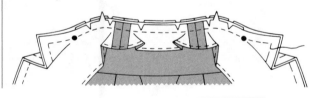

10

TRIM and CLIP seam.

11

Turn facing to inside; press. TACK at shoulder seams.

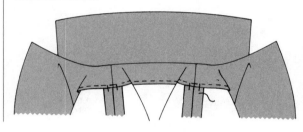

Notched Collar

WITH BACK NECK FACING

1

STAYSTITCH garment neck edge between large ●'s.

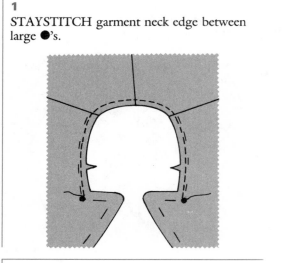

2

INTERFACE wrong side of each under collar section and garment front. Stitch under collar sections together along center back.

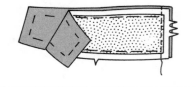

3

Pin under collar to neck edge of garment, matching large ●'s and placing small ●●'s at shoulder seams; clip garment where necessary. Baste. Stitch between large ●'s.

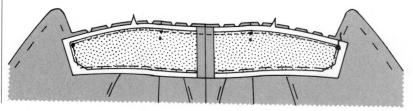

4

TRIM seam.

5

Stitch front facing sections to back neck facing at shoulders. FINISH outer edge of facing, unless garment will be lined.

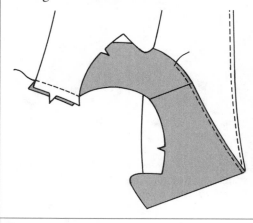

6

STAYSTITCH neck edge of facing between large ●'s.

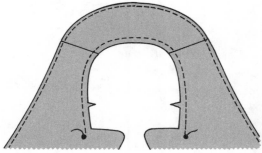

Notched Collar

7
Pin upper collar to neck edge of facing, matching large ●'s and placing small ●●'s at shoulder seams; clip facing where necessary. Baste. Stitch between large ●'s.

8
TRIM seam.

9
Pin upper collar and lapel facing to under collar and garment. Stitch front opening and lapel edges, stretching front to fit between large ●'s and ending at upper large ●'s. Stitch collar edges together between large ●'s, stretching under collar to fit.

10
TRIM seam.

11
Turn facing to inside, turning collar right side out; press.

12
Lift up facing; hand-sew neck seams together loosely.

13
Turn facing down. TACK at shoulder seams.

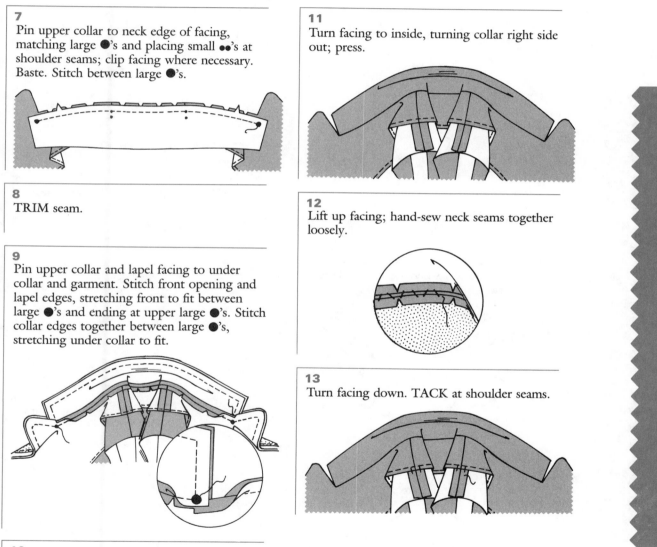

Collars

85

Notched Collar

WITHOUT BACK NECK FACING

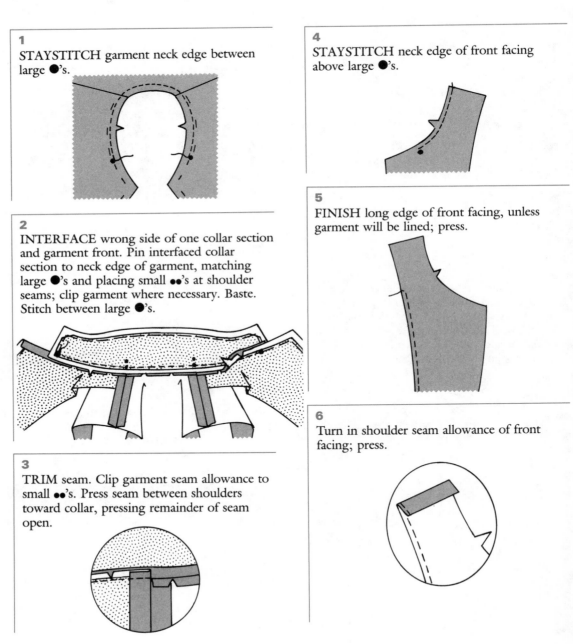

1

STAYSTITCH garment neck edge between large ●'s.

2

INTERFACE wrong side of one collar section and garment front. Pin interfaced collar section to neck edge of garment, matching large ●'s and placing small ●●'s at shoulder seams; clip garment where necessary. Baste. Stitch between large ●'s.

3

TRIM seam. Clip garment seam allowance to small ●●'s. Press seam between shoulders toward collar, pressing remainder of seam open.

4

STAYSTITCH neck edge of front facing above large ●'s.

5

FINISH long edge of front facing, unless garment will be lined; press.

6

Turn in shoulder seam allowance of front facing; press.

Notched Collar

Without Back Neck Facing, Continued

7

Pin uninterfaced collar section to neck edges of front facings, matching large ●'s and placing small ●●'s at shoulder seamlines; clip front facings where necessary. Baste. Stitch between large ●'s and ends of facings.

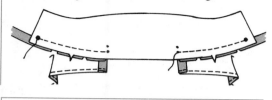

8

Press seam allowances open, turning in ⅝" (15mm) between small ●●'s. Trim seam allowances to ⅜" (10mm).

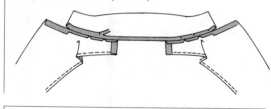

9

Pin uninterfaced collar and front facings to interfaced collar and garment, matching symbols. Stitch along front opening and lapel edges, ending at large ●'s.

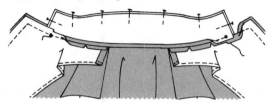

10

Stitch collar edges together between large ●'s.

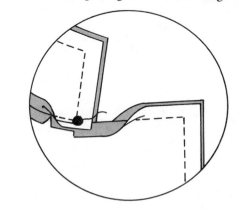

11

TRIM seam.

12

Turn front facings to inside, turning collar right side out; press.

13

Lift up front facings; hand-sew neck seams together loosely. SLIPSTITCH pressed edged of uninterfaced collar over back neck seam. Turn front facings down. SLIPSTITCH pressed edges in place.

Collars

87

Peter Pan Collar

ONE-PIECE WITH FRONT OPENING

1
STAYSTITCH neck edge between large ●'s.

2
INTERFACE wrong side of one collar section. Stitch remaining collar section to interfaced collar, leaving notched edges open.

3
TRIM and CLIP seam.

4
Turn; press. Baste raw edges together.

5
Leave collar plain or use one of the following methods to finish collar edge: EDGESTITCHING, TOPSTITCHING, or EDGESTITCHING and TOPSTITCHING (see Flat Collar, With Folded Front Opening Edges).

6
Pin collar to neck edge between large ●'s, interfaced side up, matching centers and small ●●'s to shoulder seams. Clip garment neck edge where necessary; baste.

7
Assemble and attach facing same as for Flat Collar, With Seamed Front Opening Edges.

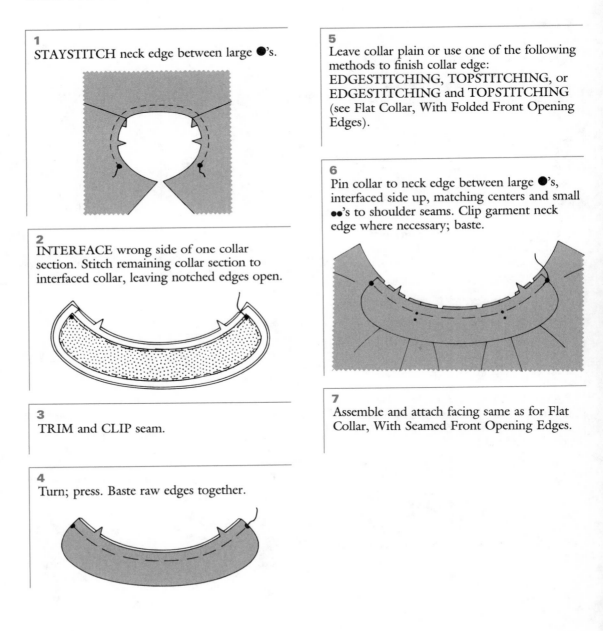

Peter Pan Collar

TWO-PIECE WITH BACK OPENING

1

STAYSTITCH neck edge.

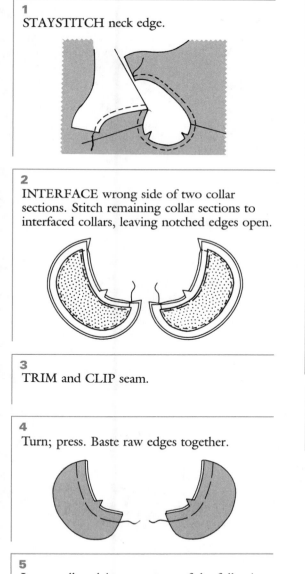

2

INTERFACE wrong side of two collar sections. Stitch remaining collar sections to interfaced collars, leaving notched edges open.

3

TRIM and CLIP seam.

4

Turn; press. Baste raw edges together.

5

Leave collar plain or use one of the following methods to finish collar edges: EDGESTITCHING, TOPSTITCHING, or EDGESTITCHING and TOPSTITCHING (see Flat Collar, With Folded Front Opening Edges).

6

TACK collar sections together at center front.

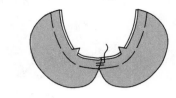

7

Pin collar to neck edge between large ●'s, interfaced side up, matching centers and small ●●'s to shoulder seams. Clip garment neck edge where necessary; baste.

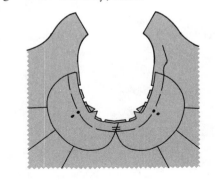

8

Assemble and attach facing same as for Flat Collar, With Folded Front Opening Edges.

Shawl Collar

WITH BACK NECK FACING

1

STAYSTITCH neck edge.

2

Stitch under collar sections together along center back.

3

Pin under collar to neck edge, matching small ••'s to shoulder seams and clipping garment neck edge where necessary. Stitch.

4

TRIM seam.

5

INTERFACE wrong side of upper collar/front facing. REINFORCE inner corner of upper collar/front facing, pivoting at small •. Clip to small •.

6

Stitch center back seam in upper collar/front facing.

7

STAYSTITCH neck edge of back neck facing.

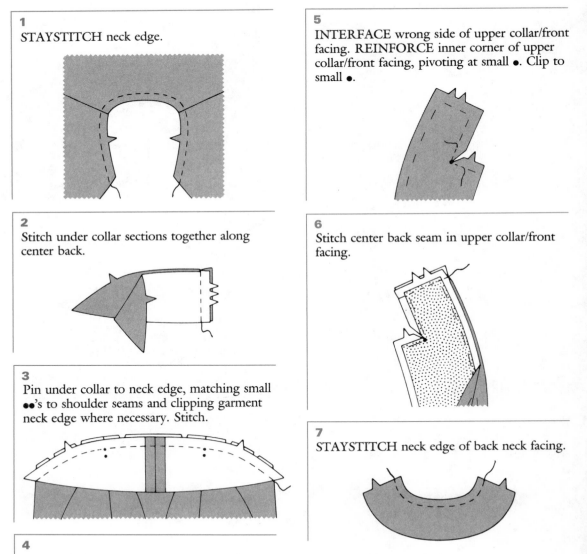

Shawl Collar

With Back Neck Facing, Continued

8
Pin back neck facing to upper collar/front facing, matching symbols at shoulders and neck edge and clipping where necessary. Stitch, pivoting at small ●'s.

9
TRIM and CLIP seam; press open.

10
FINISH long unnotched edge, unless garment will be lined.

11
Pin upper collar/front facing to garment and under collar. Stitch. If necessary, stretch under collar and garment to fit between large ●'s.

12
TRIM and CLIP seam.

13
Turn facing to inside, turning collar right side out; press.

14
Lift up facing; hand-sew neck seams together loosely.

15
Turn facing down. TACK at shoulder seams.

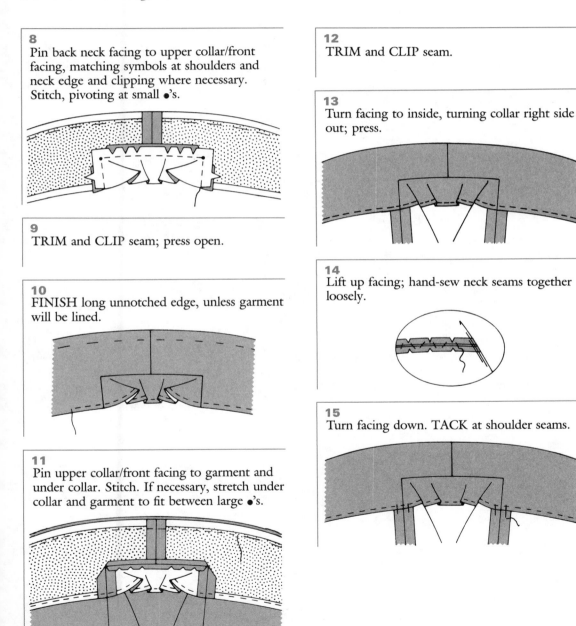

Shawl Collar

WITH BACK NECK/SHOULDER FACING

1
STAYSTITCH neck edge.

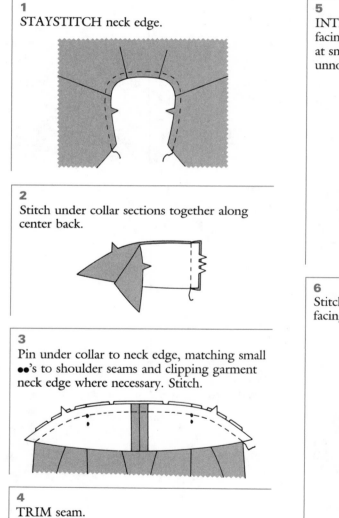

2
Stitch under collar sections together along center back.

3
Pin under collar to neck edge, matching small ●●'s to shoulder seams and clipping garment neck edge where necessary. Stitch.

4
TRIM seam.

5
INTERFACE wrong side of upper collar/front facing. REINFORCE inner corner, pivoting at small ●. Clip to small ●. FINISH long unnotched edge, unless garment will be lined.

6
Stitch center back seam in upper collar/front facing.

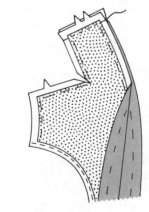

Shawl Collar

7

Stitch any darts in back facing. Press darts toward center. (For back facing without darts, omit this step). FINISH lower edge of facing, unless garment will be lined.

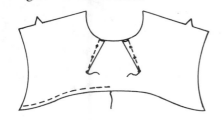

8

STAYSTITCH neck edge of back facing.

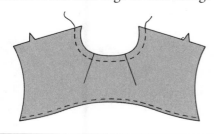

9

Pin back facing to upper collar/front facing, matching symbols at shoulders and neck edge and clipping where necessary. Stitch, pivoting at small ●'s.

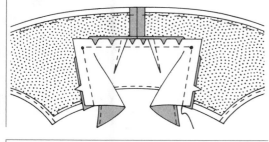

10

TRIM and CLIP seam.

11

Pin upper collar/front facing to garment and under collar. Stitch. If necessary, stretch under collar and garment to fit between large ●'s.

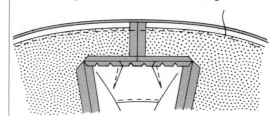

12

TRIM and CLIP seam.

Collars

93

Shawl Collar

With Back Neck/Shoulder Facing, Continued

13

Turn facing to inside, turning collar right side out; press.

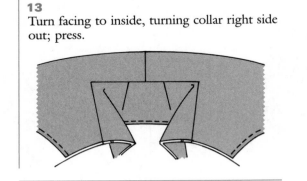

14

Lift up facing, hand-sew neck seams together loosely.

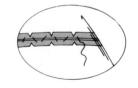

15

Turn facing down. Baste armhole edges together.

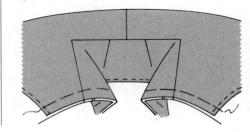

Shawl Collar

WITHOUT BACK NECK FACING

1

STAYSTITCH neck edge.

2

Stitch under collar sections together along center back.

3

Pin under collar to neck edge, matching small ●●'s to shoulder seams and clipping garment neck edge where necessary. Stitch.

4

Trim seam. Clip garment seam allowance to small ●●'s. Press seam between shoulders toward under collar; press remainder of seam open.

5

INTERFACE wrong side of upper collar/front facing. REINFORCE inner corner of upper collar/front facing, pivoting at small ●. Clip to small ●. FINISH long unnotched edge, unless garment will be lined.

6

Stitch center back seam in upper collar/front facing.

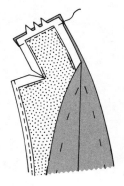

Shawl Collar

Without Back Neck Facing, Continued

7

Turn in neck and shoulder seam allowances; press. Trim pressed seam allowances to ⅜" (10mm).

8

Pin upper collar/front facing to garment, matching symbols at shoulders and neck edge. Stitch. If necessary, stretch under collar and garment to fit between large ●'s.

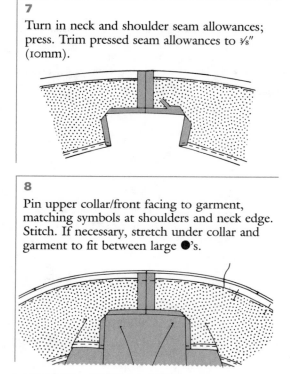

9

TRIM and CLIP seam.

10

Turn facing to inside, turning collar right side out; press.

11

SLIPSTITCH pressed neck and shoulder edges over seams.

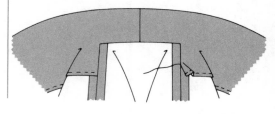

Stand-up Collar

WITH NECKLINE FACING

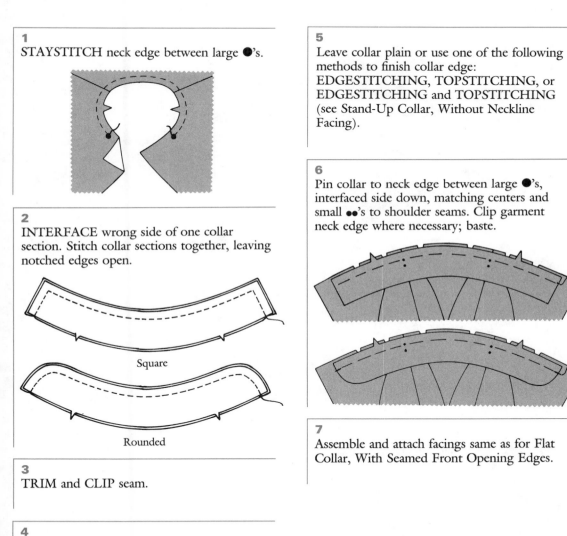

1

STAYSTITCH neck edge between large ●'s.

2

INTERFACE wrong side of one collar section. Stitch collar sections together, leaving notched edges open.

Square

Rounded

3

TRIM and CLIP seam.

4

Turn; press. Baste raw edges together.

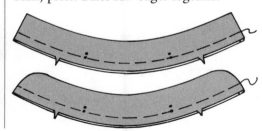

5

Leave collar plain or use one of the following methods to finish collar edge: EDGESTITCHING, TOPSTITCHING, or EDGESTITCHING and TOPSTITCHING (see Stand-Up Collar, Without Neckline Facing).

6

Pin collar to neck edge between large ●'s, interfaced side down, matching centers and small ●●'s to shoulder seams. Clip garment neck edge where necessary; baste.

7

Assemble and attach facings same as for Flat Collar, With Seamed Front Opening Edges.

Stand-up Collar

WITHOUT NECKLINE FACING

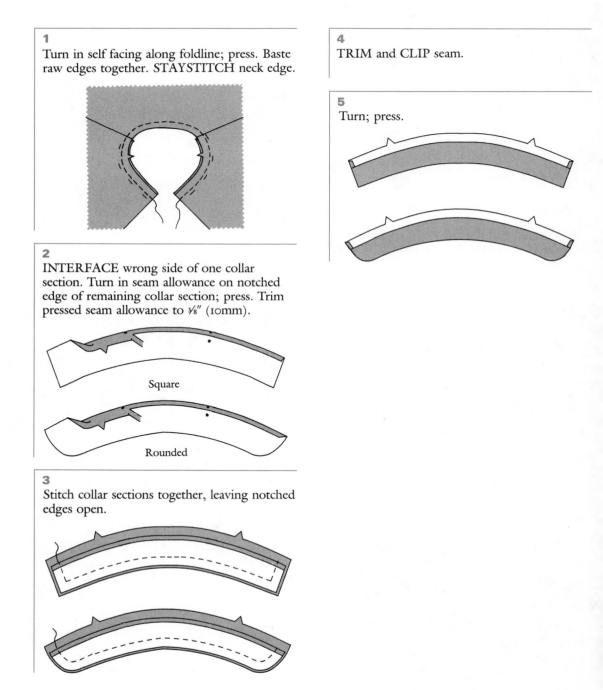

1

Turn in self facing along foldline; press. Baste raw edges together. STAYSTITCH neck edge.

2

INTERFACE wrong side of one collar section. Turn in allowance on notched edge of remaining collar section; press. Trim pressed seam allowance to ⅜″ (10mm).

Square

Rounded

3

Stitch collar sections together, leaving notched edges open.

4

TRIM and CLIP seam.

5

Turn; press.

Stand-up Collar

6

Pin collar to neck edge, interfaced side down, matching small ••'s to shoulder seams and clipping garment neck edge where necessary. Stitch, keeping pressed edge free.

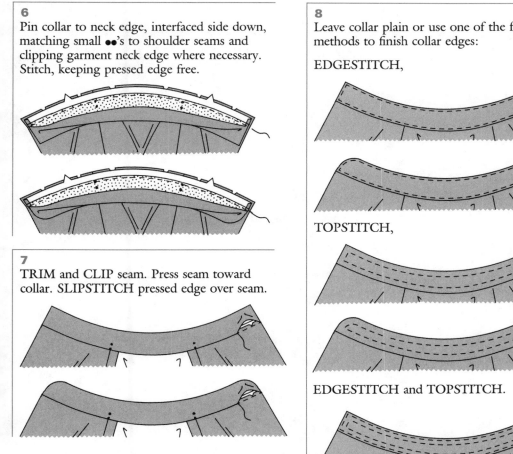

7

TRIM and CLIP seam. Press seam toward collar. SLIPSTITCH pressed edge over seam.

8

Leave collar plain or use one of the following methods to finish collar edges:

EDGESTITCH,

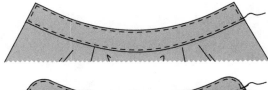

TOPSTITCH,

EDGESTITCH and TOPSTITCH.

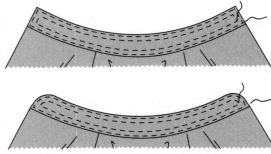

Collars

99

Making Cuff Openings

CONTINUOUS LAP

1

REINFORCE lower edge of sleeve along stitching line. Slash between stitching to upper end.

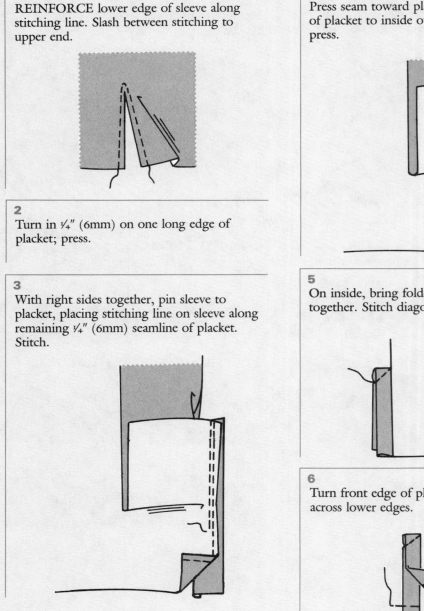

2

Turn in ¼" (6mm) on one long edge of placket; press.

3

With right sides together, pin sleeve to placket, placing stitching line on sleeve along remaining ¼" (6mm) seamline of placket. Stitch.

4

Press seam toward placket. Turn pressed edge of placket to inside over seam. SLIPSTITCH; press.

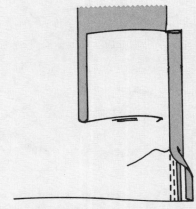

5

On inside, bring folded edges of placket together. Stitch diagonally across upper end.

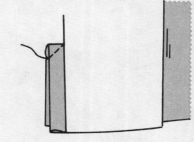

6

Turn front edge of placket to inside. Baste across lower edges.

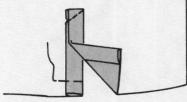

Cuffs

Making Cuff Openings

DART

1

Stitch dart in sleeve between small •'s. Cut along slash line to ▲.

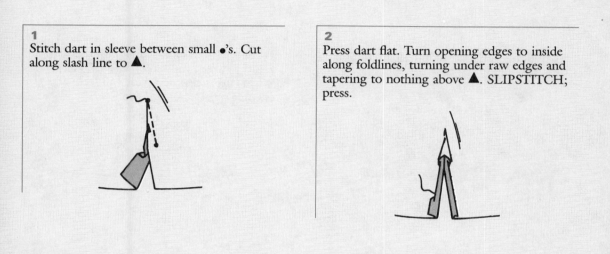

2

Press dart flat. Turn opening edges to inside along foldlines, turning under raw edges and tapering to nothing above ▲. SLIPSTITCH; press.

IN-SEAM

1

Make ⅝" (15mm) or ⅜" (10mm) NARROW HEM at sleeve opening, tapering hem to nothing above large ●.

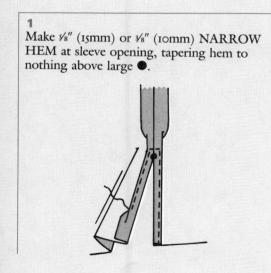

2

Stitch, pivoting across seam allowance ¼" (6mm) above large ●.

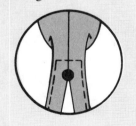

Making Cuff Openings

PLEAT

1

REINFORCE lower edge of sleeve through large ●'s. Clip to large ●'s.

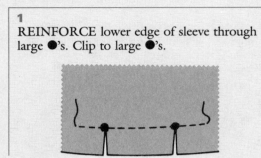

2

Hand-sew or machine-stitch a NARROW HEM between clips. WHIPSTITCH ends. When cuff is closed, a pleat will form at opening.

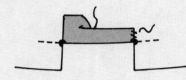

Preparing Lower Edge of Sleeve

1

Stitch sleeve seam.

2

Use one of the following methods to prepare lower edge of sleeve:

EASESTITCH,

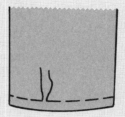

GATHER,

Pleat: On outside, crease along lines of small ●'s. Bring creases to lines of large ●'s; baste. Baste across lower edge.

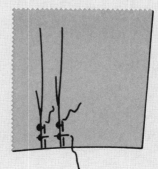

Band Cuff

WITH OPENING IN SEAM

1

INTERFACE wrong side of cuff.

2

Turn in seam allowance on long unnotched edge of cuff; press. Trim pressed seam allowance to ⅜" (10mm).

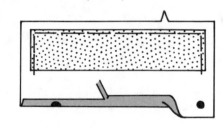

3

Pin cuff to sleeve, placing large ●'s at opening edges and matching symbols. Adjust ease or gathers, if necessary; baste. Stitch.

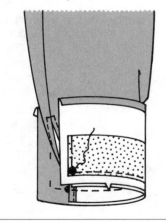

4

TRIM seam. Press seam toward cuff.

5

With right sides together, fold cuff along foldline; stitch ends.

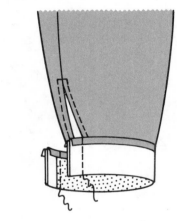

6

TRIM seams.

7

Turn; press. SLIPSTITCH pressed edge over seam and extension edges together.

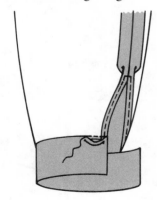

Band Cuff

With Opening in Seam, Continued

8

Leave cuff plain, or use one of the following methods to finish cuff edges:

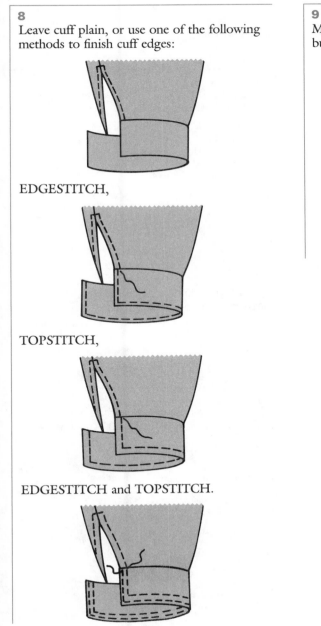

EDGESTITCH,

TOPSTITCH,

EDGESTITCH and TOPSTITCH.

9

Make buttonhole in cuff at marking. Sew button to cuff at marking on extension.

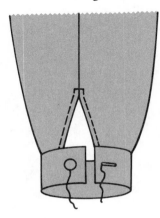

Band Cuff

WITH OPENING IN SLEEVE BACK

1
INTERFACE wrong side of cuff.

2
Turn in seam allowance on long unnotched edge of cuff; press. Trim pressed seam allowance to ⅜" (10mm).

3
Pin cuff to sleeve, placing small ●●'s at underarm seam and large ●'s at opening edges. Adjust ease or gathers, if necessary; baste. Stitch.

4
TRIM seam. Press seam toward cuff.

5
With right sides together, fold cuff along foldline; stitch ends.

6
TRIM seams.

7
Turn; press. SLIPSTITCH pressed edge over seam and extension edges together.

8
Leave cuff plain or use one of the following methods to finish cuff edges: EDGESTITCHING, TOPSTITCHING, EDGESTITCHING and TOPSTITCHING (see Band Cuff, With Opening in Seam).

9
Make buttonhole in cuff at marking. Sew button to cuff at marking on extension.

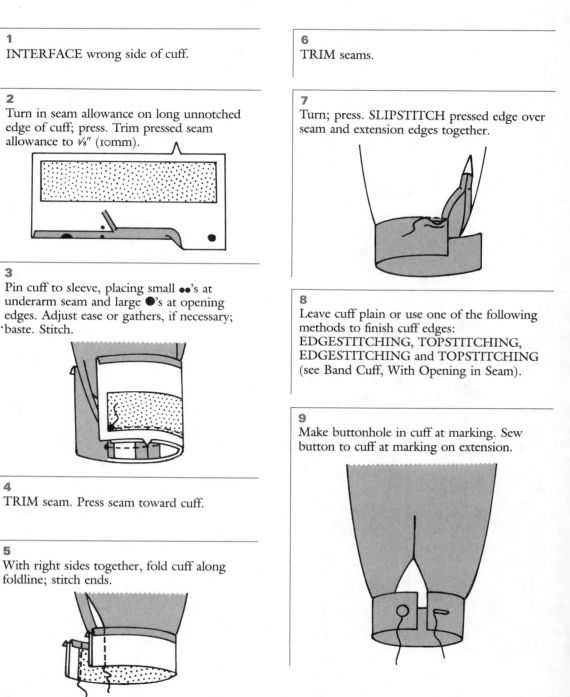

Barrel or Turned-back Cuff

1

INTERFACE wrong side of cuff.

2

Stitch ends of cuff together.

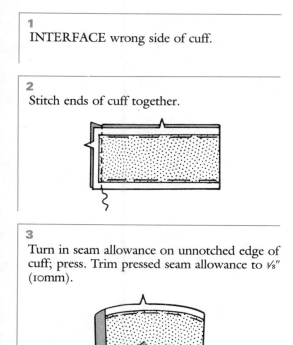

3

Turn in seam allowance on unnotched edge of cuff; press. Trim pressed seam allowance to ⅜″ (10mm).

4

Pin cuff to sleeve, matching symbols and seams. Stitch.

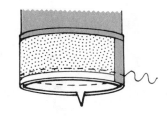

5

TRIM seam. Press seam toward cuff. Turn cuff to inside along foldline. SLIPSTITCH pressed edge over seam.

Barrel or Turned-back Cuff

Continued

6

Leave cuff plain or use one of the following methods to finish cuff edges:

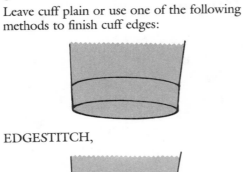

EDGESTITCH,

TOPSTITCH,

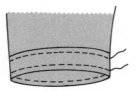

EDGESTITCH and TOPSTITCH.

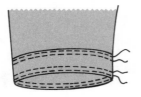

7

For turned-back cuff, turn cuff to outside along roll line; press. TACK at seam.

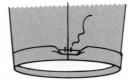

Cuff Link Buttons

FABRIC SHANK

1

Make a fabric strip (see Fabric Carrier Strips: Folded and Stitched).

2

Make strip long enough to pass through both cuff edges and turn under at ends.

3

Sew buttons to ends of strip. Fasten thread securely.

THREAD SHANK

1

Sew two buttons together. Use a length of heavy thread long enough to pass through both cuff edges and form about a ½″ (13mm) shank.

2

Work BLANKET STITCHES over thread. Fasten thread securely.

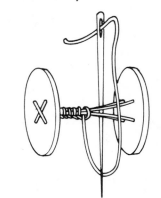

Rib Knit Band Cuff

1

For woven fabric, STAYSTITCH lower edge of sleeve or leg.

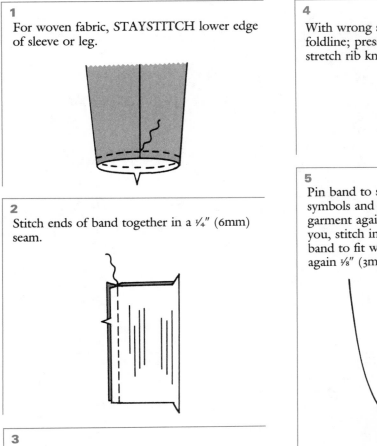

2

Stitch ends of band together in a ¼″ (6mm) seam.

3

Press seam open with fingers.

4

With wrong sides together, fold band along foldline; press lightly, being careful not to stretch rib knit. Pin raw edges together.

5

Pin band to sleeve or leg edge, matching symbols and seams. Working from inside, with garment against machine and band toward you, stitch in a ¼″ (6mm) seam, stretching band to fit without stretching garment. Stitch again ⅛″ (3mm) away in seam allowance.

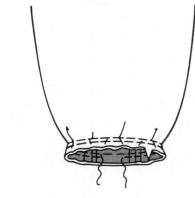

6

Press seam toward garment.

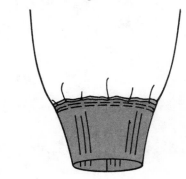

Soft Turned-back Cuff

1

FINISH raw edge. Turn lower edge to inside along foldline. Baste close to fold.

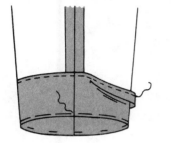

2

To form cuff, turn lower edge to outside along hemline. Baste close to fold through all thicknesses. TACK at seams.

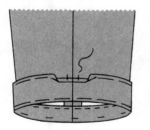

3

Sew hem in place; press.

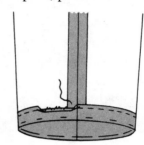

Cutting Guidelines

- Use long, bent-handled shears; cut with steady, even slashes. Never cut with pinking shears. Use pinking shears only to finish seams during construction.

- Never lift fabric from table; keep one hand flat on pattern piece while cutting.

- Use points of scissors to cut notches outward. Cut groups of notches in continuous blocks. For speed, cut off notches and CLIP-MARK no more than ¼" (6mm) into seam allowance.

- Cut each pattern piece the correct number of times. Details such as pockets, cuffs, welts, and belt carriers may need more than two pieces. This will be indicated on the pattern piece itself, as well as on the layout.

- Fold cut pieces softly; lay them on a flat surface.

- Save fabric scraps left from cutting. They may be needed for bound buttonholes, sleeve plackets, and other sections not cut from pattern pieces. Fabric scraps are also needed to test tension and stitch length, as well as fusing, marking and pressing techniques.

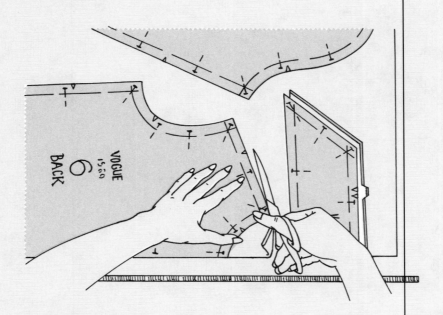

Stitching Darts

ALL DARTS

1
Begin stitching at wide end, tapering to nothing at pointed end. Take the last 2 or 3 stitches directly on the fold (do not backstitch).

2
Secure thread ends at point with a knot, working it to the very end of the dart.

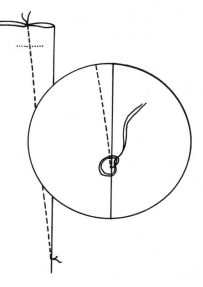

CONTOUR DARTS

1
Begin stitching just beyond center of dart, at widest point, tapering to nothing at one pointed end. Tie knot.

2
Begin stitching again at widest point, slightly overlapping stitching lines. Taper to nothing at second pointed end. Tie knot.

113

Trimming and Clipping Darts

CONTOUR DARTS

1

Clip fold along curve, as necessary, to relieve strain.

2

Allow clips to spread when pressing dart.

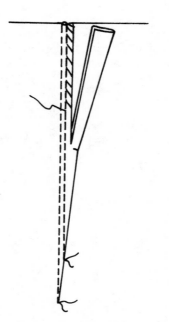

DARTS IN SHEER FABRICS

1

Stitch approximately ⅛″ (3mm) from first stitching. Trim ⅛″ (3mm) from second stitching.

2

OVERCAST, zigzag or OVERLOCK raw edges.

Trimming and Clipping Darts

1
Trim to within ½″–1″ (13mm–25mm) of point.

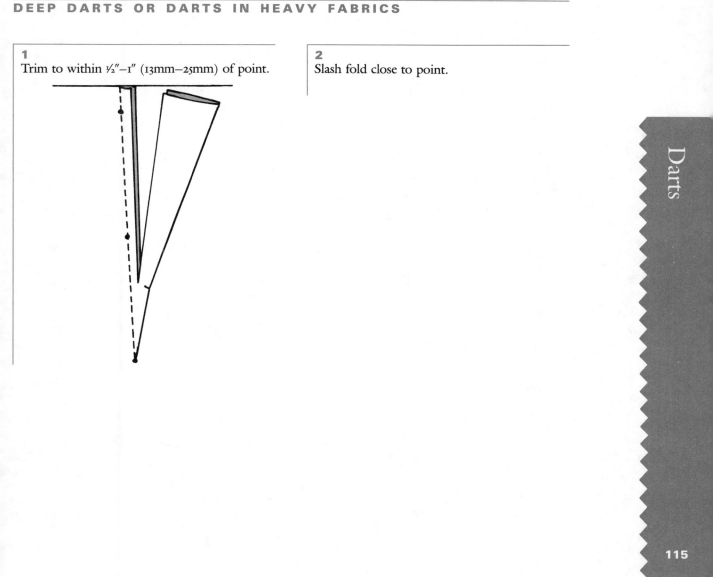

2
Slash fold close to point.

Pressing Darts

Use these guidelines when pressing darts:
Always press darts before major seams are stitched
or before intersecting by a seam.

1

Press dart fold and stitching line flat to blend stitches into fabric. Do not crease fabric beyond point.

2

Press vertical darts toward center front or center back.

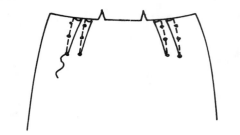

3

Press horizontal darts downward.

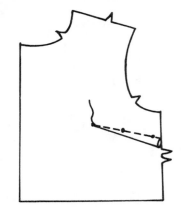

4

Press slashed area of deep darts open; press point flat.

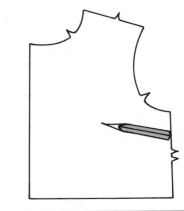

5

Spread garment open. Press dart over curved surface (tailor's ham or press mitt). Place brown paper between dart and garment to prevent ridges from forming on outside.

Drawstrings

DRAWSTRINGS WITH ELASTIC

1

Use elastic ⅛" (3mm) narrower than the finished width of casing. For tie ends, use cording, tubing, braid, leather strips or ribbon. Or, make self-fabric tie ends (see Fabric Carrier Strips: Stitched and Turned, or Fabric Loops, Making Tubing).

2

Cut elastic 5" (12.5 cm) less than body measurement at casing position.

3

Cut tie ends long enough to go around remainder of body at casing position plus an extra amount to allow for tying, as desired.

4

Pin one tie end to each end of elastic, lapping ends ½" (13mm). Stitch securely.

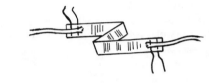

5

Use safety pin or bodkin to insert through opening in casing. If desired, knot and/or WHIPSTITCH tie ends.

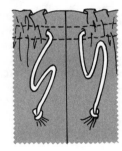

REGULAR DRAWSTRINGS

1

Use cording, tubing, braid, leather strips or ribbon for drawstring. Or, make a self-fabric drawstring (see Fabric Carrier Strips: Stitched and Turned, or Fabric Loops, Making Tubing).

2

Cut drawstring equal to body measurement at casing position plus an extra amount to allow for tying, as desired.

3

Use safety pin or bodkin to insert through opening in casing. If desired, knot and/or WHIPSTITCH drawstring ends.

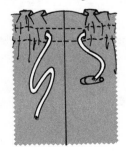

Knit Fabric Edge Finishes

FOR KNITS WHICH CURL OR RUN

There are special machine stitches to help prevent curling on lightweight knits (see Specialty Stitches, Multiple Zigzag and Overlock Stitches). Check your sewing machine manual for availability and directions.

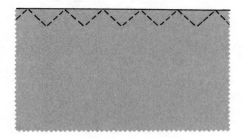

For knits which run, use an Overlock Stitch to stitch an edge or seam and finish it simultaneously (see Machine-stitched Edge Finishes, Overlock Stitch).

FOR KNITS WHICH DON'T CURL OR RUN

Leave edge unfinished since most knits don't ravel; or straight stitch ¼" (6mm) from the edge.

Woven Fabric Edge Finishes

BOUND EDGE FINISHES

Hong Kong Finish

For a nice-looking designer finish on unlined jackets or coats, or for a professional touch on fine fabrics, use the Hong Kong Finish.

1

Use 1" (25mm) wide bias strips of lining fabric or press open double-fold bias tape. With raw edges even and using small stitches, stitch bias strip to garment in ¼" (6mm) seam.

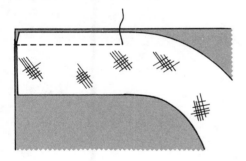

2

Press strip away from seam allowance.

3

Turn strip over seam. On right side, STITCH-IN-THE-DITCH along seam formed where binding and garment meet, catching bottom layer of binding and enclosing raw edge.

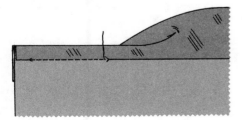

Purchased Binding

For a sturdy, attractive finish on unlined jackets, vests and coats, as well as heavyweight fabrics, use purchased binding.

1

Using purchased double-fold bias tape or nylon bias tape, encase raw edges, placing slightly narrower edge of tape on top; EDGESTITCH.

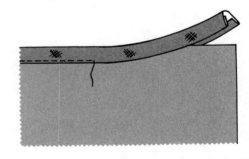

2

On curves, PRESHAPE binding first (see Single Binding, Machine-finished).

Woven Fabric Edge Finishes

HEM EDGE FINISHES

Seam Binding

To conceal a raw hem edge with a finish that is flat and will not create a ridge on the right side when pressed, use seam binding.

Place seam binding over raw edge and machine-stitch close to edge of binding.

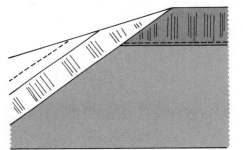

Stretch Lace

To conceal a raw hem edge with a finish that is flat and will not create a ridge on the right side when pressed, use stretch lace.

Place stretch lace over raw edge and machine-stitch close to edge of stretch lace.

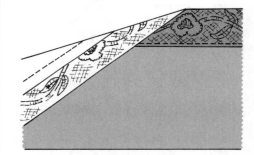

MACHINE-STITCHED EDGE FINISHES

Instead of stitching and then finishing edge with another step, use one of the following machine substitutes that does both simultaneously. Vary the stitch setting to suit the fabric weight.

Overedge Stitch

See machine manual for availability and directions.

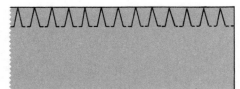

Overlock Stitch

This stitch is only available on an overlock or serger sewing machine; see machine manual for specific directions.

Woven Fabric Edge Finishes

STITCHED-AND-FINISHED EDGES

For unlined garments not worn over other garments, machine-stitch ¼" (6mm) from raw edge and finish with one of the following procedures; or see Machine-stitched Edge Finishes.

Overcasting

For fabrics which ravel easily, in a variety of weights, HAND-OVERCAST the raw edge, taking several stitches on the needle before pulling it through.

Or, use a machine zigzag stitch, instead of doing hand-overcasting.

Pinking

For tightly woven, lightweight fabrics which do not ravel easily, use pinking shears to cut along the edge, trying not to overlap cuts so pinking is evenly spaced.

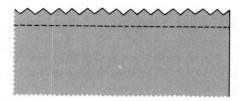

Turning and Stitching

For lightweight to medium weight fabrics, turn edge in along first stitching and machine-stitch close to fold.

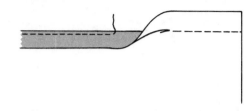

For straight seams in very lightweight or heavy weight fabrics, there are special seams which enclose the raw edges as the seam is made (see French, Mock French and Self-bound Seams).

Elastic Applications

ELASTIC APPLIED AT AN EDGE

Note: To use this method, stitch all garment seams; then apply elastic.

1

Cut elastic the measurement of body area plus 1″ (25mm), or follow elastic chart on pattern instruction sheet. Try on elastic; adjust fit, allowing for overlapping ends.

2

Overlap ends and stitch elastic together to form a circle. Divide elastic into quarters and mark.

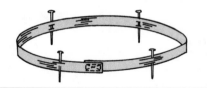

3

Trim garment seam allowance to equal the width of elastic. Divide garment edge into quarters and mark.

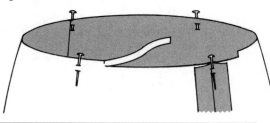

4

Matching markings, pin elastic even with raw edge on wrong side of garment.

5

ZIGZAG-STITCH or stretch-stitch (see machine manual) elastic to garment, stretching elastic to fit.

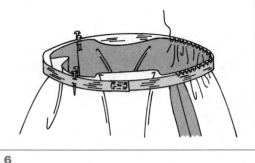

6

Turn elastic and fabric to inside of garment and pin. Straight-stitch or ZIGZAG-STITCH close to cut inner edge, stretching elastic during stitching.

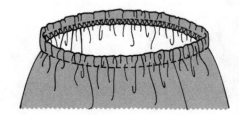

Elastic can also be applied to an edge with an overlock machine (see Overlock, Elastic).

Elastic Applications

Note: To use this method, leave the last seam of garment open until elastic is applied.

1

Cut elastic the measurement of body area plus 1″ (25mm), or follow elastic chart on pattern instruction sheet. Try on elastic; adjust fit, allowing extra for seaming.

2

Divide elastic and garment in half and mark.

Pin elastic to wrong side of garment, matching markings and centering over placement line. ZIGZAG-STITCH or stretch-stitch (see machine manual) elastic to garment, stretching elastic to fit.

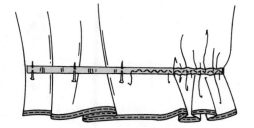

3

Stitch last seam.

To enclose elastic instead of applying it directly to garment, see Casings and Waistbands. To use decorative elastic as a waistband, see Waistbands.

Elastic

123

Embroidery Preparation

THREADS: CREWEL YARN

Wool or acrylic crewel yarn consists of three lightly-twisted plies or strands that can be separated easily. Though best used on medium weight to heavyweight fabrics, crewel yarn is also good on textured or pile fabrics because it shows up well.

Separate crewel yarn into the required number of strands before using. The instructions for crewel designs usually specify how many strands to use.

THREADS: EMBROIDERY FLOSS

The most familiar form of embroidery floss is shiny cotton, but it also comes in matte-finish cotton and in shiny, crimped rayon. Each is suitable for most fabrics and crafts.

Separate six-strand embroidery floss into one or more strands before using, depending on how bold or delicate an effect is desired. The instructions for embroidery designs usually specify how many strands to use.

THREADS: SPECIALTY THREADS

Perle cotton is twisted thread that comes in different thicknesses. The thinner ones can be used in place of embroidery floss. Narrow $\frac{1}{16}''$ (2mm) satin ribbon and very fine braid are also suitable for decorative embroidery on all but the sheerest fabrics.

Embroidery Preparation

NEEDLES: CHENILLE

Shorter than a tapestry needle, the chenille needle has a sharp point and a large eye. It is a good choice for thick threads and yarns.

NEEDLES: CREWEL

A good all-purpose needle, the crewel needle is long and sharp, with an elongated eye.

NEEDLES: SELECTION

Match the embroidery needle to the thread and fabric being used. Choose a needle that pierces fabric easily: a fine one for closely woven, lightweight fabrics; a heavier one for more coarsely woven, heavier weight fabrics. The eye of the needle should be just large enough for the thread to pass through. The point of the needle should be sharp or blunt according to the fineness or coarseness of the fabric weave. The needles come in a variety of sizes.

NEEDLES: TAPESTRY

Its blunt point makes the tapestry needle ideal for working on coarse or open-weave fabrics as well as on needlepoint canvas. Its long, rounded eye accommodates bulky threads and yarns.

Embroidery Preparation

FINISHING

Place finished piece of embroidery face down on a thick terry towel. Using a damp press cloth, press lightly with moderate heat setting. Remove press cloth and allow to dry. Repeat if necessary, being careful not to overpress, as most embroidery stitches should not be completely flat.

HOOPS

An embroidery hoop keeps fabric taut and helps to ensure smooth, pucker-free stitches. Round or oval hoops are made of wood, plastic or metal, and are available in many sizes, from tiny to very large. Choose a size a little larger than the actual design area being worked.

Embroidery Preparation

STARTING AND ENDING STITCHING

1

To thread a needle, wrap thread securely around needle. Pinch to create a crease in the thread.

2

Still holding thread, remove needle. Insert creased thread through eye of needle.

3

To start stitching, knot end of thread. On right side of fabric, insert needle a few inches away from actual starting point. Bring needle up at starting point.

4

After embroidering a few stitches, clip knot from surface of fabric.

5

Insert empty needle into stitches near end where knot was just clipped. Re-thread needle.

6

Pull through.

7

To end a length of thread, run threaded needle through stitches on wrong side of fabric.

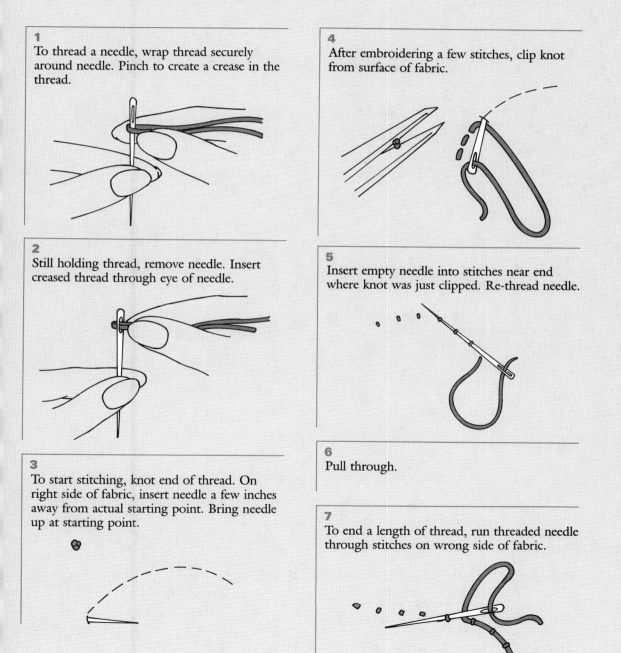

Embroidery

127

Stitches

BACKSTITCH

Work from right to left. Bring needle out of fabric at A. Insert needle at B and bring it out again at C. The distance between A and B should be equal to A and C. Start next stitch by entering at A. Continue along design line.

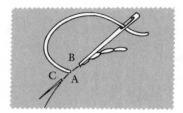

CHAINSTITCH

Bring needle out of fabric at A. Insert needle back into same hole at A then bring out at B, holding thread under point of needle. Pull needle through fabric.

Repeat the above procedure for remainder of stitches, always beginning next stitch by inserting needle into the previous hole made by the needle at B.

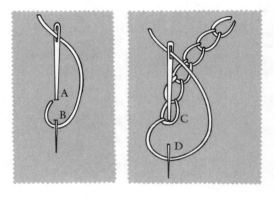

COUCHING

Thread one needle with the desired number of threads to couch over. Bring needle out of fabric at one end of design line and lay these threads along a small segment of design line.

Thread another needle with the thread to use for couching. Bring this needle out of fabric at A. Insert needle at B on other side of design line threads, and bring it out again at C. Keep distance between stitches even. Continue until threads laid along the design line are completely secure.

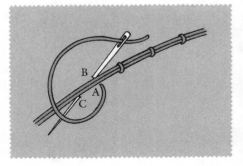

Stitches

CROSS STITCH

Work from left to right and sew one line of each cross. Bring needle out of fabric at A. Insert needle at B and bring it out again at C. Insert needle at D and bring it out again at E. Repeat across entire row.

At end of row, work back from right to left. Bring needle out of fabric at G. Insert needle at D and bring it out again at E. Insert needle at B and bring it out again at C. Repeat across entire row.

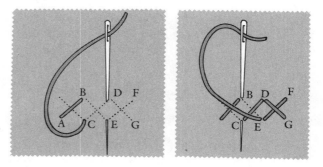

FEATHER STITCH

Mark four parallel guidelines on fabric about ¼″ (6mm) apart. Work stitches between guidelines from right to left. Bring needle out of fabric at A. Insert needle at B, above A, holding thread to the left, and bring it out at C over thread. Insert needle at D, below C, and bring it out at E over thread. Continue from right to left.

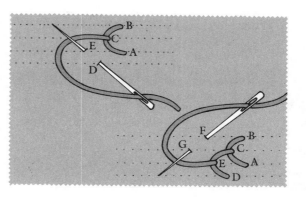

FLY STITCH

Work from left to right. Bring needle out of fabric at A. Insert needle at B and bring it out again at C, holding thread under point of needle.

Insert needle on other side of thread loop at D (to secure loop), and bring it out at E. Repeat to finish row.

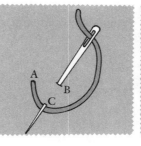
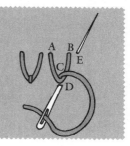

Stitches

FRENCH KNOT

Bring needle out of fabric at A. Hold thread taut and wrap thread around needle 2–3 times.

Gently pull thread so it tightens around needle. Keeping thread taut, carefully insert needle close to point A.

Pull it through to wrong side.

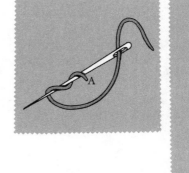

HERRINGBONE STITCH

Mark two parallel guidelines on fabric about ¼" (6mm) apart. Work from left to right. Bring needle out of fabric at A and take a stitch from B to C. Cross thread over from C to D, and take a stitch from D to E. Keep the spacing and length of all stitches even. Repeat to finish row.

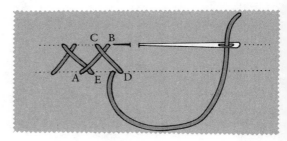

LAZY DAISY STITCH

Bring needle out of fabric at A. Insert back into same hole and come out at B, holding thread under point of needle. Pull needle through.

Insert needle at C on the other side of thread loop and bring out at D for next loop.

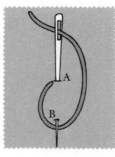
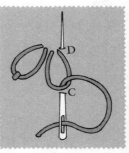

Stitches

SATIN STITCH

Bring needle out of fabric at A. Insert needle at B and bring it out again at C. Continue, keeping stitches very close together to create a solid filling.

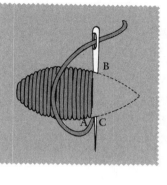

STEM STITCH

Work from left to right. Bring needle out of fabric at A. Insert needle at B and bring it out again at C. Continue along design line.

STRAIGHT STITCH

Bring needle out of fabric at A. Insert needle at B and bring it out again at C. Repeat.

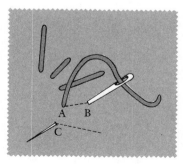

Eyelet Applications

HAND-WORKED EYELETS

1

Sew around placement marking with small RUNNING STITCHES.

2

Cut an opening the desired size or punch a hole with an awl.

3

Bring needle up through fabric from wrong side a scant ⅛" (3mm) from edge of hole. Leave 1" (2.5mm) of thread on wrong side; work around hole with BLANKET STITCHES.

4

Fasten threads securely on wrong side.

METAL EYELETS

Metal eyelet kits may be purchased at fabric stores, notion counters or craft shops. A hammer is used with the applicator tool in the kit. Work on a piece of scrap wood or hard surface that will not be damaged by hammering eyelets.

Craft shops also carry eyelet pliers which are helpful, but more of an investment than the eyelet kit. They do not require any other equipment or pounding to attach the eyelet. Apply metal eyelets where necessary, following manufacturer's instructions.

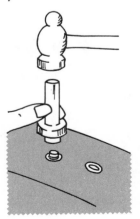

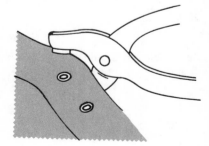

Armhole Facings

1

To prevent armhole edge from stretching, stitch ¼" (6mm) from raw edge.

2

Open out one folded edge of bias tape; lightly press out fold, but leave a slight crease. PRESHAPE tape to match curve of armhole by pressing lightly.

3

With right sides together, pin bias tape to armhole edge, placing crease along seamline. Stitch. Trim garment seam allowance even with bias tape.

4

CLIP seam allowance, if necessary.

Use one of the following methods to finish bias tape ends and stitch side seams:

Flat Construction Finish

1

Turn bias tape to inside along seam. Press. Baste tape in place and stitch close to folded edge.

2

Pin front and back together at side seam; stitch.

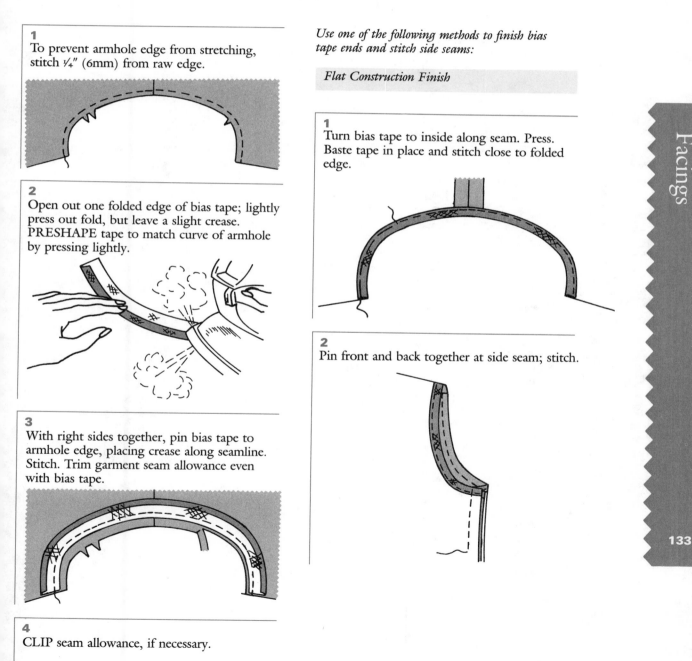

Facings

133

Armhole Facings

Bias Tape: Flat Construction, Continued

3

Turn in upper ends of seam allowances diagonally; SLIPSTITCH, OR

Round Construction Finish

1

Open out bias tape. Pin front and back together at side seam. Stitch, continuing across bias tape.

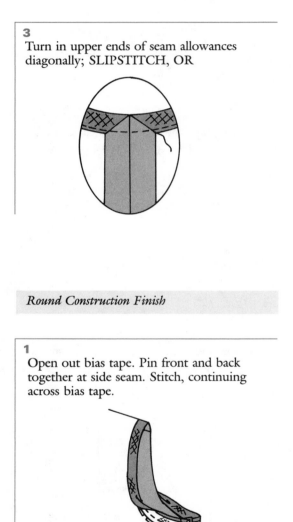

2

Turn bias tape to inside along seam. Press. SLIPSTITCH folded edge in place, OR

Baste tape in place and stitch close to folded edge.

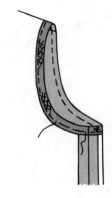

Armhole Facings

1

To prevent armhole edge from stretching, stitch ¼″ (6mm) from raw edge.

2

Open out one folded edge of bias tape; lightly press out fold, but leave a slight crease. PRESHAPE tape to match curve of armhole by pressing lightly.

3

With right sides together, pin bias tape to armhole edge, placing crease along seamline. Turn in ¼″ (6mm) on one end of bias tape and lap over remaining end. Stitch.

4

Trim garment seam allowance even with bias tape.

5

CLIP seam allowance, if necessary.

6

Turn bias tape to inside along seam. Press. SLIPSTITCH folded edge in place, OR

Baste tape in place and stitch close to folded edge. SLIPSTITCH ends.

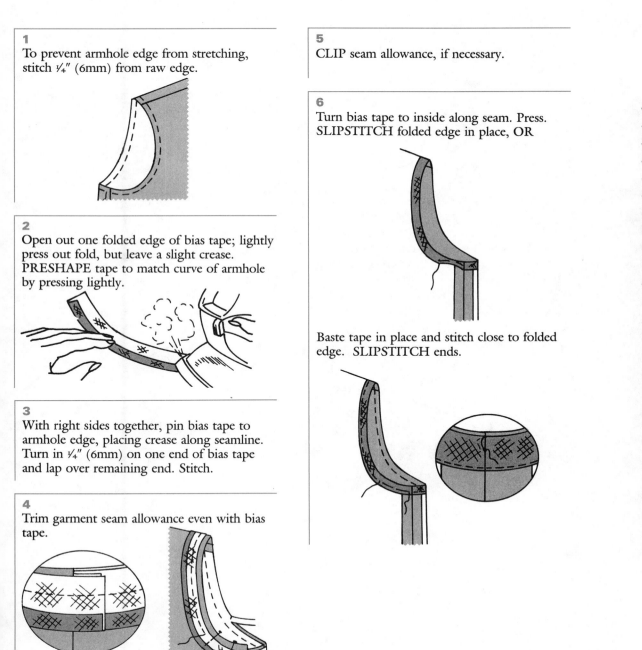

Facings

135

Armhole Facings

ROUND ARMHOLE FACINGS: FLAT CONSTRUCTION

1

FINISH unnotched edge of armhole facing.

2

With right sides together, pin facing to armhole edge, matching symbols and placing large ● at shoulder seam. Stitch.

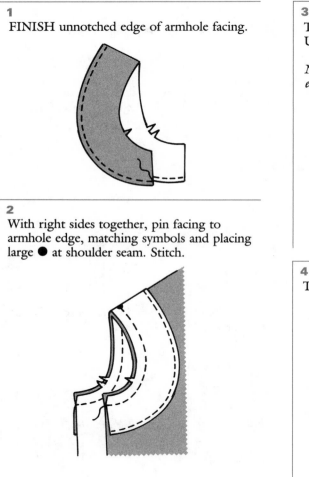

3

Trim and clip seam. Press seam toward facing. UNDERSTITCH facing.

Note: If edgestitching or topstitching armhole edge, understitching is not necessary.

4

Turn armhole facing to inside; press.

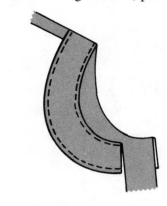

Armhole Facings

Round Armhole Facings: Flat Construction, Continued

5

Open out armhole facing. Pin front to back at sides. Stitch, continuing across facing.

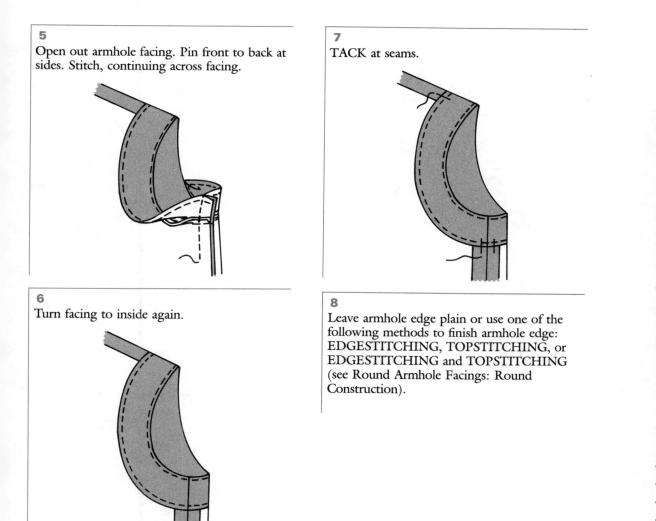

6

Turn facing to inside again.

7

TACK at seams.

8

Leave armhole edge plain or use one of the following methods to finish armhole edge: EDGESTITCHING, TOPSTITCHING, or EDGESTITCHING and TOPSTITCHING (see Round Armhole Facings: Round Construction).

Armhole Facings

ROUND ARMHOLE FACINGS: ROUND CONSTRUCTION

1

Stitch ends of armhole facing together.

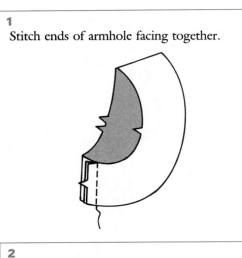

2

FINISH unnotched edge of armhole facing.

3

With right sides together, pin facing to armhole edge, matching symbols and underarm seams and placing large ● at shoulder seam. Stitch.

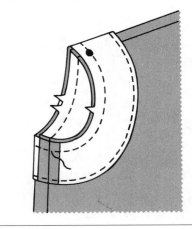

4

Trim and clip seam. Press seam toward facing. UNDERSTITCH facing.

Note: If edgestitching or topstitching armhole edge, understitching is not necessary.

Armhole Facings

5

Turn armhole facing to inside; press.

6

TACK at seams.

7

Leave armhole edge plain or use one of the following methods to finish armhole edge:

EDGESTITCH,

TOPSTITCH,

EDGESTITCH and TOPSTITCH.

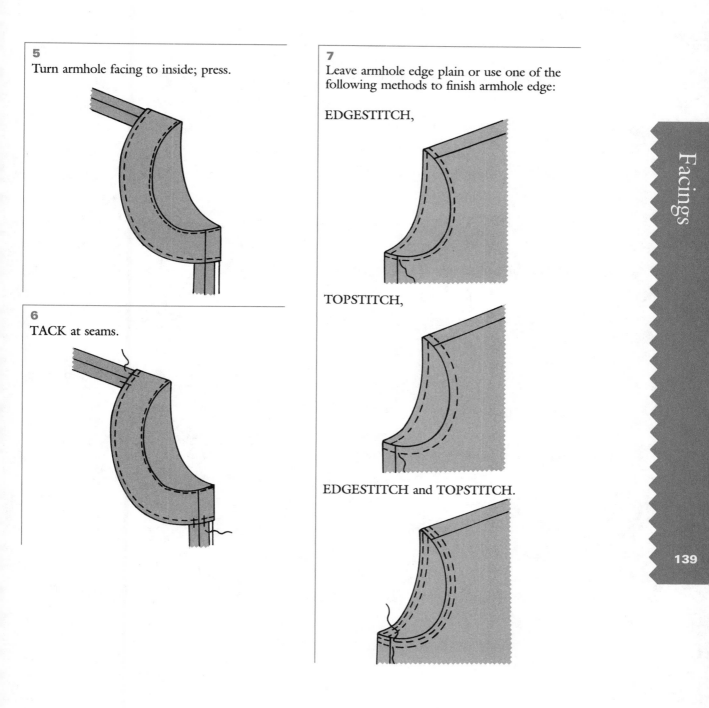

Armhole Facings

SQUARE ARMHOLE FACING

1

Stitch ends of armhole facing together.

2

FINISH unnotched edge of armhole facing.

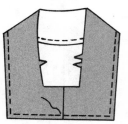

3

With right sides together, pin facing to armhole edge, matching symbols and underarm seams and placing large ● at shoulder seam. Stitch, pivoting at small ●'s. Clip corners to small ●'s.

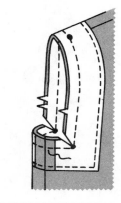

4

Trim and clip seam. Press seam toward facing. UNDERSTITCH facing.

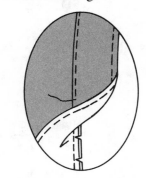

Note: If edgestitching or topstitching armhole edge, understitching is not necessary.

Armhole Facings

Square Armhole Facing, Continued

5

Turn armhole facing to inside; press.

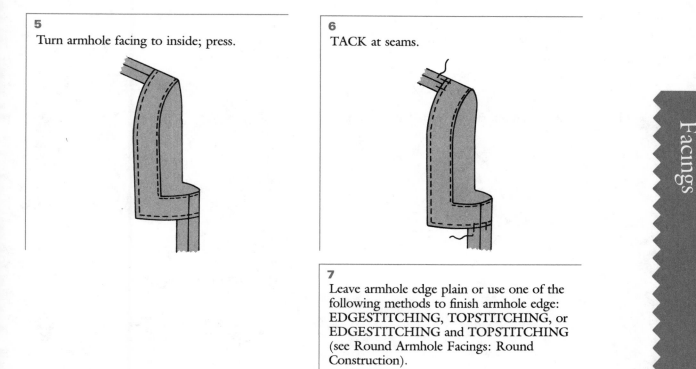

6

TACK at seams.

7

Leave armhole edge plain or use one of the
following methods to finish armhole edge:
EDGESTITCHING, TOPSTITCHING, or
EDGESTITCHING and TOPSTITCHING
(see Round Armhole Facings: Round
Construction).

Front Facings

SELF FRONT FACINGS

1

INTERFACE front and back facings or garment.

2

Stitch front self facings to back neck facing at shoulders.

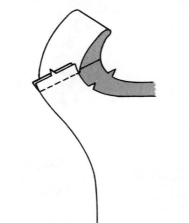

3

For unlined garments, FINISH unnotched edge of facing.

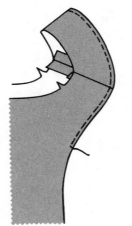

4

Turn self facings to outside along foldlines. Pin facing to neck edge. Stitch. Trim.

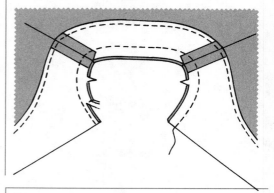

5

Turn facings to inside; press. TACK at shoulder seams.

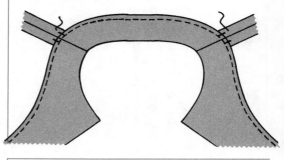

6

Complete lower garment edge (see Regular or Narrow Hems, Hem at Front Facings).

Front Facings

1

INTERFACE front and back neck facings or garment.

2

Stitch front facings to back neck facing at shoulders.

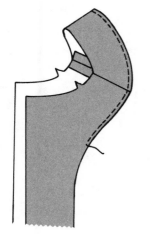

3

For unlined garments, FINISH unnotched edge.

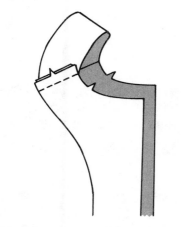

4

Pin facing to front and neck edge. Stitch front and neck edges. Trim.

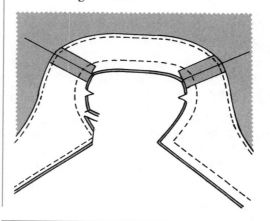

5

Turn facing to inside; press. TACK at shoulder seams.

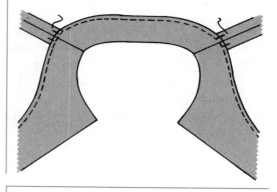

6

Complete lower garment edge (see Regular or Narrow Hems, Hem at Front Facings).

Facings

143

Neckline Facings

BATEAU: FACED

1

INTERFACE front and back neck facings or garment neck edge.

2

Stitch front neck facing to back neck facing at shoulders, ending at small •'s. FINISH unnotched edge of facing.

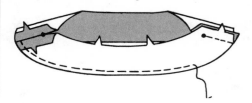

3

With right sides together, pin facing to neck edge. Stitch, pivoting at small •'s.

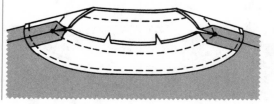

4

Trim and clip seam. Press seam toward facing. UNDERSTITCH facing.

Note: If edgestitching or topstitching neckline edge, understitching is not necessary.

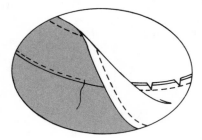

5

Turn facing to inside; press. TACK at seams.

6

Leave neckline edge plain or use one of the following methods to finish neckline edge:

TOPSTITCH,

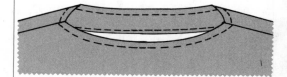

EDGESTITCH and TOPSTITCH.

Neckline Facings

BATEAU: SELF-FACED

1

INTERFACE front and back self facings.

2

FINISH long edges of front and back self facings.

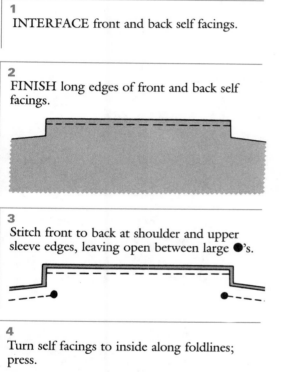

3

Stitch front to back at shoulder and upper sleeve edges, leaving open between large ●'s.

4

Turn self facings to inside along foldlines; press.

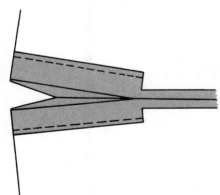

5

Leave neckline edge plain or use one of the following methods to finish edge:

TOPSTITCH,

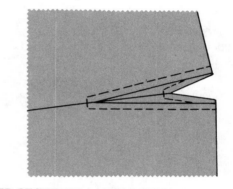

EDGESTITCH and TOPSTITCH.

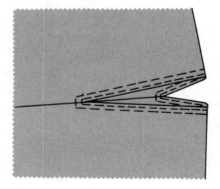

Neckline Facings

CENTER FRONT SLIT FACING

1

INTERFACE front and back neck facings or garment neck edge.

2

Stitch front facing to back neck facing section(s) at shoulders. FINISH unnotched edge of facing.

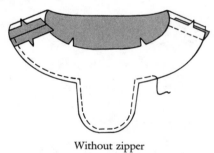

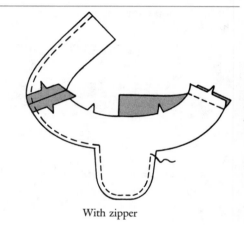

Without zipper

With zipper

3

With right sides together, pin facing to front and neck edge, matching stitching lines and shoulder seams. Stitch along neck edge seamline and front slit stitching lines.

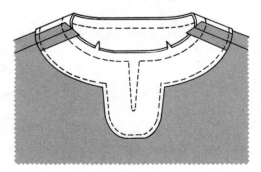

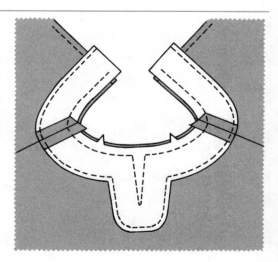

Neckline Facings

4

Slash between stitching to lower end of stitching.

5

Trim and clip neck seam. Press seam toward facing. UNDERSTITCH facing, as far as possible.

Note: If edgestitching or topstitching neckline edge, understitching is not necessary.

6

Turn facing to inside; press.

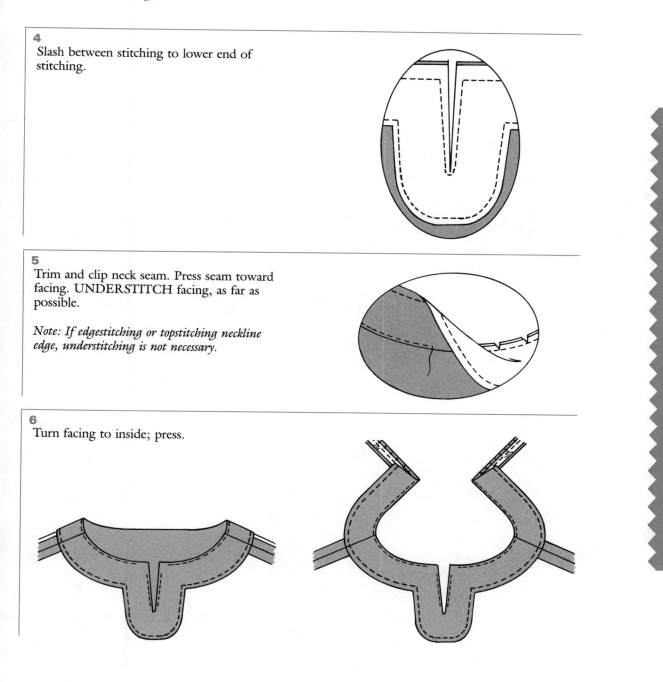

Facings

Neckline Facings

Center Front Slit Facing, Continued

7
For garment with zipper, turn in facing ends
to clear zipper teeth; press. SLIPSTITCH
facing to zipper tape.

8
Use one of the following methods to hold
facing in place:
a) TACK at seams, OR

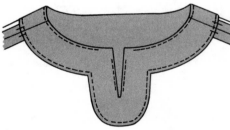

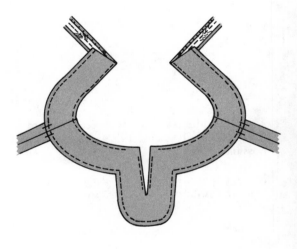

b) Baste in place along finished edge.
TOPSTITCH along basting through all
thicknesses.

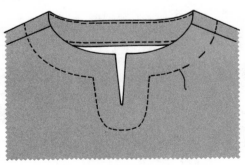

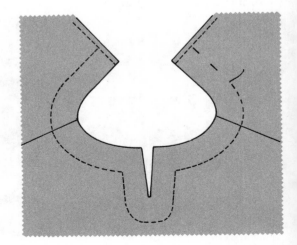

Neckline Facings

Center Front Slit Facing, Continued

8 *Continued*
If desired, TOPSTITCH again next to first stitching.

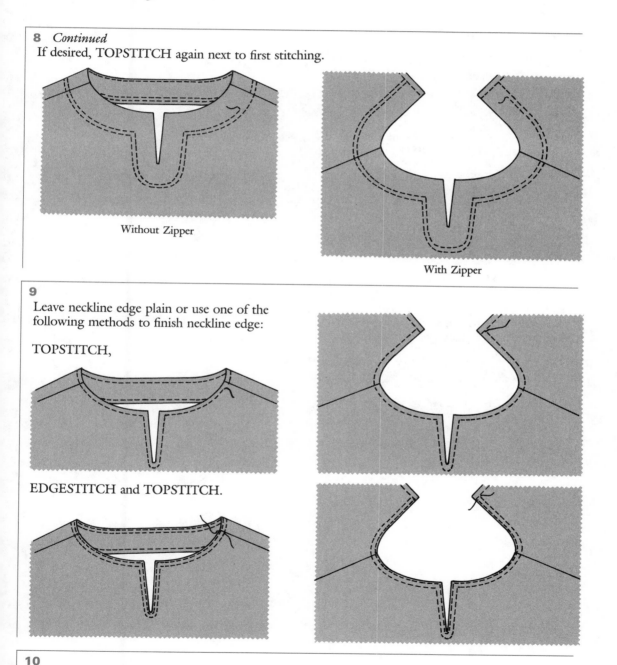

Without Zipper

With Zipper

9
Leave neckline edge plain or use one of the following methods to finish neckline edge:

TOPSTITCH,

EDGESTITCH and TOPSTITCH.

10
Sew hook and eye to opening edges above zipper.

Neckline Facings

ROUND FACING

1

INTERFACE front and back neck facings or garment neck edge.

2

Stitch front neck facing to back neck facing section(s) at shoulders. FINISH unnotched edge of facing.

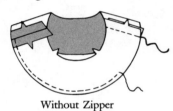

Without Zipper

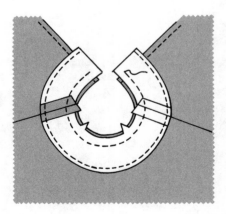

With Zipper

3

With right sides together, pin facing to neck edge, matching shoulder seams. Stitch.

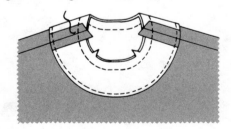

Neckline Facings

Round Facing, Continued

4

Trim and clip seam. Press seam toward facing. UNDERSTITCH facing.

Note: If edgestitching or topstitching neckline edge, understitching is not necessary.

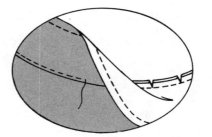

5

Turn facing to inside; press. For garment with zipper, turn in facing ends to clear zipper teeth; press. SLIPSTITCH facing to zipper tape.

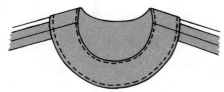
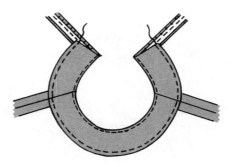

Neckline Facings

Round Facing, Continued

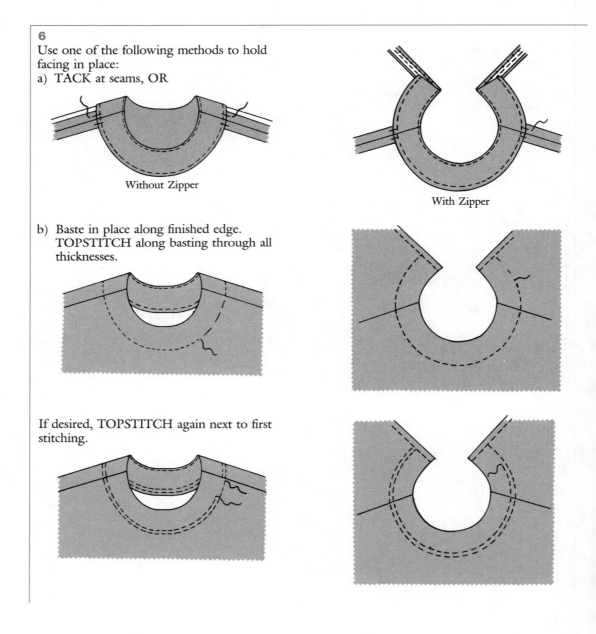

6

Use one of the following methods to hold facing in place:

a) TACK at seams, OR

Without Zipper

With Zipper

b) Baste in place along finished edge. TOPSTITCH along basting through all thicknesses.

If desired, TOPSTITCH again next to first stitching.

Facings

Neckline Facings

Round Facing, Continued

7

Leave neckline edge plain or use one of the
following methods to finish edge:

TOPSTITCH,

EDGESTITCH and TOPSTITCH.

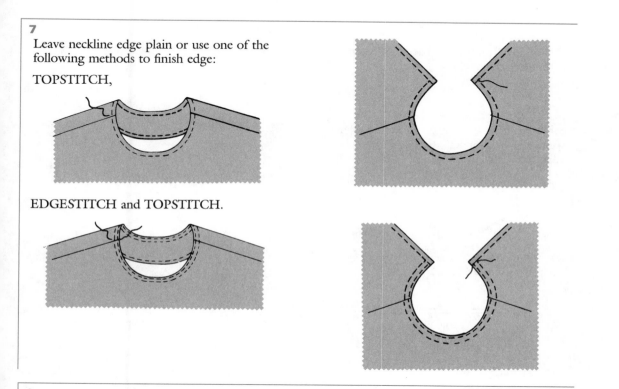

8

Sew hook and eye to opening edges above
zipper.

Neckline Facings

SQUARE FACING

1

INTERFACE front and back neck facings or garment neck edge.

2

Stitch front neck facing to back neck facing section(s) at shoulders. FINISH unnotched edge of facing.

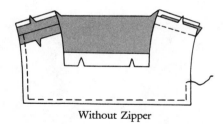

Without Zipper

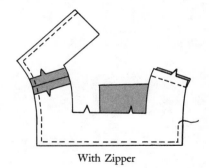

With Zipper

3

With right sides together, pin facing to neck edge, matching shoulder seams. Stitch, pivoting at small •'s. Clip to small •'s.

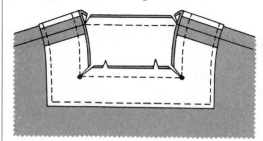

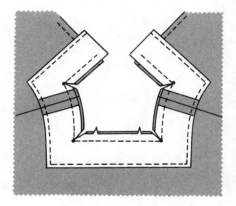

154

Neckline Facings

Square Facing, Continued

4

Trim and clip seam. Press seam toward facing. UNDERSTITCH facing.

Note: If edgestitching or topstitching neckline edge, understitching is not necessary.

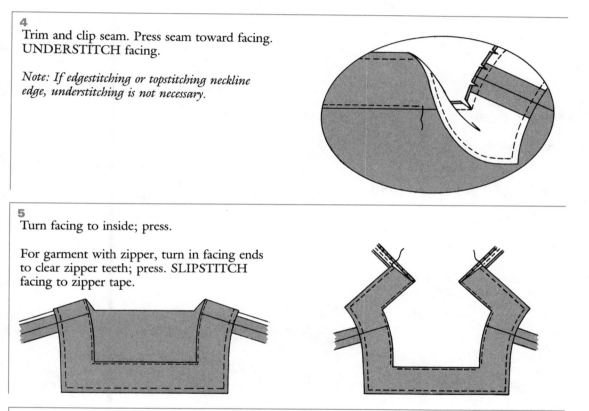

5

Turn facing to inside; press.

For garment with zipper, turn in facing ends to clear zipper teeth; press. SLIPSTITCH facing to zipper tape.

6

Hold facing in place with TACKS or TOPSTITCHING; leave neckline edge plain or use one of the following methods to finish neck edge: TOPSTITCHING, or EDGESTITCHING and TOPSTITCHING (see Neckline Facings, Round Facing).

7

Sew hook and eye to opening edges above zipper.

Neckline Facings

V-NECK FACING

1

INTERFACE front and back neck facings or
garment neck edge.

2

Stitch front neck facing to back neck facing
section(s) at shoulders. FINISH unnotched
edge of facing.

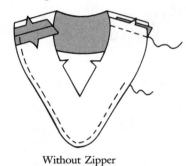

Without Zipper

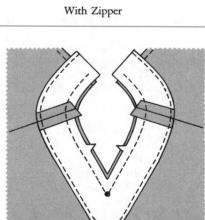

With Zipper

3

With right sides together, pin facing to neck
edge, matching shoulder seams. Stitch,
pivoting at large ●.

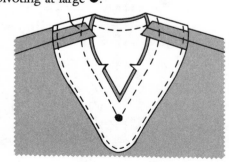

4

Clip to large ●.

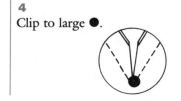

Neckline Facings

5

Trim and clip seam. Press seam toward facing.
UNDERSTITCH facing.

*Note: If edgestitching or topstitching neckline
edge, understitching is not necessary.*

6

Turn facing to inside; press.

For garment with zipper, turn in facing ends
to clear zipper teeth; press. SLIPSTITCH
facing to zipper tape.

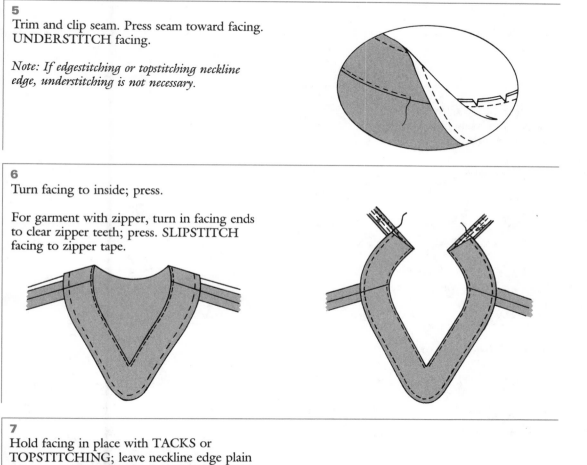

7

Hold facing in place with TACKS or
TOPSTITCHING; leave neckline edge plain
or use one of the following methods to finish
neck edge: TOPSTITCHING, or
EDGESTITCHING and TOPSTITCHING
(see Neckline Facings, Round Facing).

8

Sew hook and eye to opening edges above
zipper.

One-piece Neck and Armhole Facings

FOR NARROW SHOULDERS

1

INTERFACE front and back neck facings or garment neck edge.

2

Stitch front facing to back facing section(s) at sides. Turn in shoulder edges of facing along seamlines; press.

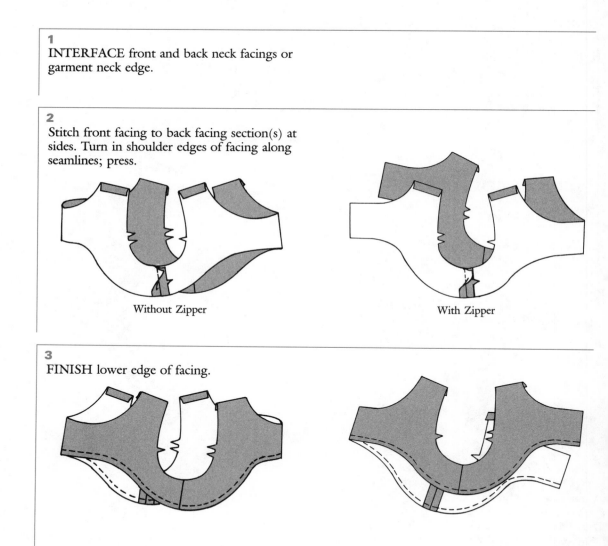

Without Zipper

With Zipper

3

FINISH lower edge of facing.

One-piece Neck and Armhole Facings

For Narrow Shoulders, Continued

4

With right sides together, pin facing to garment upper edge, matching centers and underarm seams. Stitch neck and armhole edges. Trim and clip seams.

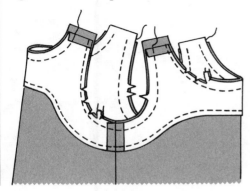
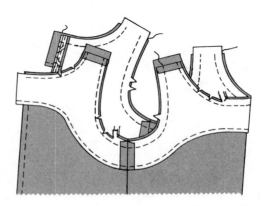

5

Turn facing to inside; press.

For garment with zipper, turn in facing ends to clear zipper teeth; press. SLIPSTITCH facing to zipper tape.

TACK at seams.

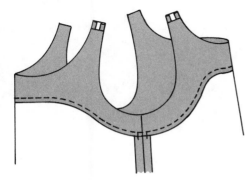
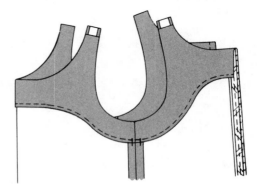

One-piece Neck and Armhole Facings

For Narrow Shoulders, Continued

6

Stitch front to back at shoulder seams, keeping facing free.

7

On inside, SLIPSTITCH pressed edges of facings together.

8

Leave neckline and armhole edges plain or use one of the following methods to finish neckline and armhole edges: TOPSTITCHING, or EDGESTITCHING and TOPSTITCHING (see One-piece Neck and Armhole Facings, For Wide Shoulders).

9

Sew hook and eye to opening edges above zipper.

One-piece Neck and Armhole Facings

1

INTERFACE front and back neck facings or garment neck edge.

2

Stitch front facing to back facing sections at shoulders. FINISH lower edges of facing.

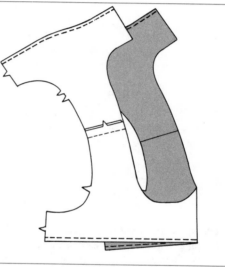

3

With right sides together, pin facing to garment, matching centers and shoulder seams. Stitch neck and armhole edges. Trim and clip seams.

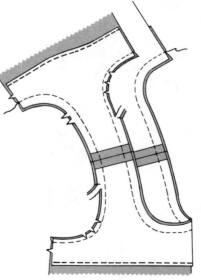

Facings

One-piece Neck and Armhole Facings

For Wide Shoulders, Continued

4

To turn right side out, pull each back section through shoulder; press.

5

For garment without zipper, open out back facings. Stitch center back seam, continuing across facings. For garment with zipper, stitch center back seam to symbols.

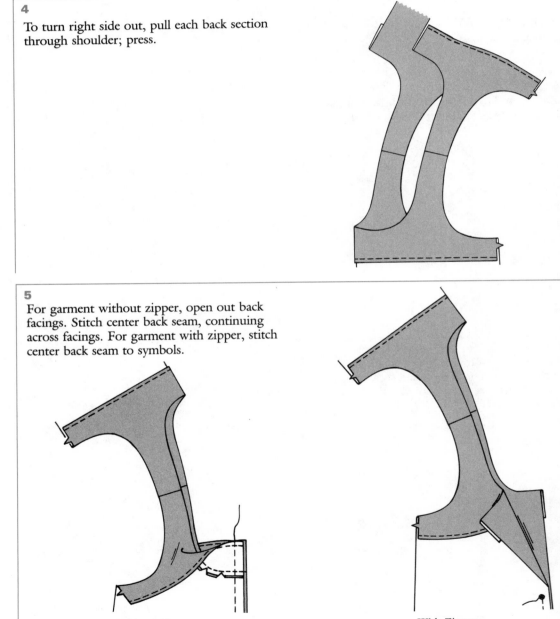

Without Zipper

With Zipper

Facings

One-piece Neck and Armhole Facings

For Wide Shoulders, Continued

6

Open out facing at back edges. Insert zipper.

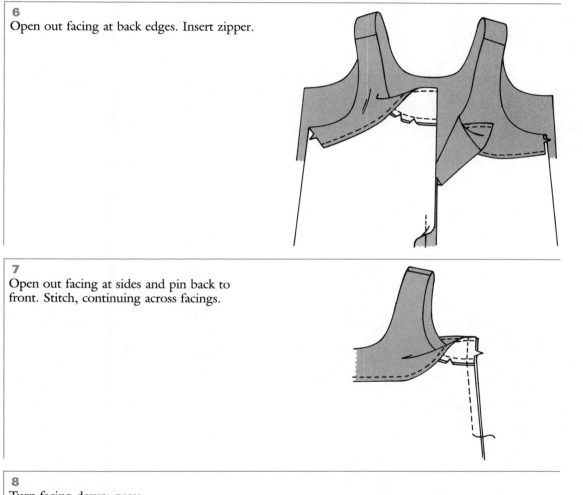

7

Open out facing at sides and pin back to front. Stitch, continuing across facings.

8

Turn facing down; press.

For garment with zipper, turn in facing ends to clear zipper teeth; press. SLIPSTITCH to zipper tape.

One-Piece Neck and Armhole Facings

For Wide Shoulders, Continued

9
TACK at seams.

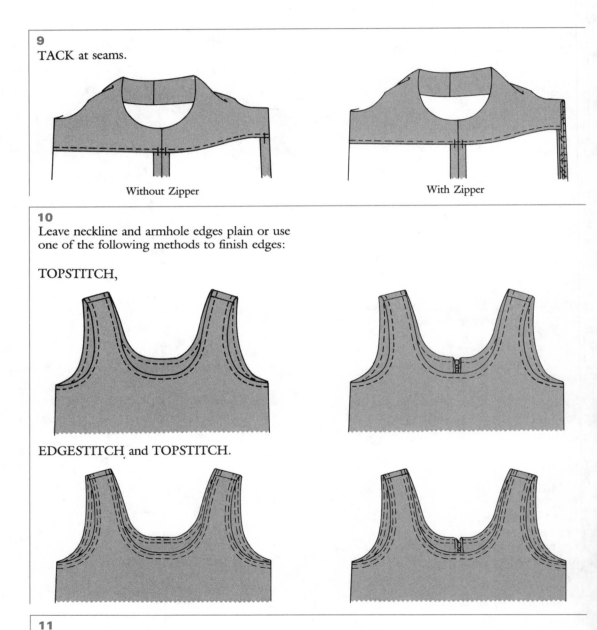

Without Zipper
With Zipper

10
Leave neckline and armhole edges plain or use
one of the following methods to finish edges:

TOPSTITCH,

EDGESTITCH and TOPSTITCH.

11
Sew hook and eye to opening edges above zipper.

Waistline Facings

FABRIC FACING

1

For raised waistline, INTERFACE wrong side of front and back facing sections.

For regular waistline, INTERFACE front and back facing sections or garment waistline.

2

Stitch front facing and back facing sections together at sides. FINISH lower edge of facing.

Raised Waistline

Regular Waistline

3

Insert zipper.

4

With right sides together, pin facing to upper edge of garment, matching centers, symbols and side seams. Stitch.

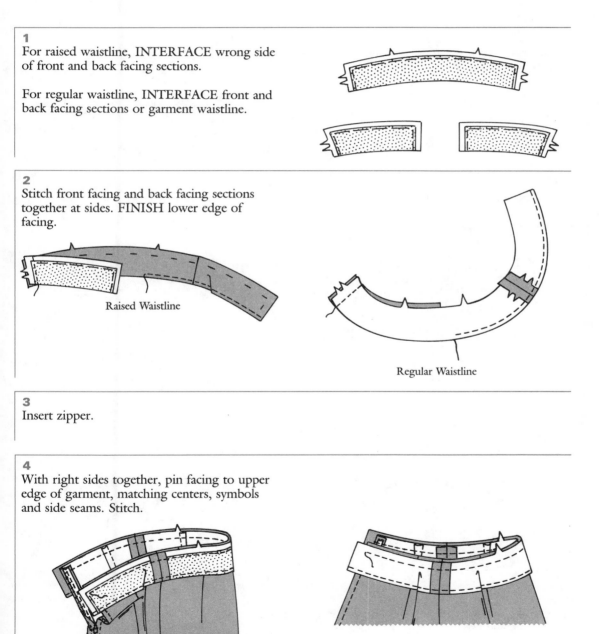

Waistline Facings

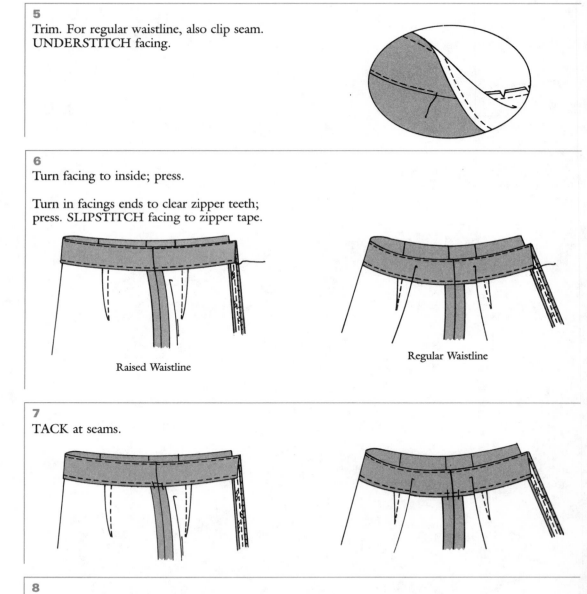

Fabric Facing, Continued

5

Trim. For regular waistline, also clip seam.
UNDERSTITCH facing.

6

Turn facing to inside; press.

Turn in facings ends to clear zipper teeth;
press. SLIPSTITCH facing to zipper tape.

Raised Waistline

Regular Waistline

7

TACK at seams.

8

Sew hook and eye to opening edges above
zipper.

Facings

Waistline Facings

RIBBON FACING

1

Insert zipper.

2

Use a ¾"–1" (20mm–25mm) wide strip of grosgrain ribbon. Cut ribbon to fit skirt waistline plus 1" (25mm).

3

STAYSTITCH garment along waist seamline. Trim seam allowance to ¼" (6mm).

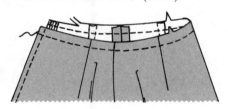

4

Pin one long edge of ribbon to right side of garment along stitching, extending ends ½" (13mm) beyond zipper edges; stitch.

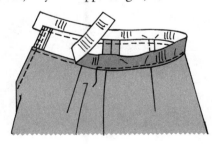

5

Turn ribbon facing to inside; press.

6

Turn in facing ends to clear zipper teeth; press. SLIPSTITCH facing to zipper tape.

7

TACK at seams.

8

Sew hook and eye to opening edges above zipper.

Godets

GODETS IN A SEAM

1

Stitch garment sections together, leaving open below symbols.

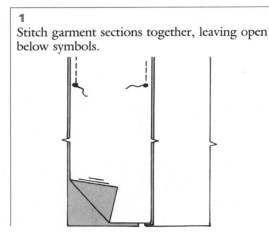

2

With right sides together, pin godet section to open edges of seam, matching symbols. Stitch godet section, breaking stitching at symbols.

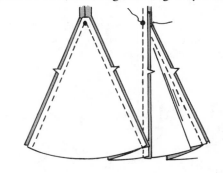

GODETS IN A SLASH

1

To reinforce inner corner, cut a 2" (5cm) square of lightweight remnant fabric.

2

On outside, center remnant over symbol. Stitch along stitching lines on garment, pivoting at symbol. Use a smaller stitch length when stitching over fabric square. Slash between stitching lines to symbol.

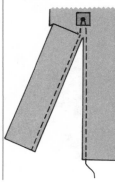
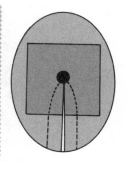

3

Turn remnant to inside; press.

4

With right sides together, pin godet section to garment, matching symbols and placing seamlines along stitching lines. Stitch along stitching lines, pivoting at symbols.

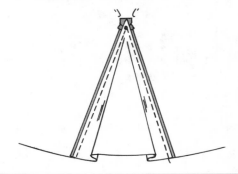

5

Trim reinforcement square even with seams. Press seams toward garment.

Gussets

1

To reinforce inner corners, cut a 2″ (5cm) square of lightweight remnant fabric for each corner.

2

On outside, center a remnant square over each symbol. Using small stitches, stitch along stitching lines, pivoting at symbols. Slash between stitching lines to symbols.

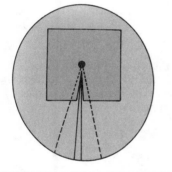

3

Turn remnants to inside; press.

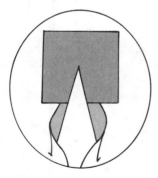

4

Stitch garment together, ending stitching at symbols for the gusset opening.

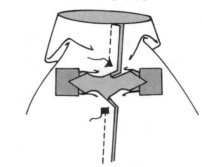

5

With right sides together, pin garment to gusset, matching symbols and placing garment stitching lines along gusset seamlines. With garment side up, stitch, pivoting at symbols and breaking stitching at seams.

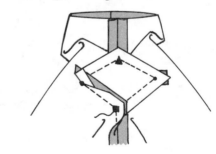

6

Press seams toward garment.

Beginning Sewing

GUIDELINES

- Work on a flat, smooth surface.

- Choose a needle size in accordance with fabric and thread. Use a single 18"–20" (46cm–51cm) length of thread, coated with beeswax for added strength and slipperiness.

- Wear a thimble on the second finger of sewing hand to make sewing hard-surfaced fabrics faster and easier.

- When sewing, pull thread taut, but not tight.

MAKING A KNOT

Cut thread at an angle; pass cut end through needle eye. Knot the same end that went through the eye as follows:

1

Using left hand, hold thread between thumb and first finger.

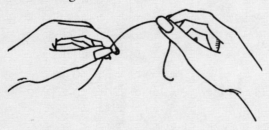

2

With right hand, bring thread over and around fingertip, crossing it over thread end.

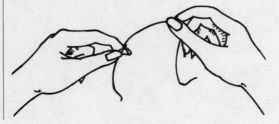

3

With thumb over crossed threads, and longer thread taut, gently push thumb toward fingertip, causing thread end to roll around loop; slide loop off finger.

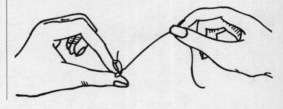

4

Lightly pinching rolled end between thumb and second finger, pull longer thread in right hand taut to set knot.

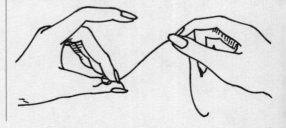

Ending Sewing

To end hand sewing, there are two choices: 1) a knot, or 2) a tack.

MAKING A KNOT

1

Begin knot by taking a tiny stitch on wrong side of fabric, directly over last stitch. Pull thread until a small loop remains.

2

Pass needle through loop, pulling thread a second time, until another small loop forms.

3

Insert needle through this second loop. Pull thread taut, forming an inconspicuous knot at the base of stitches.

MAKING A TACK

To end hand sewing or to hold two or more layers in place, make several small BACKSTITCHES over and over.

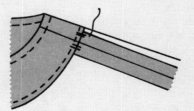

Stitches

BACKSTITCH

One of the strongest hand stitches, the backstitch is used for repairing hard-to-reach seams or for securing stitches at the beginning and end of seams.

With right sides together and following seamline, bring needle through fabric to upper side. Take a small stitch back about ¹⁄₁₆"–¹⁄₈" (2mm–3mm); bring needle out again ¹⁄₁₆"–¹⁄₈" (2mm–3mm) forward on seamline. Continue to insert needle in end of last stitch and bring it out one stitch ahead. Stitches on underside will be twice as long as those on upper side.

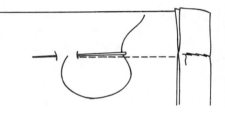

BLANKET STITCH

To make hand-finished details such as thread loops and eyelets, use a blanket stitch. Variations of the blanket stitch are used to form thread eyes, loops, belt carriers and French tacks.

Work from left to right with the edge of the fabric toward you. Secure first stitch at fabric edge. For each succeeding stitch, point needle toward you; insert it through right side of fabric and over the thread approximately ¼" (6mm) above the fabric edge and ¼" (6mm) to the right of preceding stitch. Pull thread taut, but not tight.

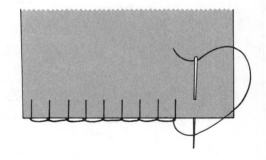

Stitches

BLINDSTITCH

For hemming and holding facings in place, use a blindstitch concealed between two layers of fabric.

Turn fabric edge down about ¼″ (6mm). Make a small diagonal stitch by first picking up one thread of garment, then one thread of hem or facing. Repeat.

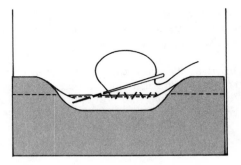

CATCHSTITCH

Use the catchstitch to hold two layers of fabric together with a degree of flexibility, such as interfacing and garment sections or hems in knit fabrics. It allows the layers to shift slightly, preventing buckling in the finished garment.

Work from left to right on two layers of fabric. Make a small horizontal stitch in upper layer of fabric a short distance from edge. Then, barely outside edge of upper layer, make another stitch in lower layer of fabric diagonally to the right of first stitch. Alternate stitching along edge in zigzag fashion, keeping threads loose.

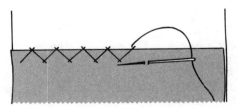

Stitches

CROSS STITCH

A decorative stitch used to hold back lining pleats closed at neck, waist, lower edges or shoulders, cross stitches show on right side of lining.

Insert needle perpendicular to edge of pleat, creating diagonal stitches through all thicknesses, then return in opposite direction, crossing stitches.

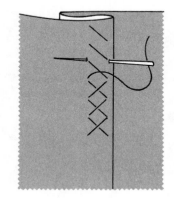

FRENCH TACK

Use a French tack to hold a free-hanging hem lining to a garment hem.

Take two or three stitches, about 1″ (25mm) long, between lining and garment.

Work BLANKET STITCHES close together over long threads covering them.

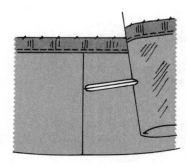

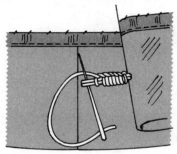

Stitches

HALF-BACKSTITCH

Suitable for sewing any seam, the half-backstitch is also used to UNDERSTITCH facings.

Make a BACKSTITCH, but carry needle back only half the length of the last stitch while continuing to bring it out of fabric one full stitch length ahead of last stitch.

HEMMING STITCH

Use the hemming stitch for all types of hemming, especially when hem is finished with seam binding.

Take a tiny inconspicuous stitch in garment, then bring needle diagonally up through edge of seam binding or hem edge. Space stitches about ¼″ (6mm) apart.

OVERCAST STITCH

Use the overcast stitch to prevent raw edges from ravelling.

Insert needle perpendicular to edge of fabric, creating diagonal stitches over the edge. Make stitches a uniform depth and space them evenly apart. It is also possible to take two or three stitches at one time to make the work go faster.

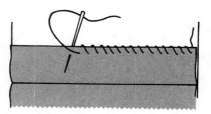

Stitches

PICKSTITCH

The pickstitch is a decorative stitch, sewn through only one layer of fabric. It may be used to accent garment edges, such as lapels, pockets and cuffs.

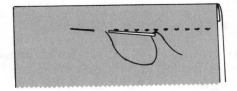

Bring needle up through the top layer of fabric the desired distance from the garment edge. Take a stitch back, picking up only one or two threads and forming a tiny surface stitch. Bring the needle out again the amount desired in front of last stitch, usually ⅛″–¼″ (3mm–6mm).

PRICKSTITCH

A variation of the BACKSTITCH, the prickstitch is used as the last step of zipper applications in fine fabrics such as velvet, velveteen, or satin, where machine stitching is not as fine or as invisible a finish.

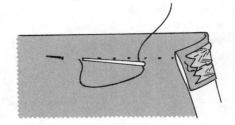

Bring needle up through all layers of fabric. Take a stitch back picking up only one or two threads and forming a tiny surface stitch. Bring the needle out again a scant ¼″ (6mm) in front of last stitch.

Stitches

RUNNING STITCH

The running stitch is the most basic stitch used to ease, gather, tuck, mend and sew seams that are not subjected to much strain.

Take several small forward stitches, evenly weaving needle in and out of fabric before pulling thread through. Pick up as many stitches each time as fabric and needle will allow.

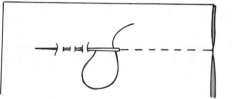

SADDLE STITCH

While strictly a decorative stitch for accenting garment edges, the saddle stitch is bolder than the PICKSTITCH.

Make RUNNING STITCHES through all layers, the desired distance from the garment edge. Stitches should be evenly spaced and at least ¼″ (6mm) long.

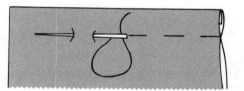

SLIPSTITCH

Use the slipstitch for an almost invisible finish to hem, or to attach linings, pockets and trims.

Slide needle through folded fabric edge, then pick up a thread of underneath fabric.

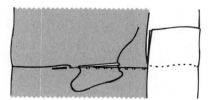

Stitches

UNDERSTITCH

Understitch finished facings to prevent the facing edge from rolling to the outside of the garment.

Use HALF-BACKSTITCHES to sew on facing close to seam through all thicknesses.

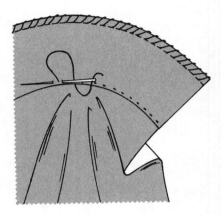

WHIPSTITCH

Use the whipstitch to hold two finished edges together, such as lace edging or ribbon to a garment.

Insert needle at a right angle from the back edge to the front edge, picking up one or two threads at a time.

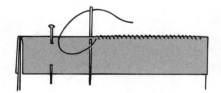

Measuring for Hems

- Determine finished garment length. Decide on hem allowance width—for a regular hem, allow 1″–3″ (2.5cm–7.5cm); for a narrow hem, allow ⅜″ (10mm) or ⅝″ (15mm). Add hem allowance to finished garment length to determine how long to cut garment piece.

- When ready to mark hem, try garment on to check length. If a belt or sash, or a certain type of shoe will be worn with the garment, put these items on before measuring the hem.

- Mark hem with pins, chalk pencil or skirt marker, placing marks every 2″–3″ (5cm–7.5cm) around the hem. Take off garment and even up marked line so hem will be straight. Trim hem allowance to an even depth.

Interfacing Hems

Interface tailored garments along lower edges of garment and sleeve. Cut bias strip of interfacing ⅝" (15mm) wider than depth of hem allowance, *piecing where necessary. For jacket, open out front facing.*

FOR CRISP EDGE

Place one long edge of interfacing along hemline. For jackets, lap ends ½" (13mm) over front interfacing. For sleeves, lap ends ½" (13mm) at one seam. HAND-BASTE close to hemline. BLINDSTITCH along upper edge. For jackets, sew ends to front interfacing. For sleeves, sew ends in place.

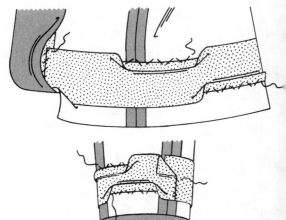

FOR SOFT, ROUNDED EDGE

Place one long edge of interfacing ⅝" (15mm) below hemline. For jackets, lap ends ½" (13mm) over front interfacing. For sleeves, lap ends ½" (13mm) at one seam. BLINDSTITCH along hemline and upper edge. For jackets, sew ends to front interfacing. For sleeves, sew ends in place.

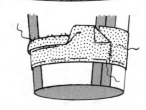

Hems

180

Narrow Hems

BIAS OR CIRCULAR HEM: KNIT FABRICS

1

Allow garment to hang for 24 hours before hemming to permit bias to set.

2

Trim hem to an even depth.

3

Stitch along hemline ⅜″ (10mm) or ⅝″ (15mm) from edge. Turn in along stitching; press, easing in fullness, if necessary. Stitch ¼″ (6mm) from folded edge. Trim close to stitching on ⅝″ (15mm) hem.

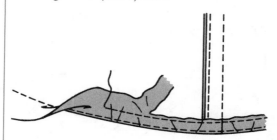

Bias or circular hems can also be stitched using an Overlock machine, but stitches will look like satin stitching (see Overlock, Hems).

BIAS OR CIRCULAR HEM: WOVEN FABRICS

1

Allow garment to hang for 24 hours before hemming to permit bias to set.

2

Trim hem to an even depth.

3

Turn in ⅜″ (10mm) or ⅝″ (15mm) hem; press, easing in fullness, if necessary.

4

Open out hem. Turn in again so raw edge is along crease; press.

5

Turn in along crease, enclosing raw edge; stitch close to upper folded edge of hem.

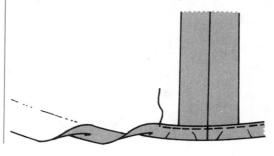

Narrow Hems

CORNERS: KNIT FABRICS

1

Stitch along hemline ⅜″ (10mm) or ⅝″ (15mm) from edge, pivoting at corner.

2

Turn in along stitching; press, easing in fullness, if necessary. Diagonally fold and trim corners to miter them before stitching.

3

Stitch ¼″ (6mm) from folded edge, pivoting at corner.

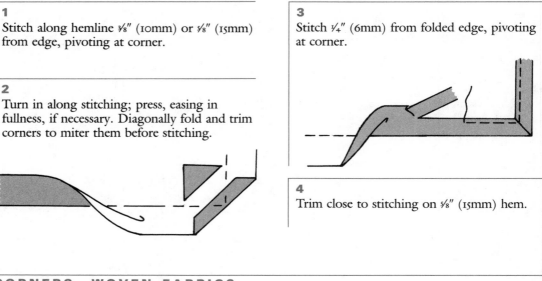

4

Trim close to stitching on ⅝″ (15mm) hem.

CORNERS: WOVEN FABRICS

1

Turn in ⅜″ (10mm) or ⅝″ (15mm) hem; press, easing in fullness, if necessary.

2

Diagonally fold and trim corners to miter them before stitching.

3

Open out hem. Turn in again so raw edge is along crease; press.

4

Turn in along crease, enclosing raw edge; stitch close to upper folded edge of hem, pivoting at corner.

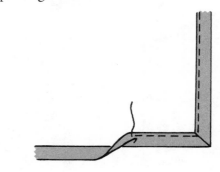

Narrow Hems

HAND-ROLLED HEM: WOVEN FABRICS

1

Trim hem to an even depth of ¼″ (6mm).

2

To hand roll, stitch along hemline ¼″ (6mm) from raw edge.

3

Trim close to stitching.

4

Roll trimmed edge toward garment; SLIPSTITCH roll in place.

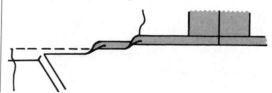

HEM AT FRONT FACINGS

1

Turn lower edge of each facing to outside along foldline or facing seam.

2

Stitch ⅜″ (10mm) or ⅝″ (15mm) from lower edge. Trim ⅝″ (15mm) seams.

Self Facing   Separate Facing

3

Turn facing to inside; press.

4

Make ⅜″ (10mm) or ⅝″ (15mm) NARROW HEM at lower edge, continuing stitching across facing.

Narrow Hems

SLIT OR SHIRT TAIL HEM: KNIT FABRICS

1

Stitch along hemline, ⅜″ (10mm) or ⅝″ (15mm) from edge.

2

Turn in along stitching; press, easing in fullness, if necessary.

3

Stitch ¼″ (6mm) from folded edge, pivoting across seam allowance ¼″ (6mm) above or below large ●.

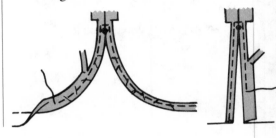

SLIT OR SHIRT TAIL HEM: WOVEN FABRICS

1

Turn in ⅜″ (10mm) or ⅝″ (15mm) hem; press, easing in fullness, if necessary.

2

Open out hem. Turn in again so raw edge is along crease; press. Turn in along crease, tapering to nothing above or below large ●.

3

Stitch close to upper folded edge of hem, pivoting across seam allowance ¼″ (6mm) above or below large ●.

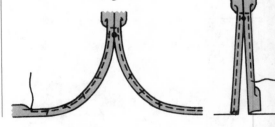

Narrow Hems

STRAIGHT HEM: KNIT FABRICS

1
Stitch along hemline ⅜″ (10mm) or ⅝″ (15mm) from edge.

2
Turn in along stitching; press, easing in fullness, if necessary.

3
Stitch ¼″ (6mm) from folded edge.

4
Trim close to stitching on ⅝″ (15mm) hem.

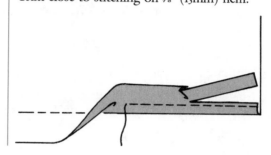

STRAIGHT HEM: WOVEN FABRICS

1
Turn in ⅜″ (10mm) or ⅝″ (15mm) hem; press, easing in fullness, if necessary.

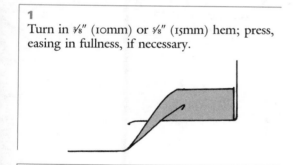

2
Open out hem. Turn in again so raw edge is along crease; press.

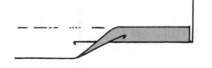

3
Turn in along crease, enclosing raw edge; stitch close to upper folded edge of hem.

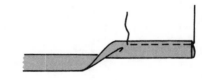

Regular Hems

BIAS OR CIRCULAR HEM

1

Allow skirt to hang for 24 hours before hemming to permit bias to set. Mark hemline.

2

Turn up hem. Baste close to fold.

3

Trim hem to an even depth.

4

EASESTITCH ¼″ (6mm) from raw edge.

5

Adjust fullness; shrink out fullness with steam iron.

6

FINISH raw edge.

7

Hand-sew hem in place. Press.

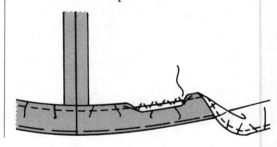

EASED HEM

1

Turn up hem. Baste close to fold.

2

Trim hem to an even depth.

3

EASESTITCH ¼″ (6mm) from raw edge.

4

Adjust fullness; shrink out fullness with steam iron.

5

FINISH raw edge.

6

Hand-sew hem in place. Press.

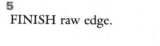

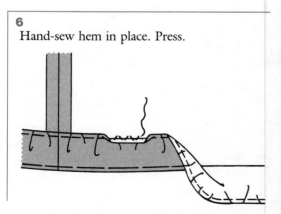

Regular Hems

HEM AT FRONT FACINGS

Machine-stitched

1

Turn lower edge of facing to outside along foldline or seam.

Stitch across facing on hemline. Trim.

2

Turn facing to inside.

3

Turn up hem. Baste close to fold. Trim hem to an even depth.

4

For unlined garments, FINISH raw edge. Hand-sew hem in place, easing in fullness, if necessary. Press. Hand-sew facing to hem.

For lined garment, use a CATCHSTITCH.

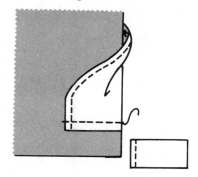

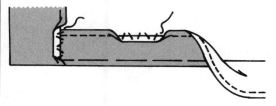

Slipstitched

1

Open out facing. Turn up hem. Baste close to fold. Trim hem to an even depth. Trim facing hem allowance.

2

For unlined garments, FINISH raw edge. Hand-sew hem in place, easing in fullness, if necessary. Press.

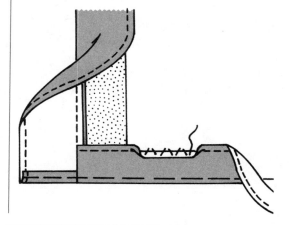

3

Turn facing to inside. Hand-sew facing to hem. For lined garments, use a CATCHSTITCH. SLIPSTITCH lower edges together.

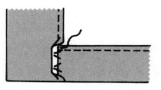

Regular Hems

PLAIN HEM

1

Turn up hem. Baste close to fold.

2

Trim hem to an even depth.

3

FINISH raw edge.

4

Hand-sew hem in place, easing in fullness, if necessary. Press.

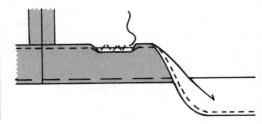

PLEAT IN HEM

1

Press pleat seam(s) open at lower edge.

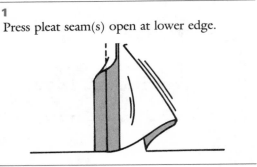

2

Turn up hem. Baste close to fold.

3

Trim hem to an even depth.

4

FINISH raw edge.

5

Clip pleat seam(s) above hem.

6

Hand-sew hem in place, easing in fullness, if necessary. Press.

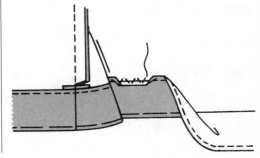

7

On inside, crease pleat seam(s) across hem. Stitch close to edge.

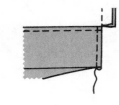

Regular Hems

SLIT IN HEM

1
Open out self facings. Turn up hem. Baste close to fold.

2
Trim hem to an even depth. Trim self facing hem allowances. FINISH raw edge.

3
Hand-sew hem in place, easing in fullness, if necessary. Press.

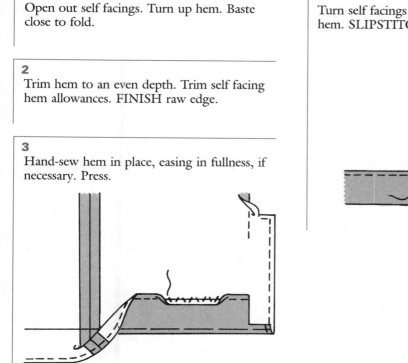

4
Turn self facings to inside and hand-sew to hem. SLIPSTITCH lower edges together.

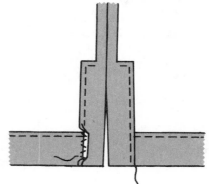

TOPSTITCHED HEM

1
Turn up hem. Baste close to fold. Trim hem to an even depth.

2
Turn in ¼" (6mm) on raw edge, easing in fullness, if necessary. Baste hem in place close to upper edge; press.

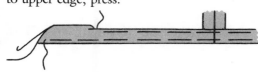

3
On outside, machine-stitch hem in place close to upper basting.

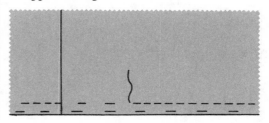

Regular Hems

VENT IN HEM

1

FINISH self facing raw edges. If right and left sides are different, NARROW-HEM right back or left front edge.

2

Open out self facings. Turn up hem. Baste close to fold.

3

Trim hem to an even depth. Trim self facing hem allowances.

4

FINISH raw edge.

5

Hand-sew hem in place, easing in fullness, if necessary. Press.

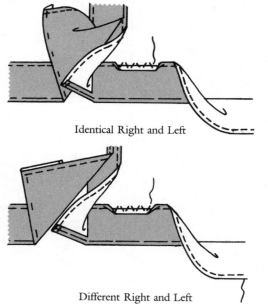

Identical Right and Left

Different Right and Left

6

Turn self facings to inside and hand-sew to hem. SLIPSTITCH lower edges together.

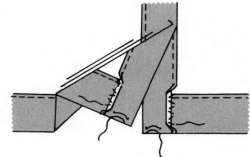

Identical Right and Left

If right and left sides are different, SLIPSTITCH right back or left front lower edges together.

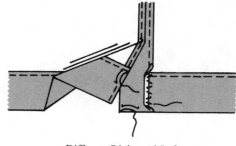

Different Right and Left

Hooks and Eyes For Edges That Meet

1

Place hook 1/16" (2mm) from one edge. Attach hook by working stitches around circular holes, picking up a garment thread with each stitch. Slip needle through fabric, surfacing to hand-sew hook end in place.

2

Place a curved eye opposite the hook, extending it slightly beyond the garment edge. Edges of garment should meet when hook and eye are fastened. Attach eye by working stitches around circular holes, picking up a garment thread with each stitch. Slip needle through fabric, surfacing to hand-sew eye in place.

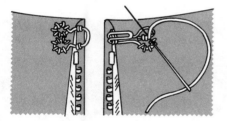

3

If desired, make a thread eye instead of using a metal eye (see Thread Loops).

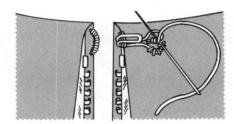

Hooks and Eyes For Edges That Overlap

HEAVY DUTY HOOK AND EYE CLOSURES

Place hook on the inside of overlapping section. Attach hook by working stitches around circular holes, picking up a garment thread with each stitch. Place eye on the outside of underlapping section. Attach eye by working stitches around circular holes.

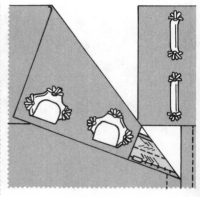

For pants with front zippers, side pocket openings and wide waistbands, position hooks and eyes as shown.

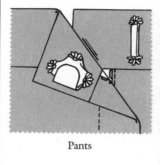

Pants

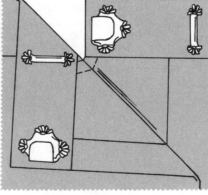

Side Pocket Openings

Wide Waistbands

REGULAR HOOKS AND EYES

Place hook(s) on the inside of overlapping section. Attach hook by working stitches around circular holes, picking up a garment thread with each stitch. Slip needle through fabric, surfacing to hand-sew hook end. Place straight eye(s) on the outside of the underlapping section. Hand-sew eye in place by working stitches around circular holes, picking up a garment thread with each stitch.

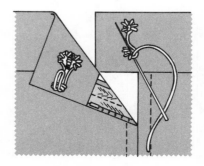

Fusible Interfacing

Always apply fusible interfacing to the facing sections, rather than garment sections, and interface the following areas:

- Facings for front and/or back garment openings

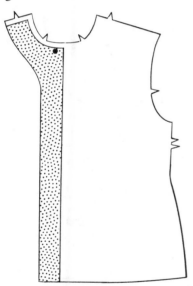

- Front and back neckline facings

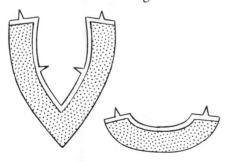

- Upper collars of dresses, blouses, and tailored jackets or coats

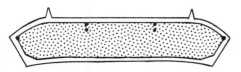

- Entire waistband or cuff

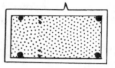

- Outer portion of detail areas such as flaps, bands, yokes, pockets, etc.

If a main garment section is interfaced with fusible interfacing, always interface the entire section. If only a portion of a section were interfaced, a ridge would show where the interfacing began.

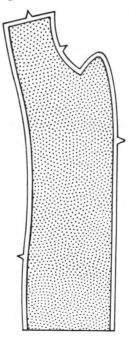

Interfacing

Fusible Interfacing

APPLYING FUSIBLE INTERFACING: ALL AREAS

1

Make a test by fusing the interfacing to a fabric sample. Check crispness of fused sample—sometimes the fusing process adds extra body or stiffness to the fabric. Change type or weight of interfacing, if necessary.

2

Cut interfacing, making sure pattern pieces are placed correctly if interfacing has grainlines or stretchability. Follow manufacturer's directions.

3

Trim ½" (13mm) from all seam allowances; trim diagonally across enclosed corners. Do not trim along foldlines.

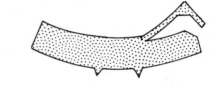

4

Fuse interfacing to wrong side of corresponding garment sections, following manufacturer's instructions. Be sure to use correct amount of steam, heat and pressure to make a permanent bond.

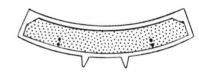

APPLYING FUSIBLE INTERFACING: FACINGS

1

Apply fusible interfacing all the way to the outer edge of facings, unless clean finishing facing edge. The interfacing bonds to the fabric during fusing, which prevents the outer raw edge from ravelling. An edge finish is not necessary.

2

However, if a more professional appearance is desired, the edge can be clean-finished or edge-finished as follows:

Fusible Interfacing

Applying Fusible Interfacing: Facings, Continued

Clean Finish

For unlined garments that might be worn open (jackets, coats, etc.), a clean finish specific to fusible interfacings gives a very finished look to garment facing edges:

1

Do not fuse interfacing yet. With right sides together, stitch outer edges of front and back neck facing and interfacing sections together in a ¼" (6mm) seam.

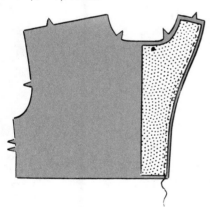

2

TRIM seam. UNDERSTITCH.

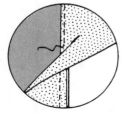

3

Turn interfacing to inside. Fuse, following manufacturer's instructions.

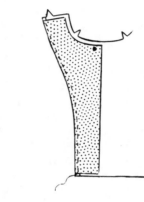

4

After shoulder seams of facings are stitched, trim outer corners of seam allowance.

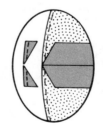

Edge Finish

1

Apply fusible interfacing all the way to the outer edge of facing.

2

Then use a regular edge finish (see Edge Finishes) suitable to fabric and type of garment.

Fusible Interfacing

Specially precut, fusible waistband interfacing is available in various widths. This interfacing is easy to apply and gives a firm, stable finish to waistbands.

1

Cut interfacing to length of waistband pattern piece.

2

Fuse to wrong side of waistband, following manufacturer's instructions.

Sew-in Interfacing

Always attach sew-in interfacing to garment sections, rather than facing sections, and interface the following areas:

• Front and/or back garment openings

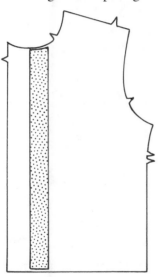

• Front and back garment necklines

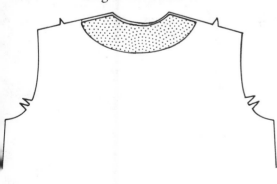

• Upper collars of dresses and blouses

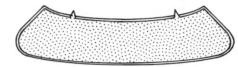

• Under collars of jackets and coats with lapels

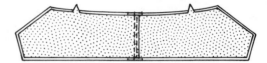

• Outer portion of detail areas such as yokes, bands, cuffs, flaps, pockets, etc.

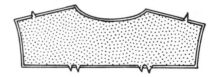

Interfacing

Sew-in Interfacing

APPLYING SEW-IN INTERFACING: ALL AREAS

1

Cut interfacing, making sure pattern pieces are placed correctly if interfacing has grainlines or stretchability. Follow manufacturer's directions.

2

For unlined garments, trim ⅜″ (10mm) from outer edge of interfacing pieces used on garment areas which will be faced.

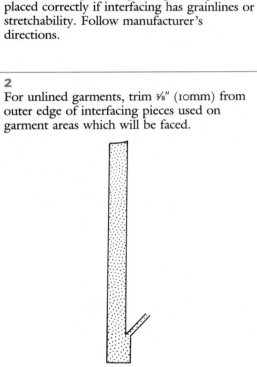

3

Pin interfacing to wrong side of fabric, matching seamlines and markings.

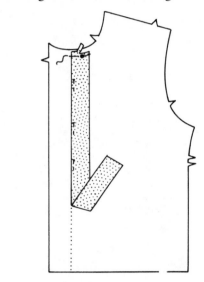

4

Trim diagonally across corner seamlines. MACHINE- or HAND-BASTE next to seamlines, on the seam allowance. Trim interfacing close to basting.

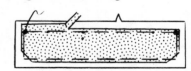

Sew-in Interfacing

Crisp Edges

When interfacing is placed along foldline or hemline of a garment section (for edgestitched or topstitched edges), CATCHSTITCH *or hand-sew invisibly to garment along foldline or hemline, with only a tiny invisible stitch catching the garment fabric.*

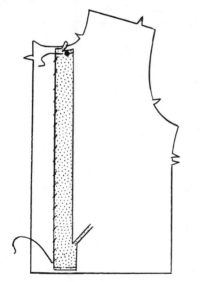

Softly Rounded Edges

When interfacing extends beyond a foldline or hemline, sew interfacing to garment along foldline or hem. Fold interfacing back and use CATCHSTITCHES or long RUNNING STITCHES with only a tiny invisible stitch catching the garment fabric.

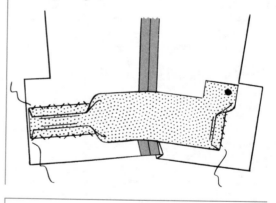

When a garment section with a foldline is completely interfaced, hand-sew interfacing invisibly to garment using long RUNNING STITCHES, with only a tiny invisible stitch catching the garment fabric.

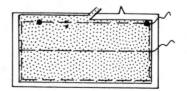

Interfacing

199

Fabric Preparation

Buy fabric according to fabric suggestions and yardage for size and view of garment. This information is usually found on the back of the pattern envelope. Additional yardage may be necessary if pattern is adjusted or if a plaid, diagonal, or striped fabric is used.

EVEN ENDS

• For woven fabrics, pull a crosswise thread until fabric puckers; cut along puckered line or tear fabric carefully along crosswise grain.

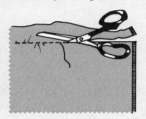

• For knitted fabrics, mark a crosswise line of loops with chalk or THREAD TRACING and cut along the line.

• Cut a tubular knit open lengthwise, following a rib or lengthwise row of loops.

CHECK GRAIN

For woven fabrics, align straightened end and one selvage edge with two edges of a square corner. If edges do not align at corner, fabric is off-grain.

Note: Knitted fabrics cannot be straightened and may be off-grain. Unless they are very off-grain they can still be used; just follow their grain as much as possible during layout.

Fabric Preparation

STRAIGHTEN GRAIN

- Permanent finish fabrics can never be straightened. Use them as they are, matching and pinning selvages only.

- Knitted fabrics cannot be straightened either. Match straightened ends of fabric only; lengthwise edges of a flat knit are not always straight.

- If a woven fabric is only slightly off-grain, steam-press threads into alignment: Fold fabric lengthwise with right sides together, pinning every few inches (cms) along selvages and straightened ends. Pin to ironing board to keep square. Press firmly, stroking from selvages toward fold.

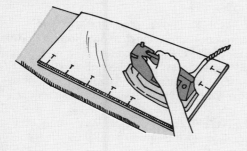

- If fabric is more than slightly off-grain, straighten by pulling fabric gently but firmly in the opposite direction from the way the ends slant, along BIAS grain, until a perfect right angle corner is formed.

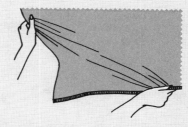

- Some printed fabrics may not be off-grain, but the print design may not coincide with grainline. Avoid these fabrics or allow print, not grain, to dictate layout.

PRESHRINK FABRIC

Note: Read label on fabric bolt to determine specifics on shrinkage and whether fabric is washable or dry cleanable.

- For washable fabrics, launder and dry fabric as you would garment. Or, fold fabric evenly and immerse in water (at a temperature suitable for fabric) for 30 minutes to an hour. Squeeze out water and dry according to fabric care instructions.

- Have dry cleanable fabrics preshrunk by a professional dry cleaner. Or, straighten ends and fold fabric in half lengthwise; baste edges together. Place on a damp sheet; fold, keeping sheet on outside. Leave fabric folded overnight. Unfold; smooth and carefully stretch fabric into right angles and on-grain. Let dry and press with a steam iron.

Understanding Terms

FABRIC AND PATTERN

Before laying pattern pieces on fabric, become familiar with the following definitions.

- BIAS: Any diagonal intersection with lengthwise and crosswise threads.

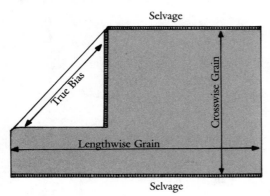

- CENTER FOLD: Pattern marking with double arrows that is used to place pattern piece along fold of fabric.

- CROSSWISE GRAIN: Threads that run from selvage to selvage.

- GRAIN: Direction in which fabric threads run.

- GRAINLINE: Pattern marking with an arrow that is used to place a pattern piece along straight grain of fabric.

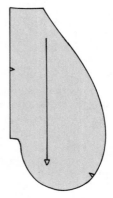

- LAYOUT: The diagram on the pattern instruction sheet which shows how to fold the fabric, and the most economical way to position pattern pieces according to the yardage recommended. Layouts are given by garment view, fabric width and garment size.

- LENGTHWISE GRAIN: Very strong and stable threads that run parallel to selvage.

- SELVAGE: Narrow, finished border along both lengthwise sides.

- TRUE BIAS: Obtained by folding on-grain fabric diagonally so crosswise threads are parallel to selvage.

Understanding Terms

TYPES OF LAYOUTS

All layouts are identified on the pattern instruction sheet by fabric width; garment view; whether the fabric has nap; and pattern size.
35" (90cm)
WITH NAP
SIZES
8-10-12

Layouts are labeled as follows:

- *CF/PT = CROSSWISE FOLD/PLIURE TRAME*
- *F/P = FOLD/PLIURE*
- *S/L = SELVAGE(S)/LISIERE(S)*

Most pattern companies produce layouts with the aid of a computer. The following types of layouts are generated for the most economical use of fabric.

- CROSSWISE FOLD: Fabric folded in half on crosswise grain with right sides together and selvages matching.

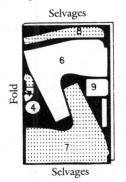

- DOUBLE FOLD: Fabric folded twice on lengthwise grain with right sides together and selvages usually meeting in the center.

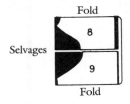

- LENGTHWISE FOLD: Fabric folded in half on lengthwise grain with right sides together and selvages matching.

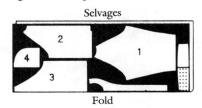

- PARTIAL-FOLD or OFF-FOLD: Fabric folded on lengthwise grain, with right sides together, only wide enough to fit width of pattern piece or pieces positioned on the fold. Other pattern pieces are placed on single layer of fabric next to folded portion.

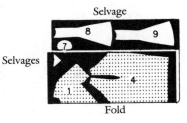

- SINGLE LAYER: Fabric opened out flat (one layer) and placed right side up.

Understanding Terms

Types of Layouts, Continued

• **STARRED LAYOUTS:** If the layout is starred with a large asterisk, fabric must be specially folded and cut:

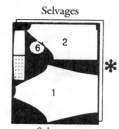

With right sides together, fold fabric crosswise. Cut along fold from selvage to selvage.

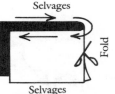

Keeping right sides together, turn upper layer completely around so nap runs in the same direction.

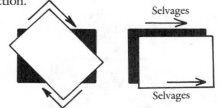

• **STARRED PIECES:** When layout shows a pattern piece extending beyond fabric fold, pattern piece is starred. Cut other pieces first; then open out fabric flat, and cut out the remaining pattern piece.

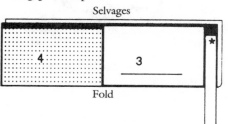

Stars are also used to indicate that pattern piece must be cut on a single layer of fabric when others are cut on a double layer;

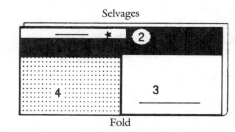

or when a pattern piece overlaps onto a second layer of fabric.

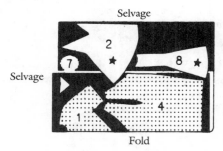

• **WITH NAP:** Layout used for cutting fabrics that have brushed surfaces (fleece), pile (velvet), woven or printed one-way designs, and texture (satin, brocade). All tops of pattern pieces and all grainline arrows should point in one direction. For richer color on velvets and velveteen, place pieces so nap runs up. Otherwise, place pattern pieces so nap runs down.

• **WITHOUT NAP:** Layout used for cutting many woven fabrics, as well as fabrics that are smooth-surfaced, or have all-over or two-way designs.

Layouts

Laying Out Pattern

Layouts are usually given for 35" (90cm), 44/45" (115cm) and 60" (150cm) fabric widths. 35" (90cm) cutting layouts are shown on pattern tissue.

1

On instruction sheet, choose correct layout according to view, pattern size and fabric width: circle.

2

Use pattern pieces designated for chosen view.

3

For double layers, fold fabric, right sides together, following chosen layout. For single layers, place fabric right side up.

4

Pin pattern tissue to fabric, following chosen layout and making sure pattern is placed on-grain. To place pattern on grain, lay tissue on fabric in position shown on cutting layout. Using a ruler or yardstick, measure from one end of grainline to selvage; pin. Measure from other end of grainline to selvage. Adjust pattern position until both measurements are the same. Pin along grainline and other edges.

5

For pattern pieces with "center fold" arrows, place edge with double arrows along fold of fabric.

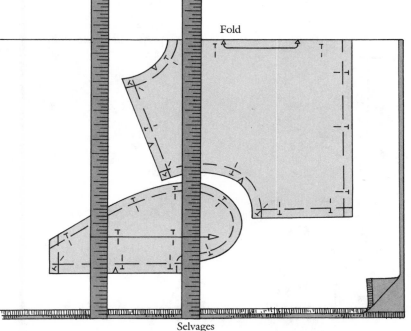

Fold

Selvages

To cut out the pattern, see Cutting.

Matching Fabric Designs

AT SEAMLINES ON PATTERN TISSUE

1

Position front pattern piece on fabric, according to most attractive position of fabric design on garment. Pin. Trace horizontal bars of plaid or stripe design onto pattern piece at side seam notch. Use colored pencils to identify colors.

2

Place reverse side of back pattern piece over front pattern piece, matching side seam notch and lapping seamlines. Trace horizontal bar design to reverse side of back pattern piece.

3

Position back pattern piece on fabric so traced bar design matches design on fabric. Pin.

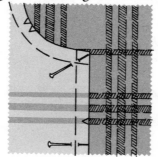

4

To match fabric design on sleeves to fabric design on front at armhole notch, place sleeve pattern piece over front pattern piece so seamlines overlap at notches. Mark point on sleeve seamline where stripe or plaid bar intersects seamline.

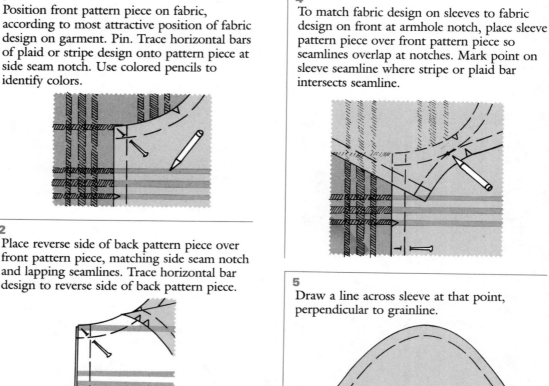

5

Draw a line across sleeve at that point, perpendicular to grainline.

6

Repeat with other pattern pieces to be matched.

Matching Fabric Designs

- If envelope illustration shows a border print or scalloped lace hem edge, the pattern will include a special layout.

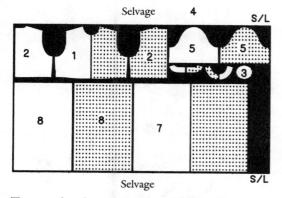

- To use a border print or lace fabric with a pattern that does not specify border prints or lace, extra yardage (metrage) may be needed. If possible, at store, lay pattern pieces out on fabric before purchasing yardage.

- For the easiest border print layout, choose a pattern with a relatively straight hemline—avoid A-line designs. Both border prints and scalloped lace require careful layout planning to achieve pleasing placement of the design on the garment and an unbroken continuation of fabric design at seams.

- Place predetermined hemline at border or scalloped edge and lengthwise arrow along crosswise grain of fabric.

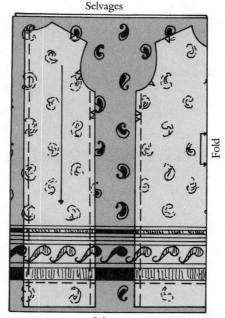

- Match design at side seams where possible (see Matching Fabric Designs, At Seamlines on Pattern Tissue). If border or lace has predominant repetitive motifs, center them at front and back where possible; sometimes, side seams will not match when this is done. Then, matching the design at center front or center back should take precedence over matching at side seams.

Matching Fabric Designs

LARGE-SCALE PRINT LAYOUTS

- The overall effect of a garment made from fabric with large-scale motifs should be totally harmonious, where nothing stands out as visually disturbing.

- Avoid placing large motifs on body curves, directly over the bust or derrière.

- Center large motifs vertically.

- If the large motifs have a definite horizontal or vertical direction, use a "with nap" layout.

- For very large motifs, select a pattern style that has only a few design lines or seams.

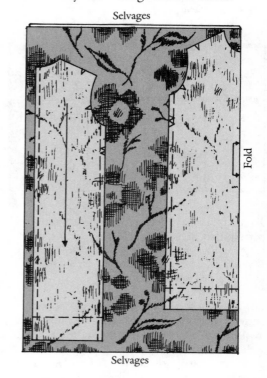

Selvages

Fold

Selvages

PLAID AND STRIPE LAYOUTS

- Determine the amount of extra yardage (metrage) needed to match the lines of plaid or stripe designs by the number of major pattern pieces needed, size of pattern tissue, and size of plaid repeat. In general, one extra plaid or stripe repeat is needed for each pattern piece that will be used.

- Follow "with nap" layouts.

- When laying the pattern pieces on fabric, always match plaid or stripe design at seamlines, not cutting lines (see Matching Fabric Designs At Seamlines on Pattern Tissue).

- Match plaid or stripe design on sleeve to fabric design on front at armhole notch; remainder of sleeve cap may not match. Match fabric design on pockets to design on garment.

- Determine the most prominent lines and colors and place them in carefully thought-out positions on each pattern piece. In plaid designs, work with the predominant stripes.

Matching Fabric Designs

- Place the dominant vertical line of a plaid or stripe at the center front or center back.

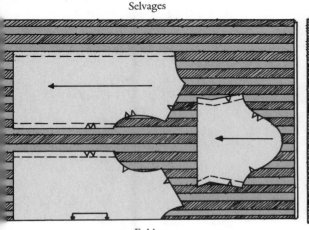

- Place dominant horizontal stripes so they are continuous from top to bottom on a garment with a waistline seam or a two-piece garment.

- Plaid or stripe lines on jackets or tops should match those of the skirt, horizontally and vertically wherever possible.

- Avoid placing a heavy, dominant horizontal stripe at the bustline or waistline. It is preferable to place it at the hemline.

- On an A-line or curved hem, place the least dominant horizontal stripe design along the hemline.

- Match plaid or stripe designs horizontally at center and side seams, starting at the bottom. It is difficult to match the designs along diagonals—darts, shoulder seams, etc. Horizontal seams above bust darts will not match.

Back Pleat

Note: Make back pleat before stitching front and back lining sections together.

1

Stitch back lining sections together, if necessary. Do not press seam open.

2

To make pleat in back lining, on inside, bring center back pleat lines together; baste. On full-length pleat, for machine-inserted lining, stitch along stitching lines above and below upper and lower small •s' and between remaining small •'s.

For pleat that tapers to seamline, stitch only above upper small •.

Full-length Pleat   Partial Length Pleat

3

For full-length pleat, press pleat toward left back; baste across upper and lower edges.

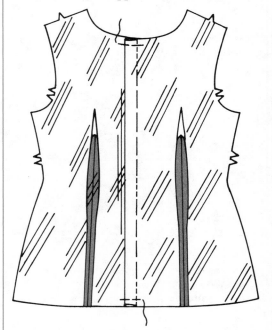

For pleat that tapers to seamline, press pleat toward left back; baste only across upper edge.

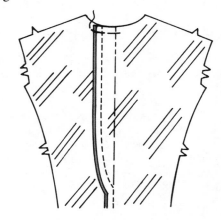

Back Pleat

Continued

4

On full-length pleat, for hand-inserted lining, on outside, CROSS-STITCH pleat above and below upper and lower small ●'s and between remaining small ●'s.

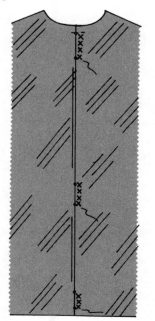

5

Eliminate cross stitch at neckline for garments with a back neck facing.

Back Vent

Note: Make back vent before stitching front and back lining sections together.

1

Trim left back lining along cut-off line for left side indicated on pattern tissue.

2

REINFORCE inner corner of left back lining, pivoting at small ●. Clip to small ●.

3

Turn in seam allowance on left back lining. Press.

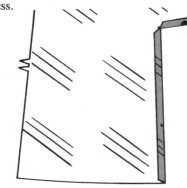

4

Turn in seam allowance on right back lining extension. Press.

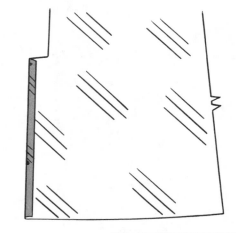

5

Machine-stitch lining sections together. Attach to garment by hand or machine.

6

After lining has been slipstitched to garment, SLIPSTITCH remainder of back lining to garment extension and self facing along seamlines.

Inserted by Hand

If lining has a back vent or pleat, refer to directions in this section.

1

Stitch front and back lining sections together.

2

STAYSTITCH front and neck edge of lining.

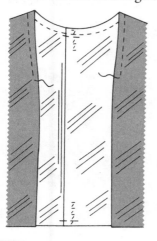

3

Turn in seam allowance on front opening and neck edge of lining, clipping where necessary; press. Hand-baste.

4

Pin lining to garment wrong sides together, matching seams. Hand-sew armhole edges together along seamlines and to shoulder pads with long RUNNING STITCHES. Trim lining armhole seam allowance even with garment. Pin basted edge of lining along facing seamline. SLIPSTITCH above lower small ●'s.

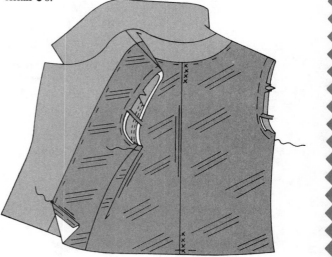

5

Turn in ⅝" (15mm) on lower edge of lining and place folded edge ⅝" (15mm) below raw edge of hem; SLIPSTITCH.

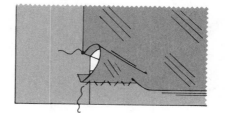

Note: A pleat will form at lower edge for wearing ease.

Inserted by Hand

Continued

6

SLIPSTITCH remainder of lining to front facing below lower small ●'s.

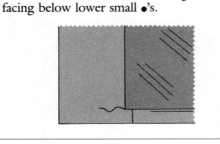

7

EASESTITCH or GATHER upper edge of sleeve lining between small ●'s. Stitch sleeve lining seam. STAYSTITCH underarm between small ●'s.

8

Turn in seam allowance on upper edge of sleeve lining, clipping where necessary; press. Hand-baste.

9

Wrong sides together, slip sleeve lining over sleeve. Pin folded edge of sleeve lining over armhole seam. For one-piece sleeve, match underarm seams and large ●'s. For two-piece sleeve, match ■'s and place large ● at shoulder seam. Adjust ease; SLIPSTITCH.

10

Turn in ⅝" (15mm) on lower edge of sleeve lining and place folded edge ⅝" (15mm) over raw edge of hem; SLIPSTITCH.

Note: a pleat will form at lower edge for wearing ease.

Linings

214

Inserted by Machine

Note: If lining has a back vent or pleat, refer to directions in this section.

1

Stitch lining sections together. To insert sleeves, see Set-In Sleeves, Round Construction.

2

STAYSTITCH front and neck edge of lining.

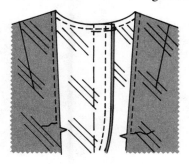

3

Open out facing. With right sides together, pin lining to garment facing, matching seams and small ●'s and clipping lining where necessary. Machine-stitch above lower small ●'s.

Inserted by Machine

Continued

4

Turn lining to inside. Slip sleeves in place. Press, turning in remaining front lining seam allowance below lower small ●'s. TACK sleeves at shoulders and underarms.

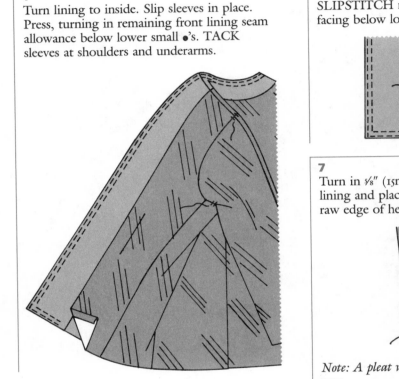

6

SLIPSTITCH remainder of lining to front facing below lower small ●'s.

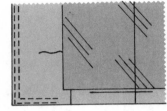

7

Turn in ⅝" (15mm) on lower edge of sleeve lining and place folded edge ⅝" (15mm) over raw edge of hem; SLIPSTITCH.

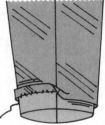

Note: A pleat will form at lower edge for wearing ease.

5

Turn in ⅝" (15mm) on lower edge of lining and place folded edge ⅝" (15mm) below raw edge of hem; SLIPSTITCH.

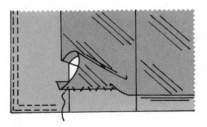

Note: A pleat will form at lower edge for wearing ease.

Lining

Fabric Loops

MAKING TUBING: CORDED TUBING

Use tubing for the loops in button closures, for spaghetti straps or for decorative closures like frogs.

1

Cut a bias strip of fabric long enough to make desired number of loops and wide enough to fit around cable cord plus ½" (13mm) for seam allowances and stretching.

2

Cut a piece of cable cord twice the length of the bias strip.

3

With right sides together, fold bias strip over cord. Stitch across short end of bias strip, at center of cord. Using a zipper foot, stitch long edge of bias next to cord, stretching bias slightly. TRIM.

4

To turn, slowly draw enclosed cord out of tubing, pushing and pulling bias over cord.

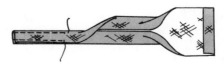

5

Cut off excess cord.

MAKING TUBING: FOLDED AND STITCHED STRIP

1

Cut a bias strip of fabric long enough to make desired number of loops and four times the desired finished width of tubing.

2

Turn in one short end. Turn in long edges of bias strip to meet at center of strip; press. Fold strip in half lengthwise; press. EDGESTITCH long edges.

Fabric Loops

MAKING TUBING: STITCHED AND TURNED TUBING

To make this tubing, use an overlock machine (see Overlock, Loops and Straps, Spaghetti Straps); or follow these directions:

1

Cut a bias strip of fabric long enough to make desired number of loops and four times the desired finished width of tubing (includes enough seam allowance to fill tubing).

2

With right sides together, fold strip in half lengthwise. Machine-stitch, leaving both ends open. Do not trim seam allowance.

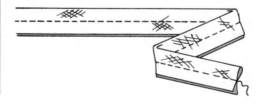

3

To turn, thread a needle with heavy thread; fasten thread securely to one end of tubing.

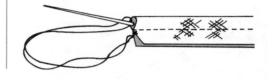

4

Push needle (eye first) through strip.

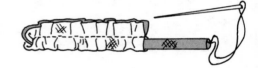

If tubing is difficult to turn, trim seam allowances a little.

Fabric Loops

APPLYING TUBING: HAND-SEWN

Note: For this method do not cut tubing or strip into sections.

1

Test pin tubing or strip to garment in position and put button through loop, adjusting length of loop so button just fits through finished loop.

2

On inside, pin loop to garment; extend ends ¼″ (6mm) at large ● and lower small ●. Remove ¼″ (6mm) of cording from each end of corded tubing. Turn under ¼″ (6mm) on ends of tubing or strips. Hand-sew securely.

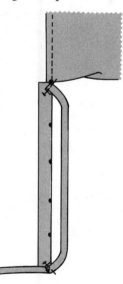

3

TACK loops in place at remaining small ●'s.

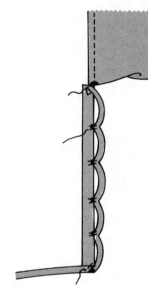

Fabric Loops

APPLYING TUBING: MACHINE-STITCHED

1

Test pin tubing or strip to garment in position and put button though loop, adjusting length of loop so button just fits through finished loop.

2

If loops are spaced apart from each other, cut tubing strip into sections, each the desired loop length plus seam allowances.

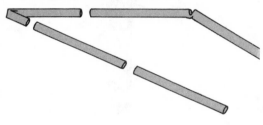

Note: For closely-spaced loops, do not cut strips.

3

On outside, for spaced loops, pin tubing or strips to garment section, centering over small ●'s with raw edges even; baste.

For closely-spaced loops, pin and baste loops as shown.

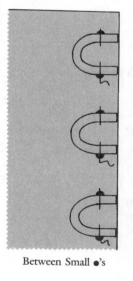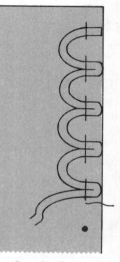

Between Small ●'s

Over Small ●'s

4

Complete garment following pattern instructions.

Frogs

1

Use tubing to form loops, face down, keeping one loop large enough to extend past garment edge and fit around button. If design is very intricate, form frog on paper with masking tape; baste.

2

TACK back of each loop in place as it is formed.

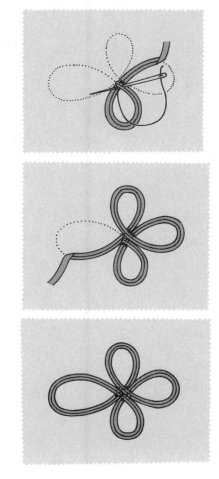

3

SLIPSTITCH to garment.

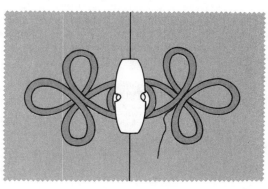

Seam Binding Dress Hanger Loops

Loops

1

Cut two pieces of seam binding, each twice the measurement from the shoulder to the waistline, plus 1″ (25mm).

2

Fold each piece of seam binding in half, lengthwise; EDGESTITCH.

3

Bring short ends of seam binding together; baste.

4

On inside, pin ends of each seam binding hanger to small ●'s at side waistline edge of skirt. Machine-stitch.

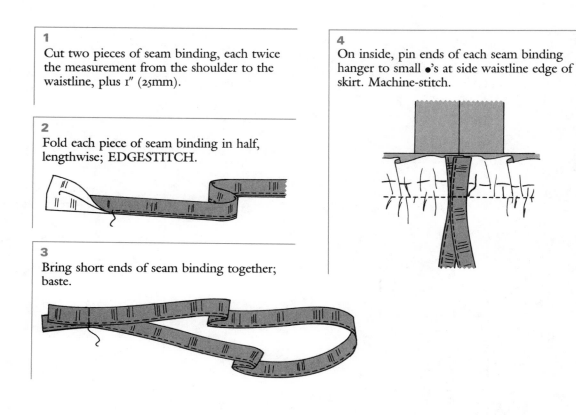

Thread Loops

Use thread loops instead of tubing for closures where there is little strain. Or, for hooks and eyes, use thread eyes instead of metal eyes.

MAKING BUTTON/LOOP CLOSURES: ON GARMENT

1

Sew button or hook to garment.

2

Place loop between symbols, if indicated. Take two or three stitches, leaving threads just long enough for button to fit through loop.

3

Work closely-spaced BLANKET STITCHES over threads to make thread loop(s).

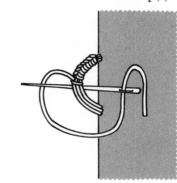

MAKING BUTTON/LOOP CLOSURES: ON OPENING EDGE

1

Sew button or hook to garment.

2

At garment opening edge opposite button(s), place loop between symbols, if indicated. Take two or three stitches, leaving threads just long enough for button to fit through loop.

3

Work closely-spaced BLANKET STITCHES over threads to make thread loop(s).

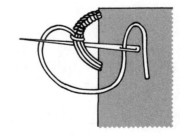

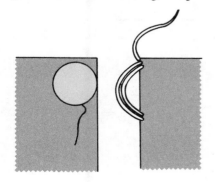

Basic Stitches

BACKSTITCH

Secure threads at end of stitching with backstitching.

Straight-stitch in reverse, following instructions in sewing machine manual.

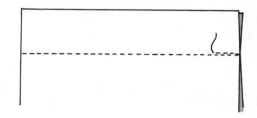

BASTING

Refer to Basting section; Specialty Stitches, Basting, in this section; and to sewing machine manual for more information on sewing machine basting methods.

Set machine on longest stitch length [6–8 stitches per inch (2–3 per cm)]. Clip stitches approximately every 1″ (25mm) to make removal easier.

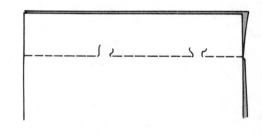

BLINDSTITCH

Do hand hemming by machine with a special automatic blindstitch. See Overlock, Hems or follow these directions.

Turn up hem; fold garment back about ¼″–⅜″ (6–10mm) beyond hem edge. Align machine blindstitch and position fabric so needle catches only one thread of folded edge. The same stitch can be used to apply elastic (see Specialty Stitches, Blind-hem or Elastic Stitches, this section).

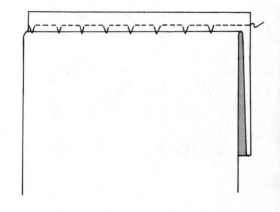

Basic Stitches

Continued

EASESTITCH: FOR AREAS WITH MODERATE EASE

To control fabric fullness in areas such as shoulders, sleeve caps and waistlines, use one of two methods:

a) Using long stitches, straight-stitch along seamline from right side of fabric. Pull thread ends and push fabric along thread, adjusting fullness to fit between symbols or markings. To provide more control on sleeve caps, make a second row of long stitches ¼" (6mm) away in seam allowance, OR

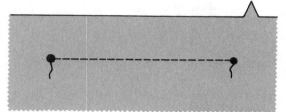
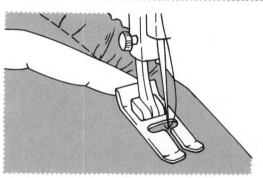

b) Press index finger against back of presser foot while straight-stitching, causing fabric to pile up against finger; do not allow tucks to form. The fabric will ease in a little fullness under the needle. Stitch several inches (centimeters) and release fabric; repeat until area between symbols or markings is eased.

Pin the two layers of fabric together; stitch seam from the eased side.

EASESTITCH: FOR AREAS WITH MORE EASE

Use the longest stitch length possible and loosen tension so bobbin threads can be pulled up easily without breaking.

Straight-stitch along seamline from right side of fabric. After distributing the fullness evenly, press seam allowance flat to avoid making tucks which could get caught in stitching. To provide more control, make a second row of stitches ¼" (6mm) away in seam allowance.

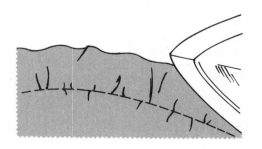

Basic Stitches

Continued

EDGESTITCH

To keep finished edges flat, hold facings to the inside of a garment and attach pockets and trims, use edgestitching.

Straight-stitch close to finished edge or seam. Some machines have a straight-stitch presser foot with a small toe that can be used as a guide for edgestitching.

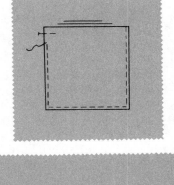

ELASTIC STITCH

Narrow elastic can be applied to garment with a special machine stitch which allows elastic to stretch without breaking stitches.

Stretch elastic to fit garment; stitch elastic in place using a multi-stitch zigzag or other elastic stitch. Refer to machine manual for specific instructions. Also see Specialty Stitches, Blind-Hem or Elastic Stitches, this section, and Pull-on Waistbands.

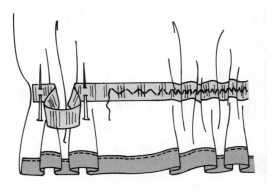

Basic Stitches

Continued

GATHERING STITCH

To control large amounts of fullness when joining a much larger section of fabric to a smaller one, use gathering stitches instead of easestitching.

Gather fabric with straight or zigzag stitches as follows:

a) For lightweight to medium weight fabrics, gather with straight gathering stitches; use medium to long stitches and loosen tension slightly. Stitch along seamline and again ¼" (6mm) away in seam allowance or along lines indicated on pattern.

Pull thread ends and push fabric along threads, adjusting fullness to fit between symbols or markings.

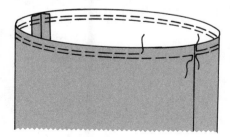

b) For heavyweight fabrics and long areas to be gathered, use zigzag gathering stitches. Place a narrow string or cord next to seamline in seam allowance. Stitch over cord with a wide zigzag, being careful not to catch cord in stitching.

Pull cord and push fabric along cord, adjusting fullness between symbols and markings. Use zipper foot to stitch along the seamline below cord. Pull out cord after seam is stitched.

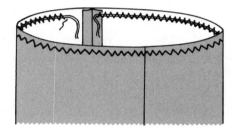

REINFORCEMENT STITCH

To prevent fabric from fraying or stretching in areas that will be clipped, reinforce seamline with machine stitching.

Use small stitches to straight-stitch along seamline where indicated in pattern sewing instructions.

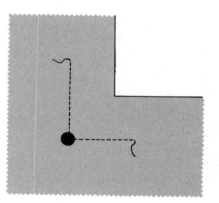

Basic Stitches

Continued

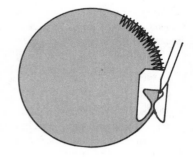

SATIN STITCH

Use a closely-spaced zigzag stitch for a bar tack to reinforce stress areas, such as pocket corners, and for stitching appliqués and buttonholes.

Set machine for zigzag stitch. Use a small stitch length. Adjust stitch width as necessary for design. Refer to machine manual for specific instructions. Also see Stitching Appliqués: Zigzag Satin Stitching.

STAYSTITCH

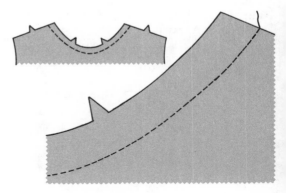

Staystitching will prevent bias or curved areas from stretching out of shape before they are stitched together.

Straight-stitch ⅛" (3mm) away from seamline in seam allowance, usually ½" (13mm) from raw edge.

STITCH-IN-THE-DITCH

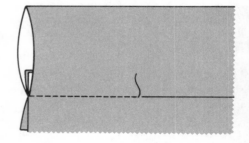

Stitching-in-the-ditch holds two seams together and eliminates hand sewing on the last step of facings, waistbands, elastic casings, pant cuffs or roll-up sleeves.

Make sure the underneath layers are aligned so seamlines match those on top. Using 10–12 stitches per inch (25mm) and spreading seam open with fingers, straight-stitch on the right side directly in the ridge or "ditch" of the seam.

Basic Stitches

Continued

TOPSTITCH

As a decorative finish, on the outside, topstitching is similar in function to edge stitching, only more noticeable.

Straight-stitch ¼" (6mm) from edge, seam or previous stitching. Use presser foot as guide, or stitch where indicated in instructions.

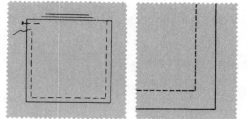

UNDERSTITCH

To prevent facings from rolling to the outside at edges, understitch.

Open out facing or underside of garment and straight-stitch facing to seam allowance, close to seam. Before stitching, trim seam and press seam and facing away from garment.

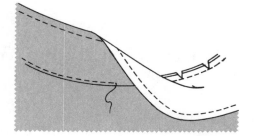

ZIGZAG STITCH

Use zigzag stitching for many different functions—as a replacement for hand sewing or as a decorative feature.

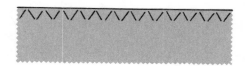

Do hand overcasting by machine, as well as many other hand-sewn details—bar tacks, buttonholes, sewing on buttons and trims.

Set the machine for a stitch length and width adjusted to the fabric weight and purpose of the zigzag. Refer to machine manual for specific instructions.

See Machine-worked Buttonholes, Elastic, Gathering, Satin Stitching, Hairline Seams, and Overcasting Edge Finish for additional information on zigzag stitching.

Specialty Stitches

Most current sewing machines have several automatic stitch designs. Some are designed with built-in strength and stretchability for sewing knit fabrics. Other specialty stitches automatically perform hand-sewing tasks. Depending on the type *of machine, these stitches will be built-in or can be added with special "cams" that fit into the machine. Be sure to follow machine manual for specific directions which vary according to type of machine.*

BASTING STITCHES

Several machines can do basting or thread tracing automatically with the option of adjusting stitch length from hand basting size to several inches (centimeters) in length.

BLIND-HEM OR ELASTIC STITCHES

Most sewing machines with special stitches have a blind hem stitch, which can be used to machine-hem almost invisibly. Some have special stretch blind-hem stitches for knits and stretch fabrics (see Basic Stitches, Blindstitch, this section). Use the same stitch, or variations of it, to apply elastic.

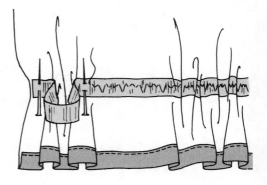

Machine Stitching

Specialty Stitches

Continued

DECORATIVE EMBROIDERY STITCHES

Most current sewing machines offer a dazzling array of embroidery stitches. To do more open machine embroidery that looks somewhat like hand embroidery, choose from the blanket, couching, cross, feather, or honeycomb stitches.

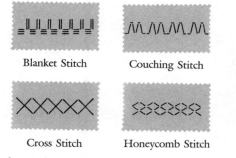

Blanket Stitch

Couching Stitch

Cross Stitch

Honeycomb Stitch

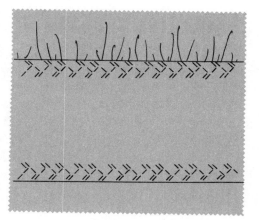

Feather Stitch

To do machine embroidery with a dense, uniform appearance, choose from scalloped or shell edge stitches, and several other satin stitch or straight-stitch designs.

Satin Stitch Designs

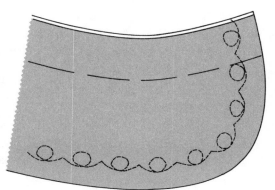

Straight Stitch Designs

MULTIPLE ZIGZAG STITCHES

Whether it is called triple zigzag, ric-rac, three-step-zigzag or multi-zigzag, this stitch is used for overcasting and finishing seams in knits which curl, in stretch and terry cloth fabrics, and for darning or patching.

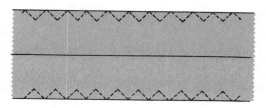

Specialty Stitches

Continued

OVERLOCK STITCHES

Also known as overedge, overcast or double-overlock stitches, depending on the sewing machine manufacturer, these stitches are all used to sew knits or stretch fabrics because they are strong, yet will stretch with the fabric. They will also prevent edges from curling.

Also see Overlock, Seams for information about sewing seams with machines that only do overlock stitching, or serging.

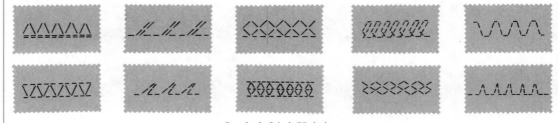

Overlock Stitch Variations

TAILOR'S TACK STITCHES

Instead of making tailor's tacks by hand, save time and make them by machine.

TRIPLE-STRAIGHT STITCHES

To stitch a very strong reinforced seam at crotch or underarms, without stitching over the seams again, use the triple-straight stitch found on most machines with specialty stitches.

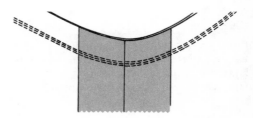

Quick Marking

CLIPS

In seams that will not be let out during fitting, make tiny clips to indicate important construction details.

Make ¼" (6mm) snips in seam allowance to mark symbols; notches; ends of darts, tucks, pleats and foldlines; and the location of zipper stop and top of sleeve.

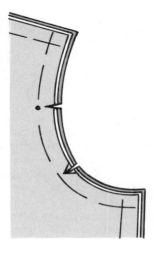

DISAPPEARING MARKING PEN

Use a disappearing marking pen to mark wrong or right side of fabric.

Place pins through pattern tissue and both layers of fabric at symbols. Carefully remove pattern tissue, leaving pins in place and tearing pattern as little as possible. Use tip of pen to mark both layers of fabric at each pin. Remove pins as they are marked.

Remove markings with water or let them disappear in 12 to 48 hours. They will also disappear when steam-pressed.

Note: Be sure to test pen on a scrap of fabric before marking to see that markings show and then disappear as expected.

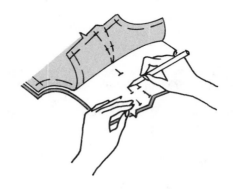

Quick Marking

MACHINE BASTING

Use machine basting to join two garment sections in a perfect point.

First MACHINE-BASTE each section along the seamlines as a stitching guide; then match the seamlines.

To mark the pivot point on a V-neckline or yoke garment section and facing, use machine basting and stitch two intersecting lines on the seamlines. Then pin both layers together at the marked points before stitching. Remove basting when garment is completed.

Use machine basting on many fabric types to mark button and buttonhole placement.

Stitch along the placement lines through pattern tissue and fabric to mark the right side. Carefully remove pattern tissue, tearing pattern as little as possible.

Or, use a disappearing marking pen, or dressmaker's carbon paper and tracing wheel to mark the wrong side of fabric first; then MACHINE-BASTE along markings so they show on the right side (see Buttonholes, Marking).

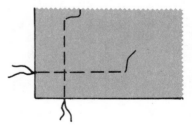

PINS

If a garment will be constructed immediately, marking with pins is a fast and easy method.

Place pins through pattern tissue and both layers of fabric at all symbols.

Turn piece over and insert additional pins at each pin. Carefully remove pattern tissue, leaving pins in place and tearing pattern as little as possible. Then, carefully separate the two fabric layers; secure pins on each layer of fabric.

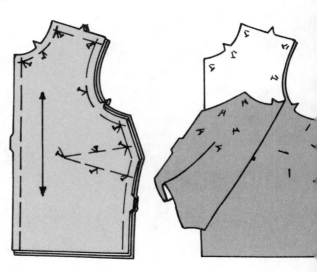

Traditional Marking

DRESSMAKER'S CARBON PAPER AND TRACING WHEEL

Some dressmaker's carbons are water soluble. If fabric is washable, mark details such as pocket or buttonhole placement on the right side of fabric; markings will wash out. They will also disappear when steam pressed.

Note: Be sure to test carbon on a scrap of fabric before marking to see that markings show and then disappear as expected.

To easily mark both layers of fabric at the same time, fold carbon paper in half and place it under pattern tissue, with carbon facing wrong side of both fabric layers (sandwich fabric between folded carbon paper). Use a tracing wheel to mark lines and symbols. A ruler will help with marking straight lines.

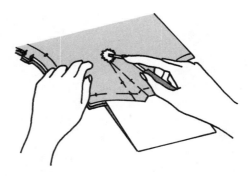

TAILOR'S CHALK OR PENCIL

For soft- or hard-surfaced fabrics, use tailor's chalk or pencil. A special marking pencil is also available. The marks it makes can be removed with a fabric eraser. Use the same marking procedures as for a chalk pencil.

Place pins through pattern and both layers of fabric at symbols. Turn piece over and chalk wrong side of fabric at each pin.

Turn piece back to pattern side. Carefully remove pattern, leaving pins in place and tearing pattern as little as possible. Chalk wrong side of fabric at each pin.

Remove pins as they are marked. Run THREAD TRACING along chalk lines if chalk tends to rub off.

Traditional Marking

TAILOR'S TACKS

Use this method on delicate fabrics that might be marred by other methods, or on spongy or napped surfaces. The technique is the same whether marking fabric in single or double layers.

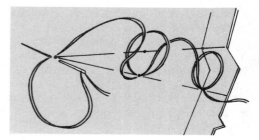

Using a long, double strand of thread without a knot, take a single, tiny RUNNING STITCH through pattern tissue and fabric at a symbol. Then, sew another stitch crossing over the first, pulling thread until a large loop is formed; do not cut thread. Go on to next symbol, leaving a loose thread in between each symbol.

Clip long threads connecting each tack and each loop. Carefully remove pattern tissue by pinching it at each symbol and pulling pattern away from thread, tearing it as little as possible.

Gently pull pieces apart and cut threads between layers, leaving tufts on either side.

THREAD TRACING

Use UNEVEN BASTING for quick marking of grainlines on all fabrics and for transferring necessary position marks to right side of fabric.

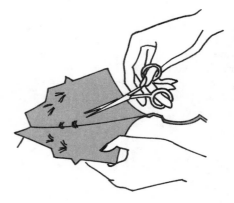

Using a single thread (do not use a knot), take a small backstitch; then use uneven basting with tiny short stitches and leave long threads in between.

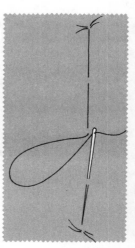

Use silk thread or basting thread on napped or pile fabrics, and light colors to avoid leaving an imprint. Thread-trace center front and center back lines, buttonhole markings, foldlines, grainlines, etc. on one garment section at a time.

Corners

INSIDE CORNERS

Stitching corners on overlock machines must be done carefully.

Pre-trim fabric to finished size. Place fabric under presser foot, aligning fabric edge to left of cutting knife. Lower presser foot and stitch, continuing into corner as far as possible.

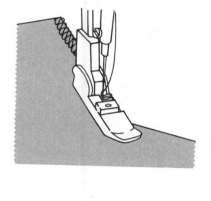

To prevent cutting into fabric, turn other edge of corner out straight in front of knife. To do this, raise needle and presser foot; turn fabric to align other corner edge with needle plate. Lower presser foot and continue stitching.

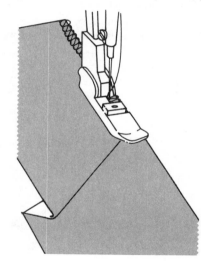

OUTSIDE CORNERS

Stitching corners on overlock machines must be done carefully.

Pre-trim fabric to finished size. Place fabric under presser foot, aligning fabric edge to left of cutting knife. Lower presser foot and stitch to end of corner. Stitch one stitch past corner. Raise needle and presser foot. Gently pull thread chain from stitch finger. Turn fabric to align other corner edges with needle plate; lower presser foot and continue stitching. On last corner, secure stitches (see Ending Seams, this section).

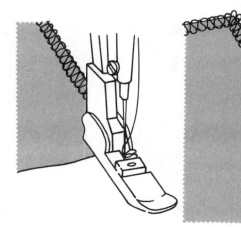

237

Curves

INWARD CURVES

When stitching curves, try to keep the fabric as straight as possible.

While stitching, keep flow of fabric even by gently pushing fabric toward presser foot. Use both hands to push fabric; knives and feed dogs on an overlock machine exert more pressure than on a regular sewing machine.

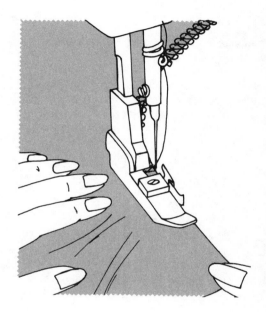

OUTWARD CURVES

When stitching curves, try to keep the fabric as straight as possible.

While stitching, keep flow of fabric even by gently pulling fabric away from presser foot. Use both hands to pull fabric; knives and feed dogs on an overlock machine exert more pressure than on a regular sewing machine.

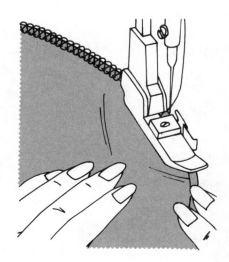

Elastic

Save the time of making a casing and inserting elastic by stitching elastic directly to the garment edge.

Follow elastic chart on pattern instruction sheet for proper width and length of elastic. Divide fabric edge and elastic into equal sections; mark with pins or water-soluble marker.

Turn in ¼" (6mm) on edge of garment; press. With wrong side up, place fabric under presser foot, aligning fabric edge with edge of needle plate. Place elastic even with folded edge of garment. Secure elastic with a few stitches; then stitch, stretching elastic and matching marks. Remove pins before they reach the cutting knife. Be careful not to cut elastic when stitching.

This elastic application will be visible on the inside and almost invisible on the outside of the garment.

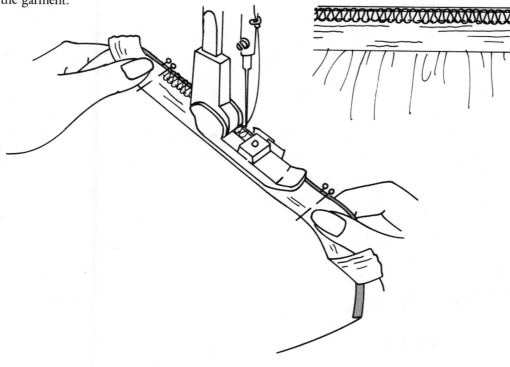

Hems

BLIND HEM

This is a good hem finish for a full skirt or dress. An optional attachment may be required.

Turn up hem; press. Fold hem to right side, forming a soft fold on garment, with the raw hem edge extending past the fold the width of the overlock stitch.

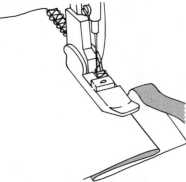

With fabric wrong side up, feed folded edge through guide on presser foot; stitch, catching a *tiny* portion of the folded edge. The excess hem allowance will be trimmed away during stitching. Stitches should be almost invisible on the right side.

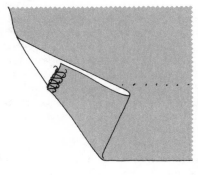

LADDER HEM

This hem is often found on ready-to-wear T-shirts and sweatshirts.

Fold fabric accordion style by turning up hem, then folding same hem back to right side.

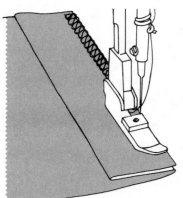

With fabric right side up, place under presser foot, aligning fabric edge to left of cutting knife. Stitch through raw hem edge and fold, being careful not to cut folded edge. Unfold fabric and pull stitches flat. The ladder effect will show on the right side.

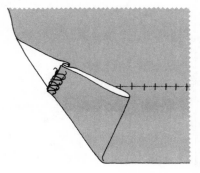

Hems

NARROW OR ROLLED HEM

Save time and use this decorative hem on all fabrics to give a uniformly stitched, raised hem finish to hems, ruffles, scarves and napkins. Good quality thread selection is important. For example, lustrous embroidery thread gives napkins and scarves a "professional" edge.

A separate attachment and stitch settings are usually necessary for this hem. Refer to machine manual to determine if the needle plate and presser foot must be changed. Practice on fabric scraps first to obtain the correct tension.

If hem allowance is wider than dust cover on machine, trim it off. With right side up, place fabric under presser foot, aligning fabric edge to left of cutting knife; overlock along hem edge.

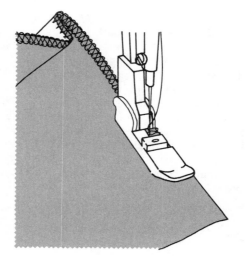

Overlock

SINGLE OR OVEREDGED HEM

For a uniformly stitched, flat hem finish that shows on the right side and eliminates the need for a hem allowance, use an overedged hem.

If hem allowance is wider than dust cover on machine, trim it off. With right side up, place fabric under presser foot, aligning fabric edge to left of cutting knife; stitch along hem edge.

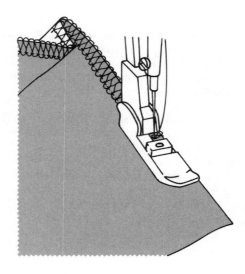

Loops and Straps

BELT LOOPS: FABRIC

Using an overlock machine is the quick way to make fabric belt loops or carriers.

Cut a strip of fabric long enough to make desired number of loops (including seam allowances) and twice the desired finished width plus seam allowances. With wrong sides together, fold strip in half lengthwise. Position folded strip to left of cutting knife. Overlock entire edge; then remove from machine.

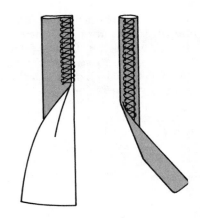

Centering overlocked edge on the underside, press strip flat.

Cut strips into number of loops needed and apply seam sealant at each end. Apply to garment (see Fabric Carrier Applications).

BELT LOOPS: THREAD CHAIN

To make inconspicuous and quick thread belt carriers, use an overlock machine.

Using a color to match fabric, stitch a thread chain long enough to make desired number and sizes of carriers. Clip chain from machine and tie a knot at one end. Place one mark on garment side seam for each belt carrier.

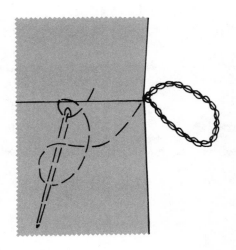

Thread a yarn needle with thread chain; at the carrier marking on the inside of the garment, insert needle and pull it through to the outside. Leaving a loop large enough to fit belt, plus a little extra, insert needle to inside near mark. Tie a knot to secure chain on inside; clip the chain. Repeat for the next carrier.

Loops and Straps

For a very easy way to make Spaghetti Straps, use an overlock machine.

Cut strips of fabric ¾" (20mm) wide and the desired finished length of strap plus seam allowances. Run a chain of stitches the length of the strip plus 2" (5cm). DO NOT CUT THE CHAIN.

Place fabric right side up, pull thread chain forward and lay it lengthwise down the center, leaving a 2" (5cm) tail at bottom. With right sides together, fold strip in half lengthwise, enclosing the thread chain; keeping thread chain at fold, overlock raw edges together.

Cut thread from machine; remove strap.

Holding strap firmly, gently pull on thread tail; fabric will turn itself right side out.

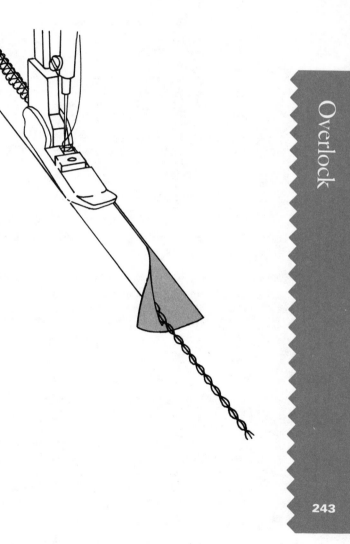

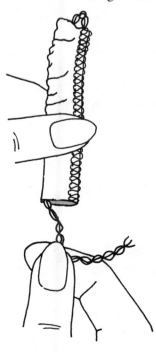

Overlock

243

Removing Stitches

TYPES OF OVERLOCK STITCHES

A four-thread machine uses two threads to make an overedge stitch and two threads to make a chainstitch.

On bottom side of stitching, pull on looper thread at end of chain stitching (it may be necessary to pull out one or more loops to "release" the chain). Then, use a seam ripper to cut overedge stitches; pull out cut threads. Use a magnifying lens to help distinguish needle and looper threads.

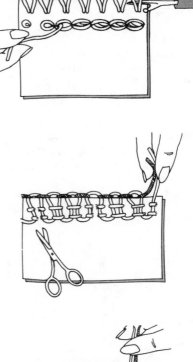

A three/four-thread machine uses the fourth thread for "safety" stitches down the middle of the longer thread.

On top side of stitching, clip two needle threads every three stitches or so. At edge of stitching, hold both looper threads and pull straight out. Remove the remaining needle threads.

On the three-thread machine, the stitching produced looks the same on both sides.

On top side of stitching, clip needle thread every three stitches or so. Hold both looper threads at edge of stitching and pull them straight out. Then, pull out needle threads.

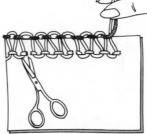

The two-thread overlock stitch looks like overedging on one side and has straight stitches perpendicular to the edge on the other.

Use a seam ripper to cut stitches; pull cut threads.

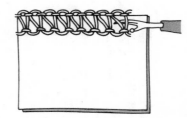

Seams

The techniques that follow may vary according to each specific overlock machine. Refer to the machine manual for further directions.

BEGINNING SEAMS

Stitch a 2" (5cm) long thread chain on the machine. Place fabric edges to left of cutting knife, bring thread chain end to left around presser foot and align chain on seam to be stitched. Secure chain by stitching over fabric and chain for about 1" (25mm). Trim excess thread by putting the chain in front of the knife—it will be cut off as the machine stitches.

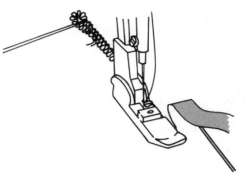

ENDING SEAMS

Although stitches in the chain are tightly locked, hanging chains and threads can make insides look messy. Following are several ways to secure ends neatly.

Encase Ends

Stitch one stitch beyond seam edge; lift presser foot, carefully pull threads off stitch finger.

Turn fabric over and bring it to the front of the machine. Re-stitch seam end for 1" (25mm), then stitch off edge at a sharp angle.

Knot tail and/or secure with seam sealant.

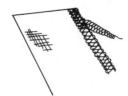

Hand-sew Ends

Thread a large-eyed needle with thread chain tail; hand-sew or weave tail back under stitching.

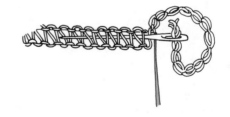

Knot Ends

Knot thread end close to seam; trim the thread chain tail.

Seams

Ending Seams, Continued

Seal Ends

Always leave a thread chain tail at ends of seams. Clip chain tail close to seam and apply a sealant, such as Fray Check™ or Fray No More™ (test on fabric first).

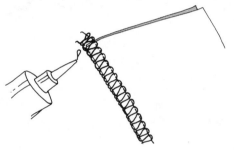

Stitch Off Ends

For circular shapes like skirt hems, stop sewing when stitching meets beginning stitches. With needle in fabric; raise presser foot and fold fabric back to left of needle.

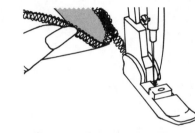

Lower foot and angle final stitches off fabric edge, being careful not to cut fabric. Trim thread chain tail or weave it back into the stitching with a needle.

FINISHING SEAMS

For neat, trim finishes, overlock garment pieces before constructing garment. This is especially helpful for fabrics that ravel. Stitch along fabric edge, being careful not to cut into seam allowances.

Seam allowances can also be finished after seaming. If using a two- or three-thread overlock machine, stitch a standard ⅝″ (15mm) seam; then overlock seam allowances, either singly or together. Be careful not to cut into seam allowances unless narrow seams are desired, on sheer fabrics, for example.

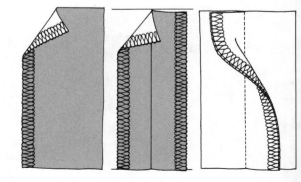

Seams

PLAIN SEAMS

To stitch and finish a seam, first hold the two fabric edges together, using a glue stick or basting tape instead of pins, which get in the way during stitching.

Adjust stitch width and length according to fabric and/or manufacturer's suggestion—as a rule of thumb, use a narrow stitch width for lightweight to medium weight fabrics and a wider stitch width for medium weight to heavyweight fabrics. Align raw edges with the ⅝" (15mm) mark on dust plate cover; stitch.

Since there is very little space on the overlock machine to maneuver fabric, use flat construction methods whenever possible. Keep one seam open on all potentially circular pieces, such as sleeves or skirts, until the garment is ready for the final seam.

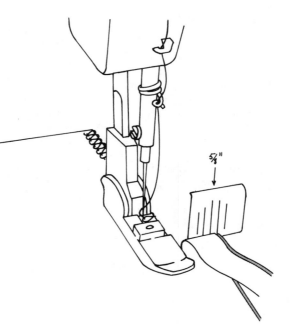

SAFETY SEAMS

Use a regular sewing machine to sew a second safety seam at stress points.

Once the seam has been overlocked on sleeves and shoulders, press it to one side and reinforce it by EDGESTITCHING close to first seam.

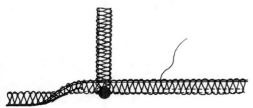

To give strength to crotch and underarm seams, sew a safety seam next to the overlocked seam.

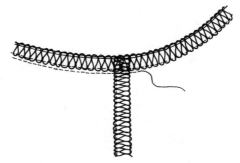

Trims

FLAT LACE AND RIBBON TRIM

With an overlock machine, lace and ribbon can be stitched on simultaneously.

Use a flat lace trim with finished edges and ⅛" (3mm) wide ribbon. Lightly mark the trim placement line on right side of fabric. Set stitch width slightly wider than width of ribbon. With wrong sides together, fold fabric on placement line. With hem edge on top, position garment to the left of cutting knife. Place straight edge of lace even with folded edge of fabric; place ribbon on top of lace. Lower presser foot; stitch over the ribbon edges, being careful not to stitch into the ribbon or cut into the fabric.

Unfold fabric and pull stitches flat.

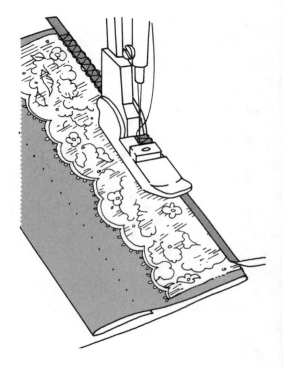

RIBBING

For sportswear, T-shirts and jogging clothes, apply rib knit trim to sleeves, necklines and legs with an overlock machine.

Divide ribbing and garment edge into equal sections; mark with pins. Place the ribbing on right side of garment, matching pin markers. With ribbing on top and making sure that both edges will fall to the left of the cutting knife, place fabric and ribbing under presser foot. Overlock the pieces together, stretching ribbing to fit. (To prevent the needle from breaking, stretch ribbing in front of the needle only.)

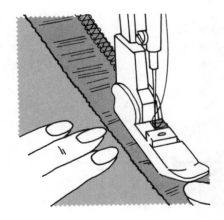

Pleat Preparation

MARKING

Three types of symbols are generally used to mark pleats. Small and large ●'s or ■'s indicate a pleat crease line or placement line. Arrows indicate direction to fold or press pleats.

Transfer all symbols and lines to fabric. If making pleats from the right side, mark on right side, using tailor's tacks or thread tracing. If making pleats from the wrong side, mark on wrong side using any marking method.

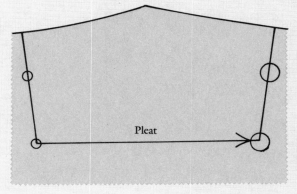

Pleat

PRESSING: PRESSED PLEATS

Make certain pleats are accurately measured and marked. Baste along each pleat fold; pin to ironing board at pleat edges.

Use a press cloth on the right side to avoid shine. To assure a sharp, lasting press, iron on both sides of each pleat fold.

To avoid creating an unattractive ridge or line on the garment beneath the pleat folds formed on the underside, insert strips of brown paper under pleat fold before light pressing.

Lightly steam unpressed pleats just to set the shape and fall of the pleat as the designer intended. This can be done most effectively while the garment hangs on a dress form.

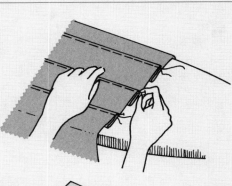

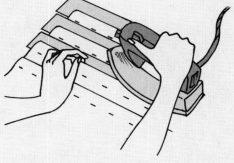

Box Pleats

Pleats

1

On outside, bring lines of large ●'s together.
Stitch to lower large ●.

2

Press pleat(s) flat. Baste across raw edges.

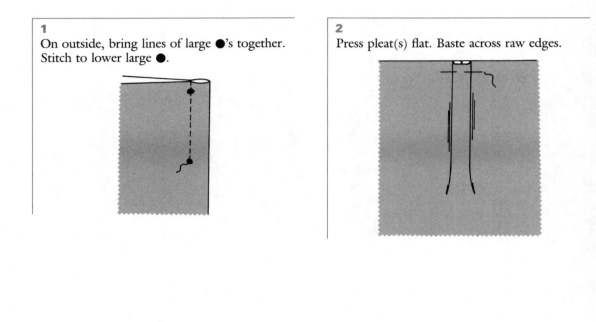

Inverted Pleats

1

On inside, bring lines of large ●'s together. Stitch or baste to lower large ●.

2

Press pleat(s) flat. Baste across raw edges. If EDGESTITCHING or TOPSTITCHING pleat(s), baste along pressed edge(s).

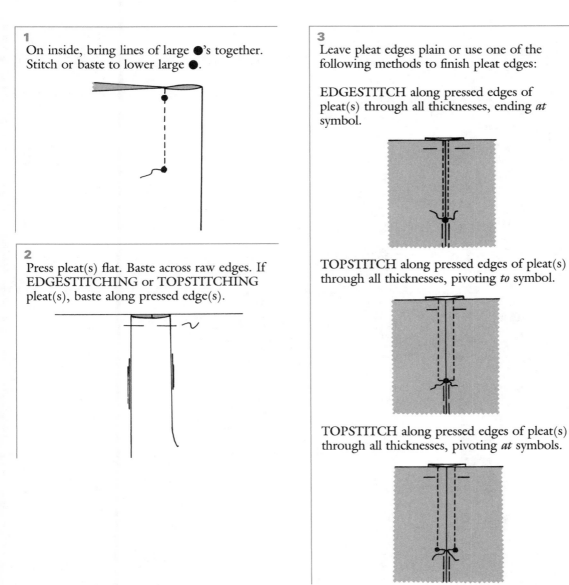

3

Leave pleat edges plain or use one of the following methods to finish pleat edges:

EDGESTITCH along pressed edges of pleat(s) through all thicknesses, ending *at* symbol.

TOPSTITCH along pressed edges of pleat(s) through all thicknesses, pivoting *to* symbol.

TOPSTITCH along pressed edges of pleat(s) through all thicknesses, pivoting *at* symbols.

4

Remove basting along pleat edge(s).

Inverted Pleats

PLEATS MADE FROM THE OUTSIDE

1
On outside, crease along line(s) of small ●'s. Bring crease(s) to line(s) of large ●'s; baste. Baste across upper edge. Press.

2
Leave pleat edges plain or use one of the following methods to finish edges: EDGESTITCHING or TOPSTITCHING along pressed edges of pleat(s) through all thicknesses (see Inverted Pleats Made From the Inside).

3
Remove basting along pleat edge(s).

PLEATS WITH UNDERLAY

1
Pin garment sections together, matching stitching lines and lines of large ●'s; baste. Stitch to ■.

2
Press extensions open.

Inverted Pleats

Pleats with Underlay, Continued

3

Pin underlay to extensions. Stitch, pivoting at small ●'s, breaking stitching at ■ and keeping garment free. Do not press seams open. Baste across underlay edge.

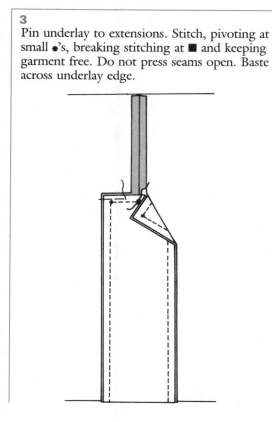

4

Leave seam above pleat plain or use one of the following methods to finish seam:

EDGESTITCH seam through all thicknesses, ending *at* ■.

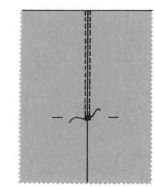

TOPSTITCH seam through all thicknesses, pivoting *to* ■.

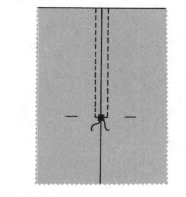

5

Remove basting across underlay edge(s).

Shaped Pleats

Pleats

1

Stitch garment sections together.

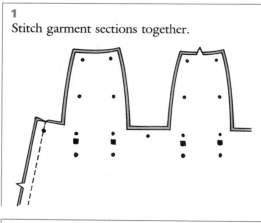

2

On inside, bring stitching lines and lines with symbols together; baste. Stitch along stitching lines to ■'s. Press pleat extensions open and press pleat(s) flat. Baste across upper edge of pleat extension.

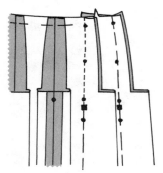

3

Stitch underlay edge of pleat(s) from folds to large ●'s, breaking stitching at large ●'s and keeping garment free.

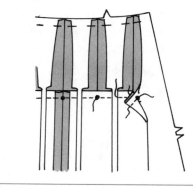

4

Leave seam above pleat plain or use one of the following methods to finish seam: EDGESTITCHING or TOPSTITCHING (see Inverted Pleats With Underlay).

5

Remove basting across pleat extension(s).

Straight Pleats (Pressed or Unpressed)

1

On inside, bring lines of large ●'s together. Stitch or baste to lower large ●.

2

Press pleat(s) to one side in direction of arrow(s). Baste across raw edges.

If EDGESTITCHING or TOPSTITCHING pleat(s), baste along pressed edge(s).

3

Leave pleat edges plain or use one of the following methods to finish edges:

EDGESTITCH along pressed edge of pleat(s) through all thicknesses, ending *at* symbol.

3 *Continued*

TOPSTITCH along pressed edge of pleat(s) through all thicknesses, pivoting *to* symbol.

TOPSTITCH along pressed edge of pleat(s) through all thicknesses, pivoting *at* symbol.

EDGESTITCH and TOPSTITCH along pressed edge of pleat(s) through all thicknesses, pivoting *to* symbol.

EDGESTITCH and TOPSTITCH along pressed edge of pleat(s) through all thicknesses, pivoting *at* symbol.

4

Remove basting along pleat edge(s).

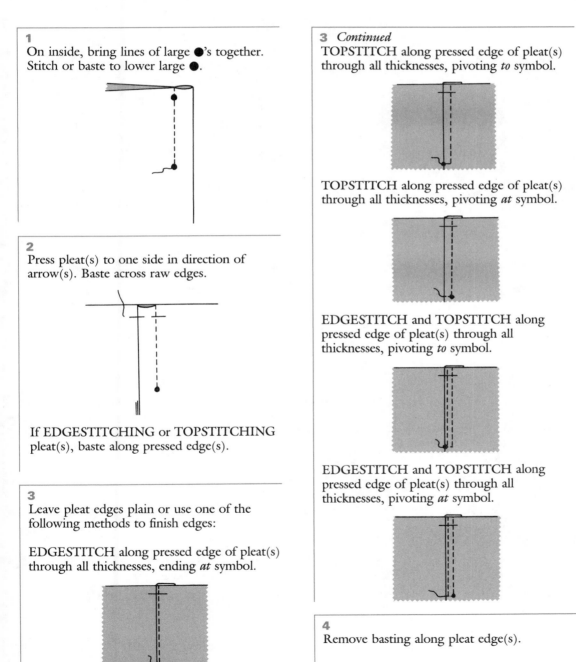

Pleats

Straight Pleats (Pressed or Unpressed)

PLEATS MADE FROM THE OUTSIDE

1

On outside, crease along line(s) of small ●'s.
Bring crease(s) to line(s) of large ●'s; baste.
Baste across upper edge. Press.

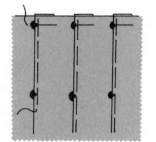

2

Leave pleat edges plain or use one of the
following methods to finish edges:
EDGESTITCHING, TOPSTITCHING, or
EDGESTITCHING and TOPSTITCHING
along pressed edge of pleat(s) through all
thicknesses (see Straight Pleats Made From
the Inside).

3

Remove basting along pleat edge(s).

Mock Flap

1

INTERFACE wrong side of one flap section.

2

For self-lined flap, with right sides together, stitch flap sections together. For lined flap, with right sides together, stitch lining to flap. For both, leave upper edge open.

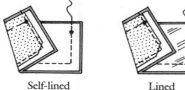

Self-lined   Lined

3

TRIM seam.

4

Turn flap; press. Baste raw edges together.

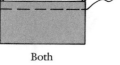

Both

5

Leave flap edges plain or use one of the following methods to finish sides and lower edge of flap: EDGESTITCHING, TOPSTITCHING or EDGESTITCHING and TOPSTITCHING (see Mock Welt).

6

Pin interfaced side of flap to garment section, placing seamline along stitching line; baste. Stitch along seamline. Trim flap seam allowance to a scant ¼" (6mm).

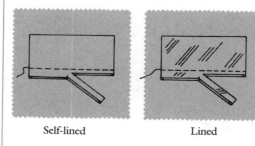

Self-lined   Lined

7

Turn flap down; press.

8

TOPSTITCH flap in place on upper edge.

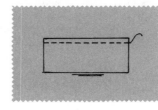

Both

Mock Welt

1

INTERFACE wrong side of welt.

2

With right sides together, fold welt along foldline. Stitch ends.

3

TRIM seams.

4

Turn welt; press. Baste raw edges together.

5

Leave edges of welt plain or use one of the following methods to finish edges:

EDGESTITCH,

TOPSTITCH,

EDGESTITCH and TOPSTITCH.

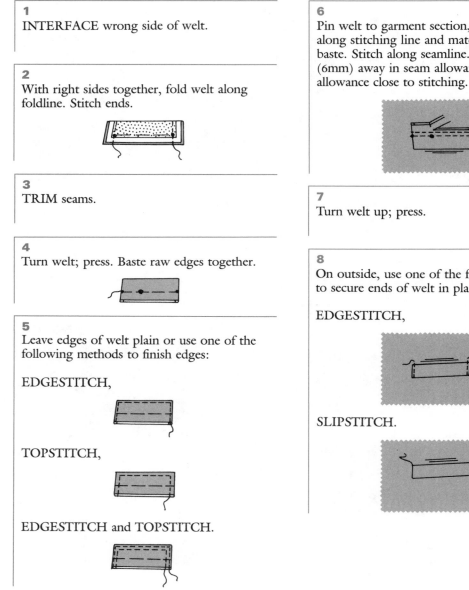

6

Pin welt to garment section, placing seamline along stitching line and matching symbols; baste. Stitch along seamline. Stitch again ¼" (6mm) away in seam allowance. Trim seam allowance close to stitching.

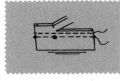

7

Turn welt up; press.

8

On outside, use one of the following methods to secure ends of welt in place:

EDGESTITCH,

SLIPSTITCH.

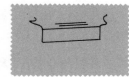

Patch Pockets

LINED

1

With right sides together, stitch pocket lining to upper edge of pocket, leaving an opening.

Square　　　　Round

2

Press seam toward lining.

3

Turn lining and upper edge of pocket to outside along foldline. Stitch sides and lower edge.

Square　　　　Round

4

Trim seam. For square pocket, also cut diagonally across corner. For rounded pocket, also notch curves.

Square　　　　Round

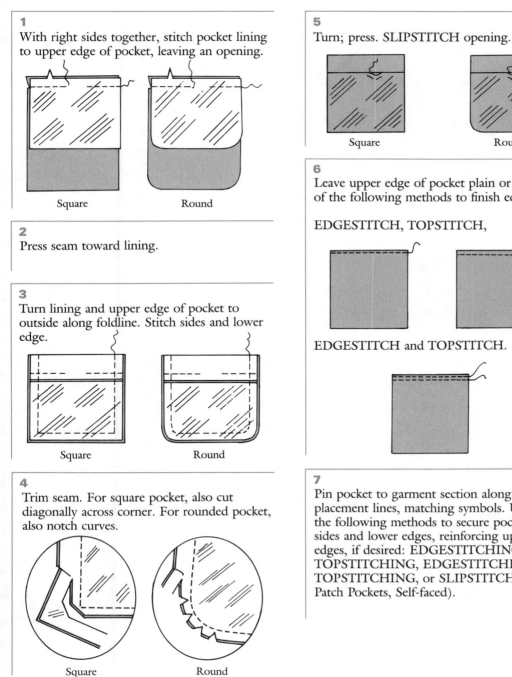

5

Turn; press. SLIPSTITCH opening.

Square　　　　Round

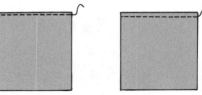

6

Leave upper edge of pocket plain or use one of the following methods to finish edge:

EDGESTITCH, TOPSTITCH,

EDGESTITCH and TOPSTITCH.

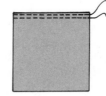

7

Pin pocket to garment section along placement lines, matching symbols. Use one of the following methods to secure pocket along sides and lower edges, reinforcing upper edges, if desired: EDGESTITCHING, TOPSTITCHING, EDGESTITCHING and TOPSTITCHING, or SLIPSTITCHING (see Patch Pockets, Self-faced).

Patch Pockets

SELF-FACED

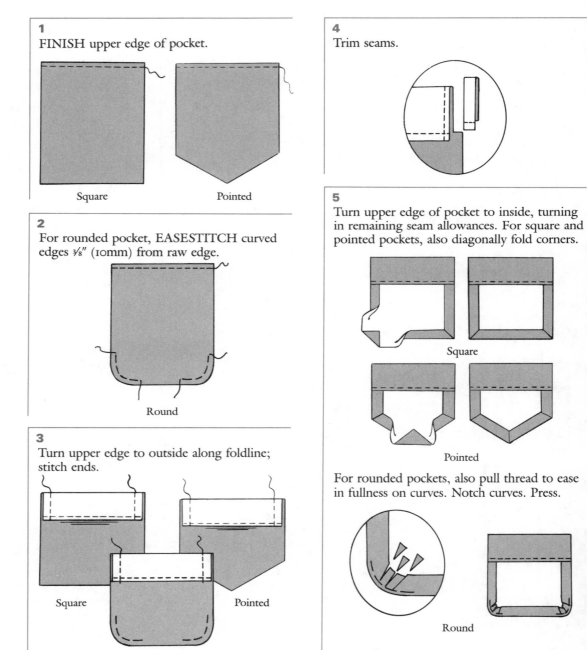

1

FINISH upper edge of pocket.

Square   Pointed

2

For rounded pocket, EASESTITCH curved edges ⅜″ (10mm) from raw edge.

Round

3

Turn upper edge to outside along foldline; stitch ends.

Square   Pointed

Round

4

Trim seams.

5

Turn upper edge of pocket to inside, turning in remaining seam allowances. For square and pointed pockets, also diagonally fold corners.

Square

Pointed

For rounded pockets, also pull thread to ease in fullness on curves. Notch curves. Press.

Round

Patch Pockets

6

Leave upper edge of pocket plain or use one of the following methods to finish edge: EDGESTITCHING, TOPSTITCHING, or EDGESTITCHING and TOPSTITCHING (see Patch Pockets, Lined).

7

Pin pocket to garment section along placement lines, matching symbols. Use one of the following methods to secure pocket along sides and lower edges, reinforcing upper edges, if desired:

7 *Continued*
EDGESTITCH and TOPSTITCH,

EDGESTITCH,

TOPSTITCH,

SLIPSTITCH.

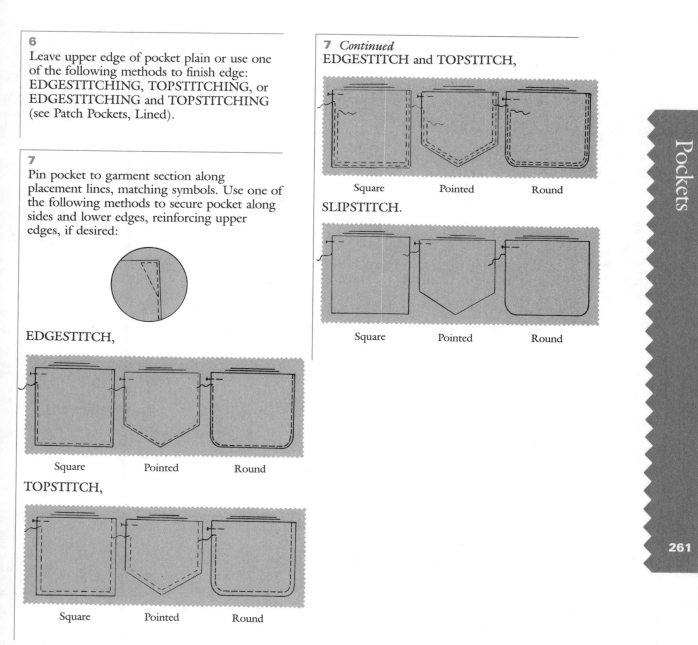

Square   Pointed   Round

Square   Pointed   Round

Square   Pointed   Round

Square   Pointed   Round

Patch Pockets

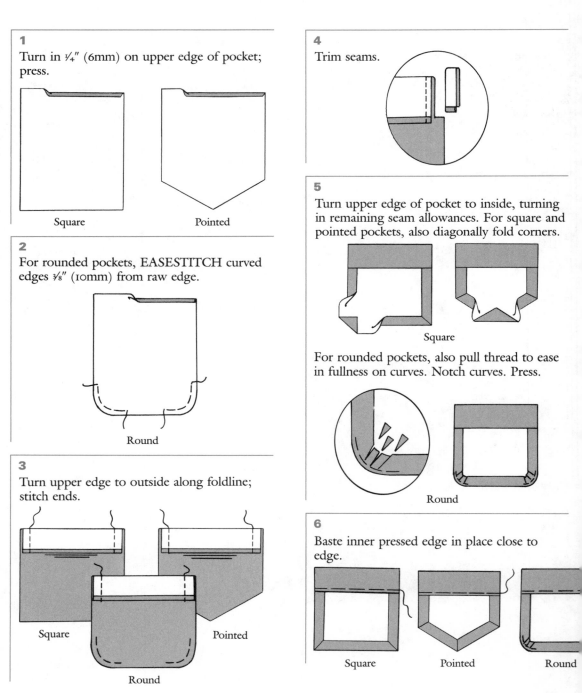

SELF-FACED AND TOPSTITCHED

1

Turn in ¼" (6mm) on upper edge of pocket; press.

Square   Pointed

2

For rounded pockets, EASESTITCH curved edges ⅜" (10mm) from raw edge.

Round

3

Turn upper edge to outside along foldline; stitch ends.

Square   Pointed

Round

4

Trim seams.

5

Turn upper edge of pocket to inside, turning in remaining seam allowances. For square and pointed pockets, also diagonally fold corners.

Square

For rounded pockets, also pull thread to ease in fullness on curves. Notch curves. Press.

Round

6

Baste inner pressed edge in place close to edge.

Square   Pointed   Round

Patch Pockets

Self-Faced and Topstitched, Continued

7

TOPSTITCH along basting through all thicknesses.

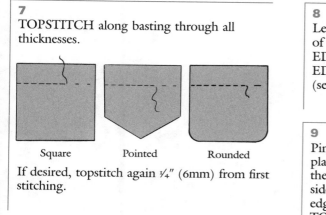

Square   Pointed   Rounded

If desired, topstitch again ¼″ (6mm) from first stitching.

8

Leave upper edge of pocket plain or use one of the following methods to finish edge: EDGESTITCHING, TOPSTITCHING, or EDGESTITCHING and TOPSTITCHING (see Patch Pockets, Lined).

9

Pin pocket to garment section along placement lines, matching symbols. Use one of the following methods to secure pocket along sides and lower edges, reinforcing upper edges, if desired: EDGESTITCHING, TOPSTITCHING, EDGESTITCHING and TOPSTITCHING, or SLIPSTITCHING (see Patch Pockets, Self-faced).

SELF-LINED

1

With right sides together, fold pocket along foldline. Stitch, leaving an opening.

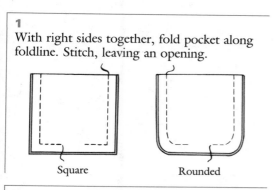

Square   Rounded

2

Trim seam. For square pockets, also cut diagonally across corners. For rounded pocket, also notch curves. Press.

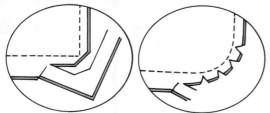

3

Turn; press. SLIPSTITCH opening.

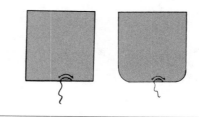

4

Pin pocket to garment section along placement lines, matching symbols. Use one of the following methods to secure pocket along sides and lower edges, reinforcing upper edges, if desired: EDGESTITCHING, TOPSTITCHING, EDGESTITCHING and TOPSTITCHING, or SLIPSTITCHING (see Patch Pockets, Self-faced).

Patch Pockets

SLANTED EDGE: NARROW-HEMMED

1

Make ⅝″ (15mm) NARROW HEM at upper side edge of pocket.

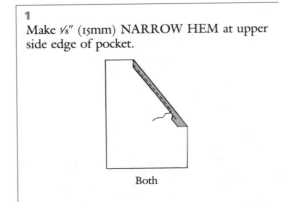

Both

2

For pocket caught in side and waistline seams, turn in seam allowances on long side edge and lower edges. For pocket caught in waistline seam only, turn in all remaining seam allowances. For both pockets, fold corners diagonally.

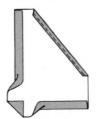 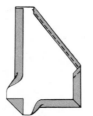

Caught in Side and Waistline Seams

Caught in Waistline Seam

3

Pin pocket to garment front section along placement lines, matching symbols. Baste raw edge(s) of pocket and garment together. Use one of the following methods to secure pocket along pressed edges:

EDGESTITCH,

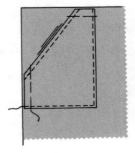 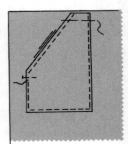

TOPSTITCH,

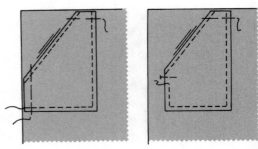

EDGESTITCH and TOPSTITCH.

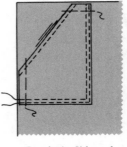 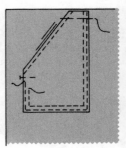

Caught in Side and Waistline Seams

Caught in Waistline Seam

Pockets

Patch Pockets

SLANTED EDGE: SELF-FACED

1

If desired, STAY upper side foldline edge of pocket.

2

FINISH upper side edge of pocket.

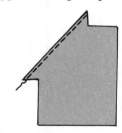

3

Leave upper side edge of pocket plain or use one of the following methods to finish edge: EDGESTITCHING, TOPSTITCHING, or EDGESTITCHING and TOPSTITCHING (see Patch Pockets, Lined).

4

For pocket caught in waistline seam only, turn upper side edge to outside along foldline; stitch side edge.

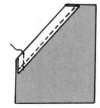

5

Trim seam.

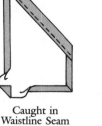

6

For pocket caught in waistline seam only, turn upper side edge of pocket to inside along foldline. Turn in seam allowances on long, lower and side edges. For pocket caught in side and waistline seams, turn upper side edge of pocket to inside along foldline. Turn in seam allowances on long and lower edges.

7

For both pockets, fold corners diagonally.

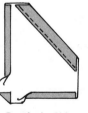

| Caught in Waistline Seam | Caught in Side and Waistline Seams |

8

Pin pocket to garment section along placement lines, matching symbols. Baste raw edge(s) of pocket and garment together. Use one of the following methods to secure pocket along pressed edges: EDGESTITCHING, TOPSTITCHING, or EDGESTITCHING and TOPSTITCHING (See Patch Pockets, Slanted Edge: Narrow-hemmed.

Patch Pockets

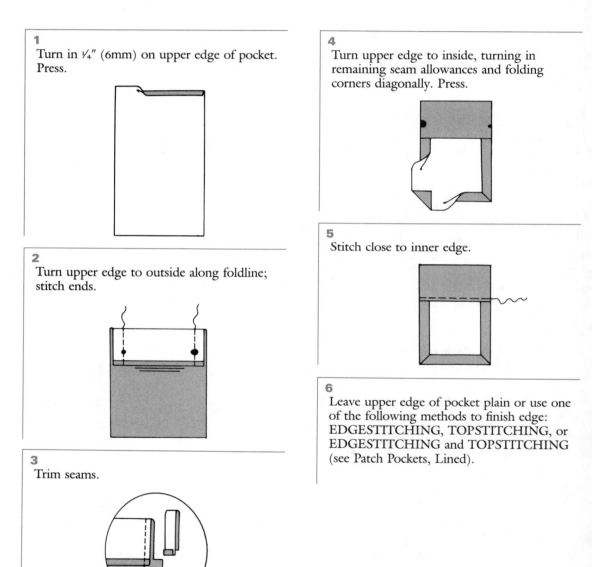

WITH SELF FLAP

1
Turn in ¼″ (6mm) on upper edge of pocket. Press.

2
Turn upper edge to outside along foldline; stitch ends.

3
Trim seams.

4
Turn upper edge to inside, turning in remaining seam allowances and folding corners diagonally. Press.

5
Stitch close to inner edge.

6
Leave upper edge of pocket plain or use one of the following methods to finish edge: EDGESTITCHING, TOPSTITCHING, or EDGESTITCHING and TOPSTITCHING (see Patch Pockets, Lined).

Patch Pockets

With Self Flap, Continued

7

Pin pocket to garment section along placement lines, matching symbols. Use one of the following methods to secure pocket along sides and lower edges (do not stitch above symbols):

EDGESTITCH,

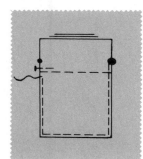

TOPSTITCH,

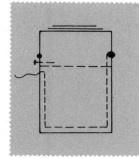

EDGESTITCH and TOPSTITCH,

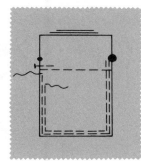

7 *Continued*

SLIPSTITCH.

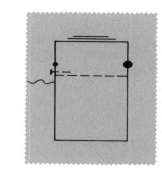

8

Turn upper edge of pocket down at symbols, forming flap. Press.

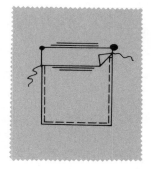

Side Seam Pockets

1

If desired, STAY side edge of pocket front foldline or seamline.

2

For pocket with extension, stitch one pocket section to each front and back extension. For pocket without extension, stitch one pocket section to front and back at each side in a ¼" (6mm) seam.

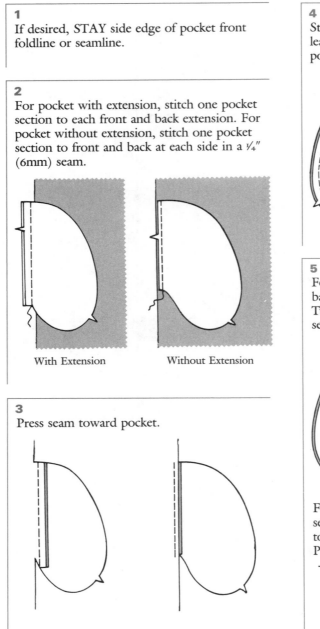

With Extension   Without Extension

3

Press seam toward pocket.

4

Stitch front and back together at side seams, leaving an opening between large ●'s. Stitch pocket edges together up to side seams.

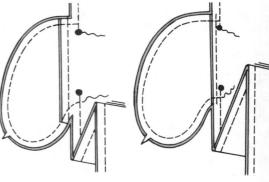

5

For pocket not caught in waistline seam, clip back seam allowance above and below pocket. Turn pocket toward front along foldlines or seamlines. Press.

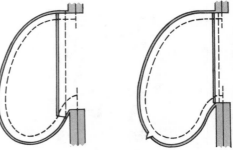

For pocket caught in waistline seam, clip back seam allowance below pocket. Turn pocket toward front along foldlines or seamlines. Press. Baste upper raw edges together.

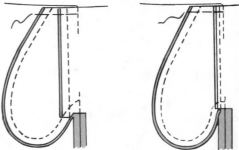

Side Slant Pockets

WITH OPENING IN BOTH POCKETS

1

If desired, STAY upper side seamline edges of garment front.

2

Make ⅝" (15mm) NARROW HEM on long straight unnotched edge of each pocket section.

3

Stitch pockets to upper side edges of garment front.

4

Press seams toward pockets. TRIM seams, being careful not to cut any stays. UNDERSTITCH pockets.

5

Turn pockets to inside along seamlines; press.

6

Leave upper side edges of pockets plain or use one of the following methods to finish edges: EDGESTITCHING, TOPSTITCHING, or EDGESTITCHING and TOPSTITCHING (see Patch Pockets, Lined).

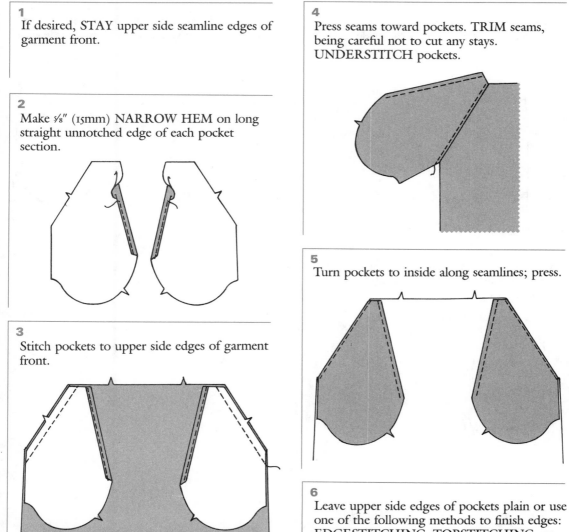

Side Slant Pockets

With Opening in Both Pockets, Continued

7
Make ⅝″ (15mm) NARROW HEM on long straight unnotched edge of each side front section.

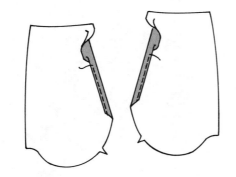

8
With right sides together, stitch side fronts to pockets along outer edges, keeping garment front free.

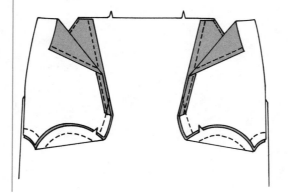

9
Baste waistline edges of pockets to garment front, keeping side front free. Baste side edges.

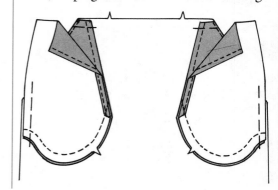

Side Slant Pockets

1

If desired, STAY upper side seamline edges of garment front.

2

Make ⅝″ (15mm) NARROW HEM on straight unnotched edge of left pocket section.

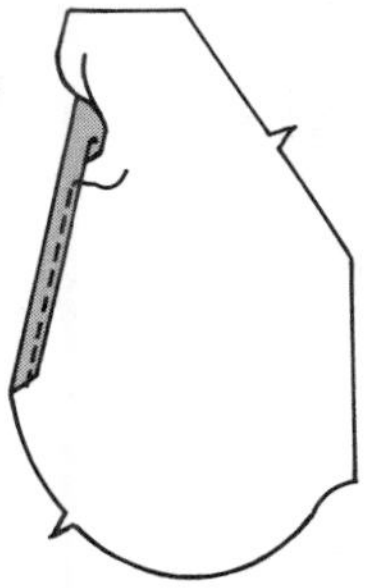

3

Stitch pockets to upper side edges of garment front.

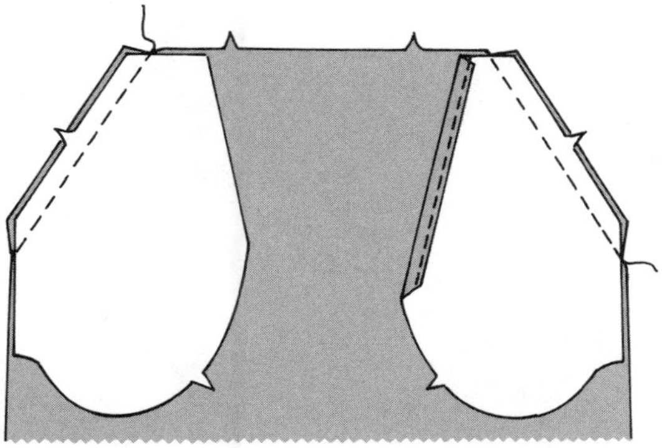

4

Press seams toward pockets. TRIM seams, being careful not to cut any stays. UNDERSTITCH pockets.

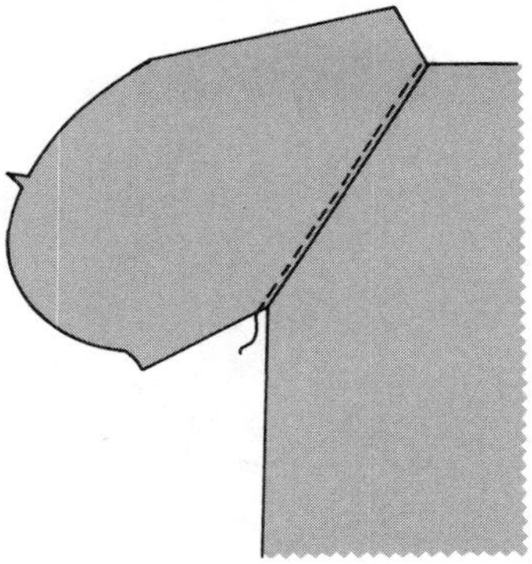

5

Turn pockets to inside along seamlines; press.

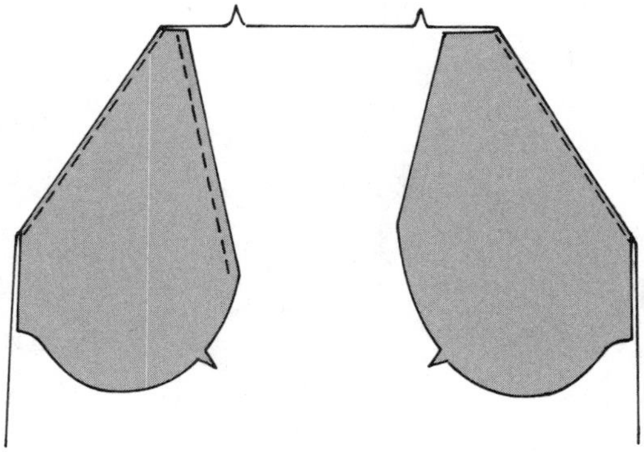

6

Leave upper side edges of pockets plain or use one of the following methods to finish edges: EDGESTITCHING, TOPSTITCHING, or EDGESTITCHING and TOPSTITCHING (see Patch Pockets, Lined).

Pockets

271

Side Slant Pockets

With Opening in Left Pocket, Continued

7

Make ⅝" (15mm) NARROW HEM on long straight unnotched edge of left side front section.

8

With right sides together, stitch side fronts to pockets along outer edges, keeping garment front free.

9

Baste waistline edges of pockets to front, keeping left side front free. Baste side edges.

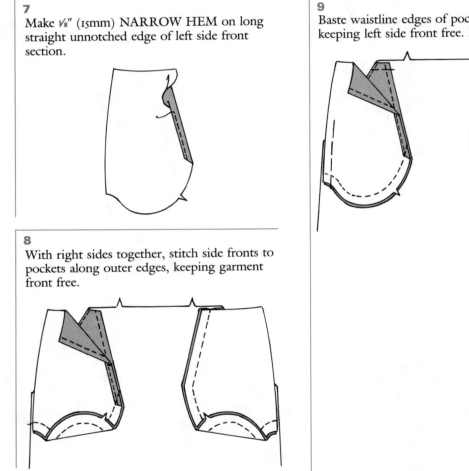

Side Slant Pockets

WITHOUT SIDE OPENINGS

1
If desired, STAY upper side seamline edges of garment front.

2
Stitch pocket to upper side edges of garment front.

3
Press seams toward pockets.

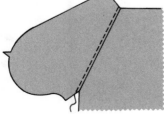

4
TRIM seams, being careful not to cut any stays. UNDERSTITCH pockets.

5
Turn pockets to inside along seamlines; press.

6
Leave upper side edge of garment front plain or use one of the following methods to finish edge: EDGESTITCHING, TOPSTITCHING, or EDGESTITCHING and TOPSTITCHING (see Patch Pockets, Lined).

7
With right sides together, stitch one side front to each pocket along outer edge, keeping garment front free.

8
Baste waistline and side edges.

Welt Pocket

1

INTERFACE wrong side of welt.

2

With right sides together, fold welt along foldline. Stitch ends.

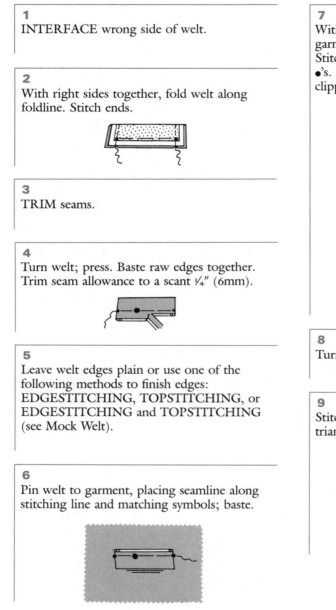

3

TRIM seams.

4

Turn welt; press. Baste raw edges together. Trim seam allowance to a scant ¼″ (6mm).

5

Leave welt edges plain or use one of the following methods to finish edges: EDGESTITCHING, TOPSTITCHING, or EDGESTITCHING and TOPSTITCHING (see Mock Welt).

6

Pin welt to garment, placing seamline along stitching line and matching symbols; baste.

7

With right sides together, pin pocket to garment over welt, matching stitching lines. Stitch along stitching lines, pivoting at small ●'s. Slash along line between stitching, clipping diagonally to small ●'s.

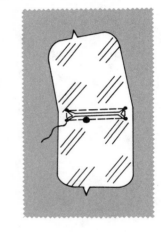

8

Turn pocket to inside, turning welt up; press.

9

Stitch pocket edges together, catching triangular ends.

Welt Pocket

Continued

10

On outside, use one of the following methods
to secure ends of welt in place:

EDGESTITCH,

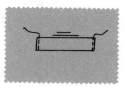

SLIPSTITCH.

Pressing Guidelines

Use these procedures for best results when pressing:

- Press garment as each seam is sewn for well-defined edges and contours—the mark of a professional-looking garment.

- Test a scrap of fabric first for reaction to steam and heat.

- Remove basting before pressing.

- Press with grain of fabric; be careful not to stretch edges of curves by pulling.

- Press on wrong side of fabric. To press on right side, always use a press cloth.

- Do not over-press, creating shine, bumps or ridges in fabric.

ESSENTIAL PRESSING TOOLS

The following items are standard pressing equipment:

- Sturdy ironing board with thickly padded cover

- Steam/spray iron with a surge-of-steam feature

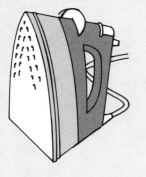

- Several different press cloths made from scraps of self fabric, non-woven fabric, lightweight cotton fabric such as a man's handkerchief, wool and heavy duty fabric such as cotton twill, as well as disposable and see-through press cloths which are easy to use and are good for most basic sewing tasks.

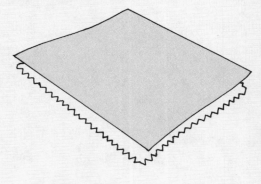

OPTIONAL PRESSING TOOLS

The equipment below will help in pressing specific garment areas or fabrics:

- Dress form, for steaming garment sections, such as roll of collar, into correct position.

- Needle board, for pressing pile fabrics such as velvet or corduroy.

Pressing Guidelines

Optional Pressing Tools, Continued

- Point presser or pressing board, a smaller board with multicurved edges, for pressing seams in small areas such as collars.

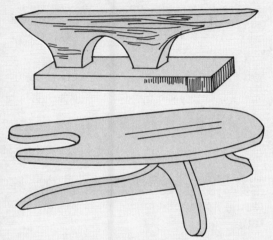

- Press mitt which fits over one hand, for shaping sleeve caps and other rounded areas.

- Press pad, purchased or made with thick woolen scraps or a heavy towel, and used to prevent unwanted ridges from appearing when you press.

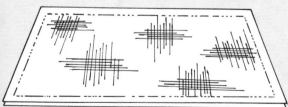

- Pounding block or tailor's clapper, for pounding sharper creases on edges after steaming.

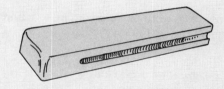

- Seam roll, for pressing long, straight seams.

- Sleeve board, a mini-ironing board for pressing narrow garment sections.

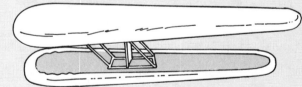

- Soleplate cover, a rigid cover with perforations for steaming, which fits over soleplate of iron and is used in place of a press cloth.

- Tailor's or dressmaker's ham, for pressing curved areas such as darts or princess seams.

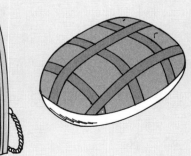

Pressing Guidelines

USING A PRESS CLOTH

To prevent shine and to prevent fabric from getting too much heat, use a press cloth when pressing the right side of fabric.

• Choose press cloth fabric according to nature of fashion fabric—wool for wool, cotton for cotton, for example.

• A good size for a press cloth is 12″ x 18″ (30.5 × 46cm).

• Use a dry press cloth with a dry or steam iron.

• To dampen a press cloth, moisten it with a sponge or immerse in water, wring out and press until proper dampness is achieved. Never place a very wet press cloth on fabric. It may cause shrinkage.

USING STEAM

Steam provides the slight amount of dampness needed to get truly flat seams or edges.

• Set the shape of curved sections or the hang of draped sections by steaming them into position after they are hung on a hanger or dress form.

• Use a press cloth whenever touching an iron directly to right side of fabric. If iron is held 3″ (7.5cm) from fabric surface, no press cloth is necessary.

• Steam, then mold fabric with fingers while fabric is still damp. Allow steam to dissipate and fabric to dry before resuming work.

FINAL PRESSING

Final pressing is a touch-up job.

• Set soft pleats, godets, collars, etc. by lightly steaming and patting garment into position on dress form or hanger.

• Use tissue paper under collars, inside sleeve caps and other areas to hold them in place while fabric dries.

Pressing Garment Sections

BOUND BUTTONHOLES

1
On wrong side of fabric, place brown paper strips under edges of buttonholes.

2
On right side, press buttonholes lightly, merging fabric and threads.

3
Touch up garment between buttonholes on wrong side, if necessary.

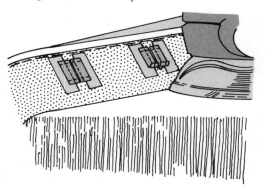

GATHERS

1
Press from the wrong side, if possible.

2
Hold gathers along the stitching, using tip of iron to press between folds of fabric.

Pressing Garment Sections

HEMS

1

Mark hem, turn up, and baste close to fold.

2

Place paper between hem and garment.

3

Hold iron over hem; steam lightly to shrink out excess fullness.

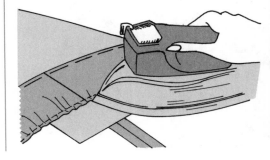

4

Sew hem in place. Remove basting. Steam lightly.

POCKETS

1

Press from right side, using a press cloth.

2

For welt or flap pockets, put paper between the garment and welt or flap on wrong side. Press, using a press pad.

3

From wrong side, lift up pocket and touch up garment area.

Pressing Garment Sections

SEAMS

1

Press along stitching line in same direction seam was stitched to merge stitches with fabric.

2

Open seam flat with tip of iron.

3

To prevent ridges on the right side, steam-press flat seams with paper strips under seam allowances or over a seam roll.

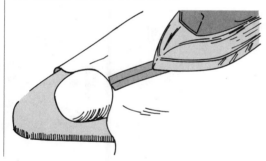

4

Curved or round seams should be pressed flat first, but when pressed open, seam area should maintain built-in roundness. Use a tailor's ham, press mitt or dressmaker's ham and tip of iron to preserve shape of seam.

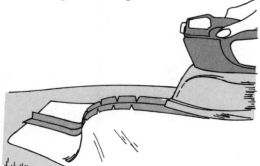

5

Press seams at finished edges open (when seam allowances are completely enclosed within parts of a garment such as cuffs, collars, etc.) and then press flat before turning right side out as follows:

a) Stitch garment section. Place seam over edge of a point presser or tailor's board. Press open with tip of iron.

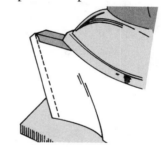

b) Next, lay section flat on ironing board, underside up. Turn both pressed seam allowances toward section until stitching shows; press lightly.

c) Turn section right side out; press with cloth from underside, keeping seam on underside.

Pressing Garment Sections

SLEEVES

1
Press sleeve seam open, using sleeve board.

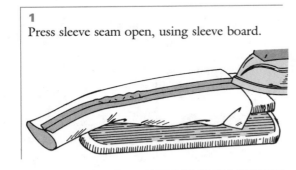

2
Ease and fit sleeve cap into garment seam; remove.

3
Place on narrow end of sleeve board. Use tip and side of iron to shrink fullness from seam allowance.

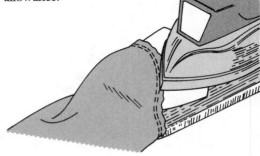

4
Stitch sleeve to armhole. Press along seam over tailor's ham to blend stitches into fabric.

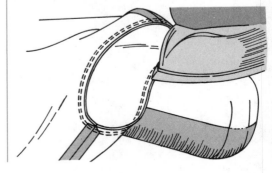

ZIPPERS

1
Work from wrong side over a pressing pad, using a press cloth and limited moisture. Excess dampness creates puckers. To avoid scratching the soleplate or melting plastic teeth, do not press directly on zipper teeth, hooks and eyes or snaps. Touch up right side of fabric lightly.

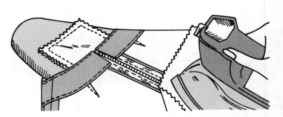

Also see Darts, Pleats, and Tucks for additional pressing information.

Pressing Special Fabrics

Note: Always test pressing method, using scraps of fashion fabric, before pressing garment.

BEADED, SEQUINNED OR METALLIC FABRICS

Note: Never steam beaded or sequinned fabrics—backing could curl or sheen may be lost from sequins or beads. Metallic fabrics may tarnish or discolor from steam.

1

Use a low heat setting because beads or sequins may melt and metallic fabric may melt or become brittle if iron is too hot.

2

Press seams and edges with tip of iron or finger-press, covering finger with thimble.

FAKE FUR FABRICS

Note: Never press on the right side; hairs may melt or mat from steam.

1

Press fake fur fabrics on the wrong side with a dry iron.

2

Finger-press seams open before pressing.

Pressing Special Fabrics

PILE FABRICS

Press pile fabrics, such as velvet, corduroy, plush, velour, bouclé, melton and fleece, over a needle board, terry towel or self fabric.

1

Use a self-fabric press cloth on inside if pile is exposed on both sides, OR

2

Cover iron with a damp cloth, hold fabric lightly. Run inside of garment across covered iron to press seam open and steam out wrinkles.

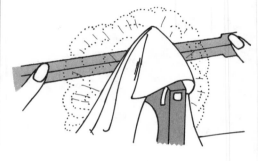

SYNTHETIC SUEDE, LEATHER AND VINYL

Note: Generally, these fabrics need only light pressing. Major pressing is not necessary.

1

Press on wrong side, using a press cloth and a warm, dry iron on a "synthetic" setting.

2

For synthetic suedes, use a piece of self fabric against right side to prevent flattening the nap.

3

Press to imbed stitches.

4

Glue or stitch seam allowances in place.

Quilting Preparation

1

For padding, use a layer of batting, polyester fleece or outing flannel.

2

For backing, use a firmly-woven, lightweight fabric such as muslin or broadcloth.

3

Use matching or contrasting thread or, for a more pronounced stitching line, use topstitching thread or buttonhole twist.

4

Mark quilting lines on right side of fabric with chalk, disappearing marking pencil or thread tracing as follows:

If quilting design lines are evenly spaced and a quilting foot is being used, mark only one or two lines.

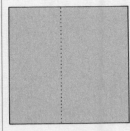
Evenly-spaced Marking

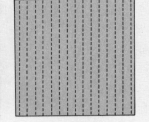
Evenly-spaced Design

Evenly-spaced Marking

Evenly-spaced Design

4 *Continued*

If quilting lines will outline the sections of a fabric design, no marking is necessary.

Fabric Design

If design is irregular, mark all lines.

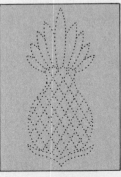
Irregular Design Marking

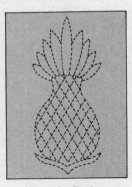
Irregular Design

Experiment on a sample of all fabric and padding layers to determine the proper machine tension, pressure and stitch length.

Complete quilting before cutting out garment sections because quilting may reduce the size of the fabric.

Corded Quilting

Note: Make corded quilting on a garment section, such as a neck band or hem band, before it is joined to the garment.

1

Machine-stitch through two layers of fabric in parallel lines spaced evenly apart. If ends will not be enclosed in a seam, turn in seam allowances before stitching.

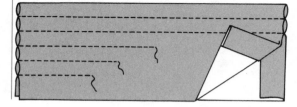

2

Thread a blunt tapestry needle with several strands of yarn and insert between stitching lines to create the corded effect.

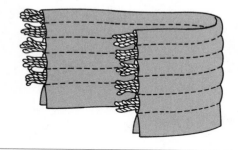

3

If ends will be enclosed in a seam, baste along seamlines and trim yarn out from seam allowances before stitching sections.

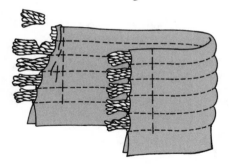

4

If ends will not be enclosed in a seam, trim excess yarn and SLIPSTITCH the openings.

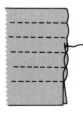

5

Complete garment following pattern instructions.

Machine Quilting

Note: Complete machine quilting before cutting out garment sections.

1

Place padding over wrong side of backing; place wrong side of fabric over padding; pin. HAND-BASTE around edges and along lengthwise grain every few inches (cm) to prevent shifting.

2

On right side, carefully machine-stitch along marked quilting lines or if design lines are evenly spaced, use a quilting foot as a guide. Work from the center of the piece to the outside edges.

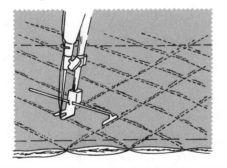

3

When quilting is complete, cut out garment sections.

4

To reduce bulk in seams, remove quilting stitches on seam allowances and trim away padding.

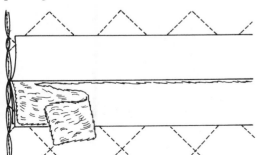

5

Slash darts open, trim away padding and press open.

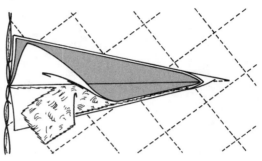

6

Complete garment following pattern instructions.

Trapunto Quilting

Note: Do trapunto after cutting out a garment section.

1

Use a lightweight, soft fabric (such as organdy) for backing and strands of yarn for padding. BASTE backing to wrong side of garment section in the desired location.

2

On outside, machine-stitch along quilting lines with small stitches; tie thread ends on wrong side.

3

Thread strands of matching yarn through a blunt tapestry needle. Insert needle through backing; carry yarn between fabric and backing from the stitching line for one design area to the stitching line of the other area. Clip ends of yarn close to stitching. Pass needle as far as possible before bringing it up, and do not pull tightly.

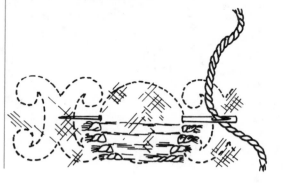

4

For large areas, angles, and sharp curves, bring needle out and back through backing. When changing directions, leave some slack to fill out the angle. Continue until entire area is padded.

5

Slightly stretch the fabric around each section of pattern to make the tiny yarn ends recede into the backing.

6

Press lightly on wrong side over a turkish towel or pressing pad.

7

Complete garment following pattern instructions.

Circular Ruffles

DOUBLE LAYER

Note: Assemble garment area where ruffle will be applied.

1

Stitch seams on ruffle and ruffle facing sections.

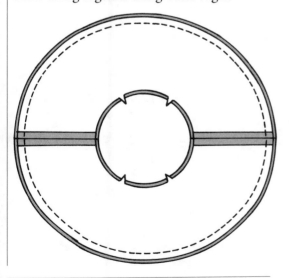

2

With right sides together, stitch ruffle and ruffle facing together along outer edges.

3

TRIM seam and NOTCH curve.

4

Turn. Press. Baste raw edges together. Stitch inner edge along seamline.

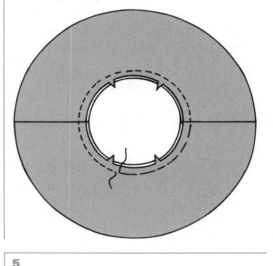

5

Leave outer ruffle edge plain, or if desired, use one of the following methods to finish outer edge:

EDGESTITCH, TOPSTITCH,

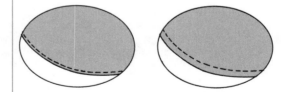

EDGESTITCH and TOPSTITCH.

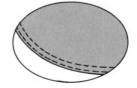

Circular Ruffles

Double Layer, Continued

Ruffles Finished by Double-stitched Seam

With right sides together, pin ruffle to garment, matching symbols. Clip ruffle where necessary, being careful not to clip stitches; baste. Stitch. Stitch again ¼" (6mm) away in seam allowance. Trim close to stitching. Lightly press ruffle away from garment and seam toward garment.

Ruffles Finished by Other Garment Sections

If another garment section, band or facing will be applied over ruffle, pin ruffle to right side of garment, matching symbols. Clip ruffle where necessary, being careful not to clip stitches; baste.

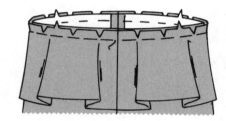

Complete ruffle as directed by pattern instructions.

SINGLE LAYER

Note: Assemble garment area where ruffle will be applied.

1
Cut ruffle along cutting line indicated on pattern.

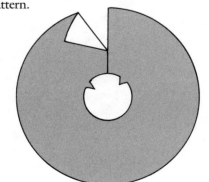

2
STAYSTITCH or EASESTITCH inner edge of ruffle along seamline between symbols.

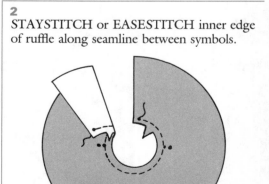

Circular Ruffles

NARROW HEM outer edge and ends of ruffle, easing where necessary and diagonally folding and trimming corners.

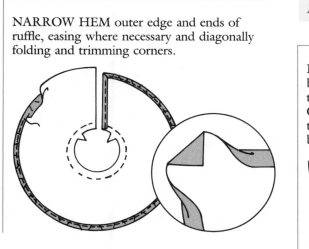

Ruffles Finished by Double-stitched Seam

With right sides together, pin ruffle to garment, matching symbols. Clip ruffle where necessary, being careful not to clip stitches. Adjust ease, if applicable; baste. Stitch. Stitch again ¼″ (6mm) away in seam allowance. Trim close to stitching. Lightly press ruffle away from garment and seam toward garment.

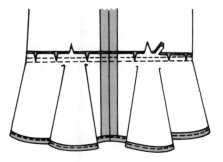

Ruffles Finished by Other Garment Sections

If another garment section, band or facing will be applied over ruffle, pin wrong side of ruffle to right side of garment, matching symbols. Clip ruffle where necessary, being careful not to clip stitches. Adjust ease, if applicable; baste.

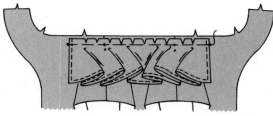

Complete ruffle as directed by pattern instructions.

Straight Ruffles

DOUBLE LAYER

Note: Assemble garment area where ruffle will be applied.

1

Stitch ruffle sections together.

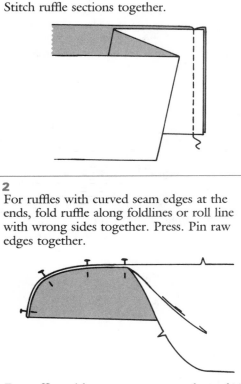

2

For ruffles with curved seam edges at the ends, fold ruffle along foldlines or roll line with wrong sides together. Press. Pin raw edges together.

For ruffles with square corners at the end(s), fold ruffle along fold line or roll line with right sides together. Stitch end(s).

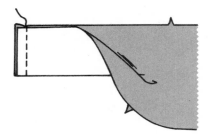

2 *Continued*

TRIM seam. Turn. Press. Pin raw edges together.

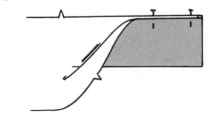

3

Make two rows of GATHERING stitches along remaining edge of ruffle.

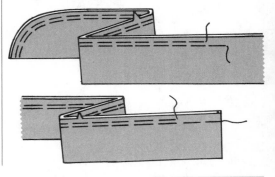

4

Leave folded ruffle edge plain, or use one of the following methods to finish folded edge:

EDGESTITCH,

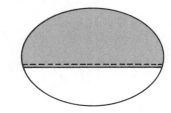

Straight Ruffles

Double Layer, Continued

**4 *Continued*
TOPSTITCH,**

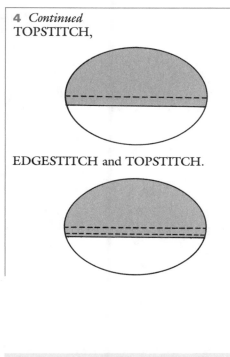

EDGESTITCH and TOPSTITCH.

Ruffles Finished by Double-stitched Seam

Pin ruffle to right side of garment, matching symbols. Adjust gathers; baste. Clip ruffle and garment if necessary, being careful not to clip stitches. Stitch. Stitch again ¼" (6mm) away in seam allowance. Trim seam close to stitching. Lightly press ruffle away from garment and seam toward garment.

Ruffles Finished by Other Garment Sections

If another garment section, band or facing will be applied over ruffle, pin ruffle to right side of garment, matching symbols. Adjust gathers; baste.

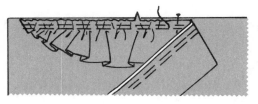

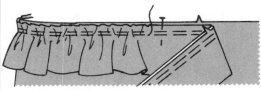

Clip ruffle and garment if necessary, being careful not to clip stitches.

Complete ruffle as directed by pattern instructions.

Ruffles

293

Straight Ruffles

DOUBLE LAYER, ARMHOLE RUFFLES

Note: Assemble garment area where ruffle will be applied.

1

Stitch seams on ruffle and ruffle facing sections.

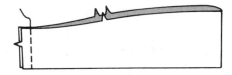

2

Press seam open. With right sides together, stitch armhole ruffle sections to armhole ruffle facings along unnotched edge.

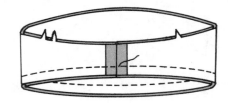

3

Turn. Press. Pin raw edges together. Make two rows of GATHERING stitches along notched edge of armhole ruffle.

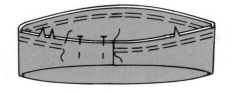

4

Leave seamed ruffle edge plain, or use one of the following methods to finish seamed edge: EDGESTITCHING, TOPSTITCHING, EDGESTITCHING and TOPSTITCHING (see Straight Ruffles, Double Layer).

Ruffles Finished by Double-stitched Seam

Pin ruffle to armhole edge, matching symbols. Adjust gathers; baste. Clip ruffle and garment if necessary, being careful not to clip stitches. Stitch. Stitch again ¼" (6mm) away in seam allowance. Trim. Lightly press ruffle away from garment and seam toward garment.

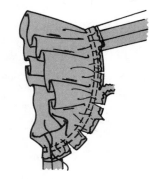

Ruffles Finished by Other Garment Sections

If garment section, band or facing will be applied over the ruffle, pin ruffle to armhole edge, matching symbols. Adjust gathers; baste. Complete ruffle as directed by pattern.

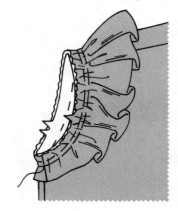

Straight Ruffles

SINGLE LAYER WITH BOTH EDGES HEMMED

Note: Assemble garment area where ruffle will be applied.

1

Stitch ruffle sections together.

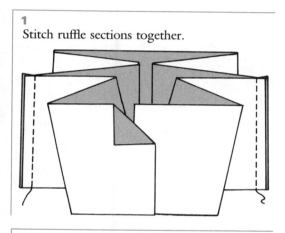

2

NARROW HEM upper and lower edges. If ruffle has free ends, diagonally fold and trim corners.

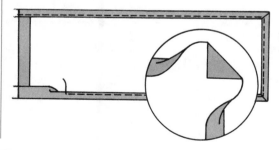

3

Make a row of GATHERING stitches on ruffle along stitching line and again ⅛" (3mm) above and below first row.

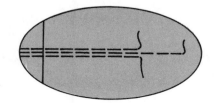

4

Pin wrong side of ruffle to right side of garment, matching ●'s. Adjust gathers; baste.

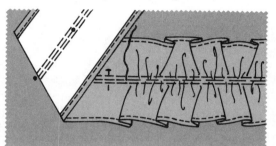

5

Stitch ruffle along stitching line, through all thicknesses. Remove basting.

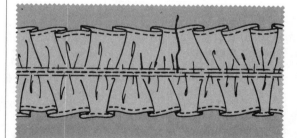

Straight Ruffles

SINGLE LAYER WITH ONE EDGE HEMMED

Note: Assemble garment area where ruffle will be applied.

1

Stitch ruffle sections together.

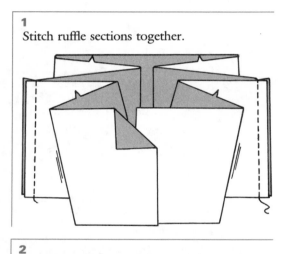

2

NARROW HEM edge(s) without symbols. If ruffle has free ends, diagonally fold and trim corners.

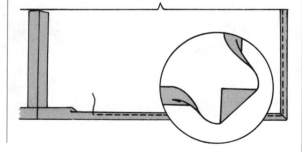

3

Make two rows of GATHERING stitches along remaining edge.

Ruffles Finished by Double-stitched Seam

With right sides together, pin ruffle to garment, matching symbols. Clip ruffle and garment if necessary, being careful not to clip stitches. Adjust gathers; baste. Stitch. Stitch again ¼" (6mm) away in seam allowance. Trim seam close to stitching. Lightly press ruffle away from garment and seam toward garment.

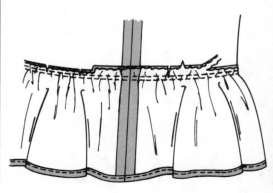

Straight Ruffles

Single Layer with One Edge Hemmed, Continued

Ruffles Finished by Other Garment Sections

If another garment section, band or facing will be applied over the ruffle *and the ruffle will hang down or be pressed away from the garment section* (e.g., ruffle at hem), pin ruffle to garment, right sides together, matching symbols. Clip ruffle and garment if necessary, being careful not to clip stitches. Adjust gathers; baste.

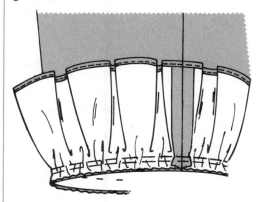

Complete ruffle as directed by pattern instructions.

If another garment section, facing or band will be applied over the ruffle *and the ruffle will be left in the same position* (e.g., a vertical ruffle on a blouse front), pin wrong side of ruffle to right side of garment, matching symbols. Clip ruffle and garment if necessary, being careful not to clip stitches. Adjust gathers; baste.

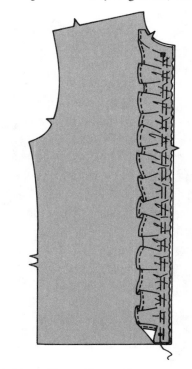

Complete ruffle as directed by pattern instructions.

Seam Guidelines

PLAIN SEAMS

To stitch a perfect seam, adjust machine tension, pressure and stitch length to suit fabric texture and weight; then follow the tips below. Refer to sewing machine manual for specific information.

1

Test stitching on fabric scraps of the actual garment before sewing.

2

With right sides together and raw edges even, BASTE seams, matching notches, symbols and raw edges.

3

Stitch seams in direction of fabric grain to prevent stretching (generally from widest to narrowest part of each piece).

With Grain
Stitch This Way   Against Grain

4

Start and end stitching in one of the following ways:

• Begin at the seam end, stitch forward with edges of fabric along seam allowance guide or lines on machine needle plate. Secure thread ends with knots; OR

4 Continued

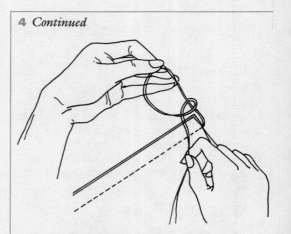

• To omit tying a knot, begin stitching ½″ (13mm) from seam end, put needle into fabric; then lower presser foot. BACKSTITCH to end of seam; then stitch forward, with edges of fabric along seam allowance guide or lines on machine needle plate. To stop stitching at opposite end, stitch to seam end and BACKSTITCH ½″ (13mm).

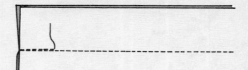

• To secure thread ends when ending stitching before reaching an edge, pull one thread end through to the other side and knot ends.

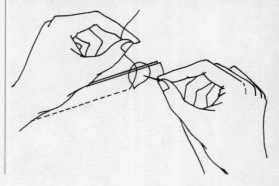

Seam Guidelines

Plain Seams, Continued

5

Clip thread ends after backstitching or knotting.

6

Press seams flat, or press in direction specified by pattern (see Pressing).

SEAM ALLOWANCE GUIDES

⅝" (15mm) is the standard seam allowance used on most patterns. The pattern tissue is always marked when the seam allowance is different than ⅝" (15mm).

Use one of the following guides to help stitch an even seam:

• Place edges of fabric along ⅝" (15mm) marking on needle plate; OR

• Measure out ⅝" (15mm) from needle. Set a machine seam guide at ⅝" (15mm) from needle; OR

• Measure out ⅝" (15mm) from needle. Place straight edge of masking tape along ⅝" (15mm) marking on needle plate.

To mark a guide for stitching square corners, measure ⅝" (15mm) from needle toward front of presser foot. Place edge of tape along ⅝" (15mm) marking.

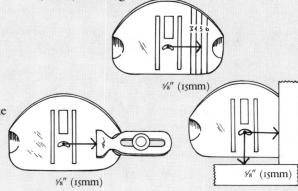

⅝" (15mm)

⅝" (15mm)

⅝" (15mm)

TRIMMING SEAMS

To help make edges flat and to help prevent seam allowances from making a ridge on the garment during pressing, trim seam allowances.

1

Trim enclosed seams (inside collars, cuffs, etc.) to ¼" (6mm) and GRADE them to cut down on bulk.

2

Cut diagonal corners from the ends of seams and trim enclosed seam allowances diagonally at points and corners.

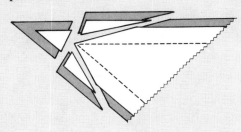

Seam Guidelines

GRADING SEAMS

Grade seam allowances when they are turned in one direction or enclosed. To grade means to trim each fabric layer in the seam to a different width. This technique is most commonly used on medium weight to heavyweight or thick fabrics to cut down on bulk. Also grade seam allowances to prevent seam edges from making a ridge on the garment during pressing and to help seams lie flat.

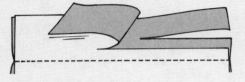

1
Trim enclosed seams narrower than exposed seams.

2
Leave garment section seam allowances wider than facing seam allowances.

CLIPPING SEAMS

To allow seam allowances on one garment section to be spread to fit the corresponding section, clip certain curved seam allowances before stitching seams.

1
STAYSTITCH curved edge of garment section.

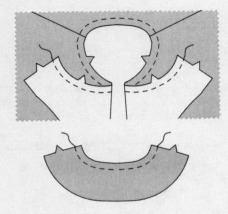

2

With right sides together, pin edge of corresponding garment section to curved edge, clipping to staystitching at even intervals until curved edge fits corresponding edge easily.

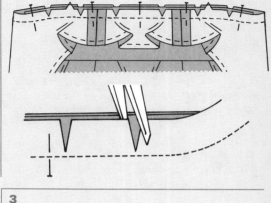

3
Stitch seam.

Seam Guidelines

NOTCHING SEAMS

Notch seam allowances on curves of pressed open or enclosed seams to allow seam to lie flat without bumps.

To notch, cut small wedges from seam allowance at even intervals.

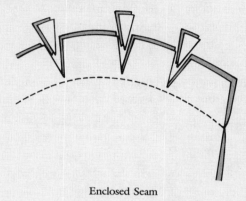

Enclosed Seam

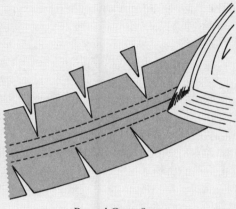

Pressed Open Seam

CONTINUOUS STITCHING

To save time, stitch as many pieces together as possible without stopping to remove each piece from the machine and cut threads.

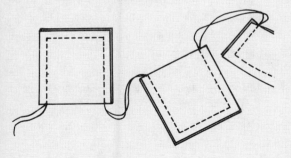

1

Stitch from one piece right into the next one, leaving a length of thread between pieces.

2

Then cut threads and tie knots to secure threads

Seam Guidelines

MATCHING FABRIC DESIGNS

Note: Lay out pattern tissue pieces on fabric and cut, matching print, stripe or plaid design at seamlines (See Layouts, Matching Fabric Designs at Seamlines).

1

With right sides together, match seam edges and fabric design by using pin basting, basting stitches, glue stick or basting tape to hold layers in position so fabric design matches.

2

Stitch seam with an Even Feed Foot™ or a roller foot for best results. These attachments can be purchased from sewing machine dealers.

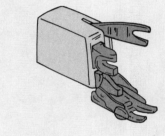

TISSUE PAPER UNDER SEAMS

To stabilize fabrics that tend to stretch or shift (bias seams on crepe or satin), or stick (vinyl, leather) during stitching, use tissue paper or tear-away stabilizer.

1

Place tissue paper or tear-away stabilizer on machine bed under seams and stitch through fabric and tissue paper or stabilizer.

2

Tear away paper.

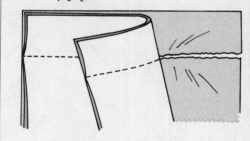

Also see Machine Stitching for more information on stitching procedures mentioned here.

Types of Seams

BIAS SEAMS

Since bias tends to stretch, it is important to use pinning and basting as well as the methods mentioned under Bias Skirt Seams below.

1

To join a bias edge to a straight edge, with right sides together, pin and baste bias edge to straight edge.

2

To control stretching of bias edges, stitch seam with bias side up.

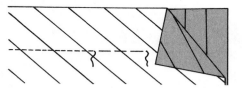

BIAS SKIRT SEAMS

Traditional bias skirt seam allowances on pattern pieces are 1 ½" (3.8cm) in width, beginning 2" (5cm) below the waist.

1

With right sides together, stitch skirt sections together, leaving open below symbols. Do not stitch seam where zipper will be inserted. Pin seams below symbols, spacing pins approximately 3" (7.5cm) apart.

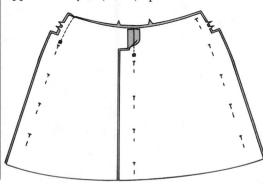

2

Allow skirt to hang for 24 hours, permitting bias to set. Then, try on skirt to check the fit. Adjust and re-mark construction lines if necessary.

3

To prevent seams from stretching while stitching, cut 1" (25mm) wide strips of tissue paper or tear-away stabilizer, the length of seamlines, using pattern tissue as a guide. Transfer markings. Pin paper over seamlines before stitching.

4

Stitch seams below symbols. BASTE zipper opening above large ●. Trim all seam allowances except zipper seam allowance to ⅝" (15mm).

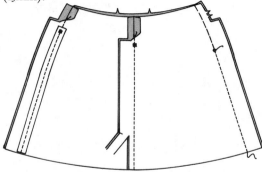

5

Insert zipper. Trim seam allowance to ⅝" (15mm).

Types of Seams

CURVED SEAMS

Depending on the type of curve, clip seam allowances to allow them to spread or notch seam allowances to allow them to lie flat without bumps.

1

With right sides together, stitch seam, using seam allowance guide.

2

Clip inner curves.

Inner Curve

Notch outer curves.

Outer Curve

3

Press seams flat and then in direction specified by pattern.

For Princess Seams

1

STAYSTITCH curved edges.

2

Clip inner curved edge to staystitching when pinning.

3

With right sides together, stitch seam.

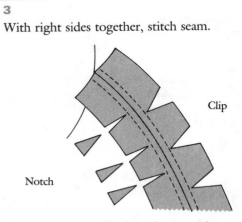

Clip

Notch

Notch outer curved edge when pressing, staggering notches between the clips.

For Scallops

1

With right sides together, stitch curved seam, using small stitches (15–20 per 1"/6–8 per cm). Take one stitch across each point to make turning easier.

2

Clip to each point.

3

Grade and notch curves.

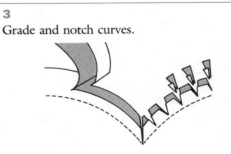

Types of Seams

DOUBLE-STITCHED SEAMS

To stitch a strong seam in stretchy fabrics or a fine, narrow seam in laces and sheers, use a double-stitched seam. If an overlock machine is available, use an overlocked seam instead of a double-stitched seam. This machine stitches, trims and finishes the seam in one step (see Overlock, Plain Seams).

For Lace or Sheer Fabrics

1
With right sides together, stitch seam.

2
Stitch again ⅛" (3mm) away in seam allowance.

3
Trim close to second stitching.

4
OVERCAST raw edges with a fine zigzag stitch or HAND-OVERCAST.

For Soft Knits

Use double-stitched seams when fabric edges tend to curl.

1
With right sides together, stitch seam.

2
Then straight-stitch again ⅛"–¼" (3mm–6mm) away in seam allowance. Or, zigzag-stitch next to first stitching.

3
Trim close to second stitching.

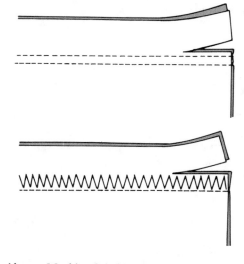

Also see Machine Stitching, Specialty Stitches, Multiple Zigzag or Overlock Stitches.

305

Types of Seams

DOUBLE-TOPSTITCHED SEAMS

To accent a seam and make it more durable, use double-topstitching.

1
With right sides together, stitch seam.

2
Press open.

3
TOPSTITCH ¼″ (6mm) on both sides of seam, through all thicknesses.

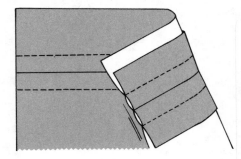

EASED SEAMS

The pattern tissue and instructions will indicate when seams need to be eased.

1
From right side, EASESTITCH where indicated on pattern tissue.

2
Pin two layers together with eased side face up, matching symbols.

3
Pull on ease thread and slide fabric along ease thread, distributing fullness evenly to fit between symbols.

4
Pin; stitch seam.

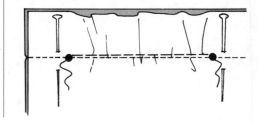

Types of Seams

EDGESTITCHED SEAMS

To accent a seam and make it more durable, use Edgestitching.

1
With right sides together, stitch seam.

2
Press both seam allowances to one side.

3
EDGESTITCH close to seam through all thicknesses.

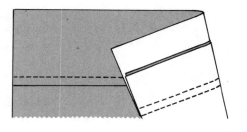

FLAT-FELL SEAMS

For sportswear, men's wear and heavyweight fabrics, the flat-fell seam is very sturdy as well as decorative.

Made on the Inside

1
With right sides together, stitch seam. Press both seam allowances to one side.

2
Trim underneath seam allowance to ⅛″ (3mm). Turn other seam allowance under ¼″ (6mm); press. Place over trimmed edge. EDGESTITCH pressed edge in place.

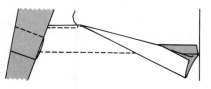

Note: On bulky fabrics, SLIPSTITCH pressed edge in place.

Made on the Outside

1
With *wrong* sides together, stitch seam. Press both seam allowances to one side.

2
Trim underneath seam allowance to ⅛″ (3mm).

3
Turn other seam allowance under ¼″ (6mm); press.

4
Place over trimmed edge. EDGESTITCH pressed edge in place.

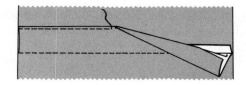

Types of Seams

FRENCH SEAMS

For straight seams on sheer or lightweight fabrics, make a French seam—a neat, narrow seam which encloses the raw edges.

1
With *wrong* sides together, stitch ⅜" (10mm) from seamline in seam allowance.

2
Trim close to stitching, being careful not to cut stitches. Press seam open; then, with right sides together, crease along seam; press.

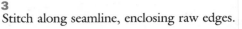

3
Stitch along seamline, enclosing raw edges.

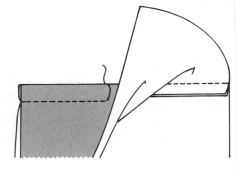

GATHERED SEAMS

Note: To gather, use this method or see Machine Stitching, Gathering.

1
To gather, loosen needle tension and from right side, stitch rows of GATHERING stitches where indicated on pattern tissue.

2
With right sides together, pin edge to be gathered to corresponding edge, matching raw edges, centers, notches, seams or symbols.

3
Pull up bobbin threads and slide fabric along them, distributing fullness until gathered edge fits adjoining edge. Depending on amount of gathers and length of straight piece, this may need to be done more than once.

4
Secure gathers by winding thread ends around pin in a figure eight.

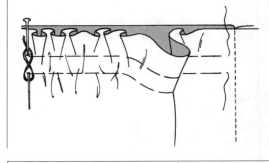

5
Adjust gathers, distributing fullness evenly. With gathered side up, stitch on seamline.

Seams

Types of Seams

HAIRLINE SEAMS

For a narrow enclosed seam on sheer or lightweight fabrics when a regular width seam allowance would be distracting, use a hairline seam.

1

With right sides together, OVERLOCK the seams.

2

If the overlock stitch is not available, use one of two other hairline seams:

a) With a short stitch length and right sides together, stitch along seamline. Using a narrow ZIGZAG stitch, stitch again close to first stitching. Trim close to second stitching.

2 *Continued*

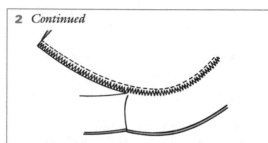

b) Using a short stitch length and right sides together, stitch along seamline. Stitch again close to first stitching. Trim close to second stitching. HAND-OVERCAST raw edges if desired.

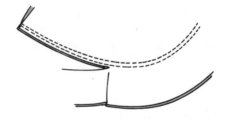

INTERSECTING SEAMS

With seams that cross, it's important to match all seamlines so they are a continuous line.

1

With right sides together, stitch seam in one garment section; press open. Stitch seam in second garment section in same manner.

2

With right sides together, pin the two garment sections together, using the point of a pin to match crossed seams exactly at seamline. Pin on either side of seams and stitch seam.

3

Trim corners diagonally.

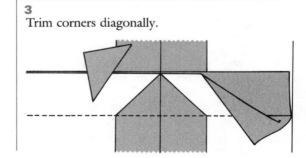

Types of Seams

LAPPED SEAMS

The lapped seam looks similar to the Edgestitched Seam, but is made in a different way. It is particularly useful when the section to be lapped on top is so intricately cut that it would be very difficult to use a plain seam.

1

Turn in seam allowance of garment section which will be lapped on top of adjoining garment section; press.

2

On right side, place pressed edge along seamline of corresponding garment section; baste or pin. EDGESTITCH the pressed edge.

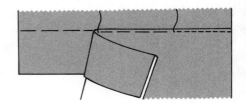

MOCK FRENCH SEAMS

For straight seams with edges finished at the same time, use a mock French seam.

1

With right sides together, stitch seam. Do not press open. Turn in ¼" (6mm) on each seam allowance; press.

2

EDGESTITCH the pressed edges together. Press seam to one side.

PIPED SEAMS

To accent garment seams and stiffen the edge, use purchased piping in the seam.

1

With a zipper foot, MACHINE-BASTE piping to right side of fabric section along seamline, making sure raw edges of piping are on seam allowance.

2

With right sides together, place second fabric section over piping; baste. With piped side up, use a zipper foot to stitch along basted seamline through all thicknesses.

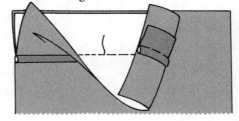

Types of Seams

SELF-BOUND SEAMS

For straight seams with edges finished at the same time, use the self-bound seam.

1

With right sides together, stitch seam.

2

Trim one seam allowance to ⅛″–¼″ (3mm–6mm), depending on fabric (trim bulky fabrics more).

3

Turn edge of other seam allowance under; press.

4

Fold pressed edge down, encasing trimmed seam allowance and SLIPSTITCH or EDGESTITCH.

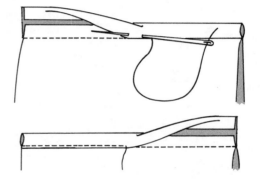

SLOT SEAMS

For a decorative effect on tailored garments, use the slot seam.

1

With right sides together, BASTE seam; press open.

2

Cut a fabric strip as long as seam and slightly wider than both seam allowances.

3

With wrong side up, place strip over seam and BASTE in position.

4

On outside, TOPSTITCH on both sides of seam.

5

Remove basting.

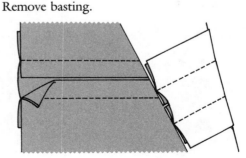

Types of Seams

STAYED SEAMS

Stay seams to strengthen them (kimono underarm) or to prevent stretching (waistline and shoulder seams in knit fabrics, pocket edges), using nylon stabilizing tape, woven seam binding or twill tape.

Foldlines

1

Use one of two methods:

a) Place tape edge along foldline on facing side; EDGESTITCH one edge; OR

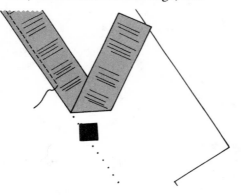

b) Center tape over foldline; sew tape invisibly to foldline, catching only a thread of garment fabric.

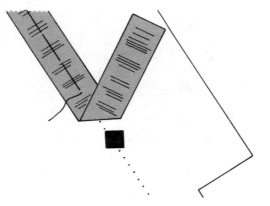

Seamlines

1

Center tape over seamline and pin.

2

Baste in place over, or between, symbols if indicated.

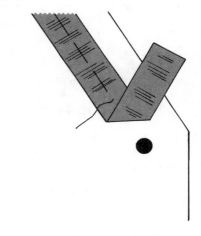

Types of Seams

TOPSTITCHED SEAMS

To accent a seam and make it more durable, use topstitching.

1

With right sides together, stitch seam.

2

Press both seam allowances to one side.

3

TOPSTITCH through all thicknesses the desired distance from seam, usually ¼" (6mm).

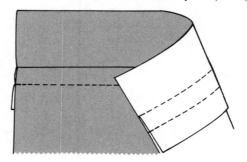

WELT SEAMS

To accent a seam and make it more durable, use a welt seam.

1

With right sides together, stitch seam.

2

Press both seam allowances to one side.

3

Trim underneath seam allowance to ¼" (6mm).

4

TOPSTITCH through all thicknesses.

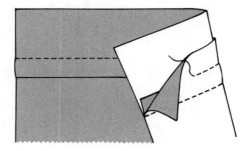

To understitch seams, see Hand Sewing, Understitching and Machine Stitching, Understitching.

Shoulder Pad Guidelines

SHOULDER PADS FOR RAGLAN SLEEVES

These pads cup the top of the arms at the shoulders. They are made from combinations of batting, interfacing and foam.

Regular Shoulder Pads

In garments that have dolman, raglan or kimono sleeves or dropped shoulders, regular raglan shoulder pads give a softly-rounded shoulder shape.

Extended Shoulder Pads

For raglan, kimono, dolman or dropped shoulder styles, extended shoulder pads project beyond the natural shoulder line to give a soft, exaggerated shoulder shape.

SHOULDER PADS FOR SET-IN SLEEVES

These pads are triangular shapes which sit on top of the shoulders. They are made from combinations of batting, interfacing and foam.

Regular Shoulder Pads

In dresses, jackets or coats with set-in sleeves (regular armhole), regular shoulder pads give a flattering "squared look".

Extended Shoulder Pads

Designed to project beyond and broaden the natural shoulder line, extended shoulder pads are suitable for any pattern with slightly extended shoulders.

Thin Pads/Shoulder Shapes

In blouses, lightweight dresses and sweaters, these smaller pads provide smooth shaping.

Shoulder Pad Guidelines

SIZE (THICKNESS) OF SHOULDER PADS

• Shoulder pads come in a variety of sizes (or thicknesses). Standard shoulder pad sizes are ¼″ (6mm), ½″ (13mm) and 1″ (25mm). Some pads are thicker or thinner than the standard size. Generally, thinner pads are used for lightweight garments—blouses and dresses. Thicker pads are used for heavier weight garments—jackets, coats and medium weight to heavyweight dresses.

• The specific type and thickness of shoulder pads will always be given in the notions listing on the back of the pattern envelope. It is important to use the correct shoulder pad. The pattern has been designed for that particular size; height has been added to the armhole and the sleeve to accommodate it. If the shoulder pad is omitted, the garment will collapse in the shoulder area because it is missing the proper inner support.

Shoulder Pads

Attaching Shoulder Pads

Most shoulder pads have notched edges or other markings to help position the pad at the shoulder. Be sure to match shoulder pad line markings to the shoulder seam or garment markings. If shoulder pads are removable, be sure to remove them before cleaning.

REMOVABLE SHOULDER PADS

Attached to Garment With Hem Tape™

1

Apply double-sided transparent Hem Tape™ along upper shoulder line of shoulder pad.

2

Try on garment for shoulder pad placement; pin pad in place. Look in a mirror and adjust placement of pad, if necessary, so placement complements the garment shape and the body.

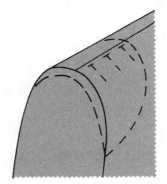

3

On inside, remove tape backing. Finger-press pad to seam allowances, smoothing fabric toward neck edge and armhole.

Note: Tape is temporary and will only last through a few washings. Replace tape when it does not stick any longer.

Attached to Garment With Velcro ®

1

Cover shoulder pad (see Covering Shoulder Pads).

2

Cut two strips of Velcro, each 2-½" (6.5 cm) long.

3

For each shoulder pad, place a hook section on pad with one end ½" (13mm) from outer (straightest) edge. Hand-sew in place.

Attaching Shoulder Pads

Removable Shoulder Pads, Continued

4

Try on garment for shoulder pad placement; pin pad in place. Look in a mirror and adjust placement of pad, if necessary, so placement complements the garment shape and the body.

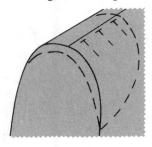

5

Mark placement for loop section of Velcro. On inside of garment, hand-sew loop section to shoulder seam allowances.

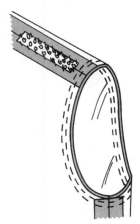

Attached to Lingerie Strap With Velcro ®

1

Cover shoulder pads (see Covering Shoulder Pads).

2

Cut four strips of Velcro, each 2-¼" (5.7cm) long.

3

For each shoulder pad, place two loop sections of Velcro on pad, approximately 3" (7.6cm) apart and 1" (25mm) away from outer (straightest) edge. Hand-sew in place.

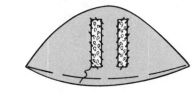

4

Place hook sections on loop sections. At straightest edge of shoulder pad, hand-sew ends together.

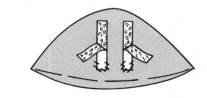

5

To wear, open out Velcro. Place shoulder pad on shoulder. Slip hook section under lingerie strap; press Velcro sections together.

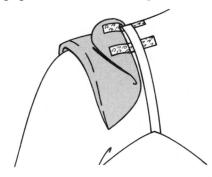

Attaching Shoulder Pads

SEW-IN SHOULDER PADS

If desired, cover shoulder pads (see Covering Shoulder Pads).

1

Try on garment for shoulder pad placement; pin pad in place, following pattern or package instructions.

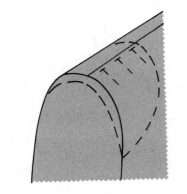

2

Look in a mirror and adjust placement of pad, if necessary, so placement complements the garment shape and the body.

3

Hand-sew pad to shoulder seam allowance as indicated in pattern or package instructions so stitches do not show on outside of garment. TACK ends to armhole seam.

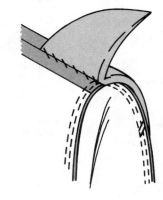

Covering Shoulder Pads

Shoulder pads can be purchased covered or uncovered. Uncovered shoulder pads are used in lined garments. Attach these pads permanently.

The shoulder pads used in unlined garments should be covered. For lightweight garments, use self fabric. For heavier garments, use a matching lining fabric. Try to match the fabric to the dominant color of the garment so the shoulder pad won't show through. If the fabric color can't be matched, or if self fabric isn't available, use beige or flesh-tone fabric.

1

Cut two squares of lining or self fabric large enough to cover the pads plus seam allowances.

2

Place shoulder pad on wrong side of square. Fold square over shoulder pad, folding in fullness, where necessary.

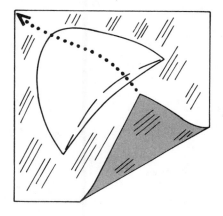

3

Stitch close to edge of shoulder pad.

4

FINISH shoulder pad edge.

5

Trim close to stitching.

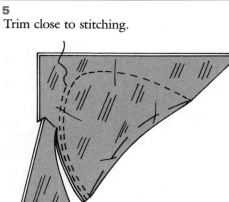

Kimono Sleeves

CUT-IN-ONE WITH YOKE: FLAT CONSTRUCTION

1

With right sides together, pin lower edge of
yoke front to garment front, matching centers
and notches. Stitch seam.

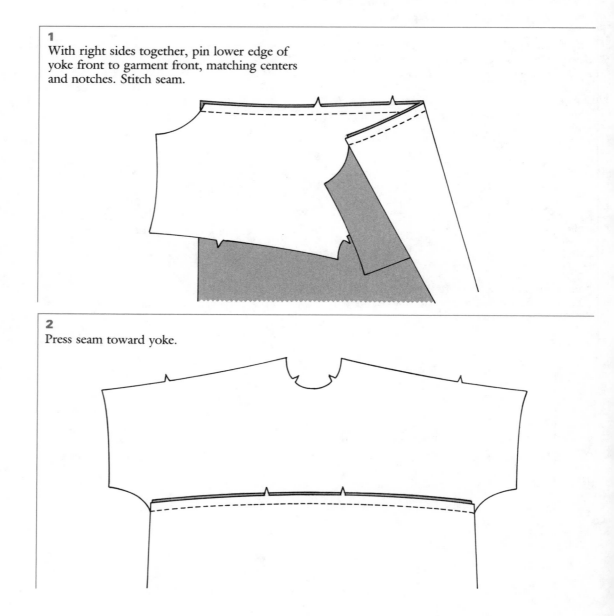

2

Press seam toward yoke.

Kimono Sleeves

Cut-in-One with Yoke: Flat Construction, Continued

3

With right sides together, pin lower edge of yoke back(s) to garment back(s), matching centers and notches. Stitch seam.

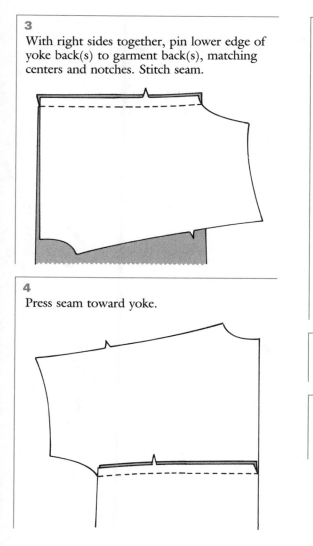

4

Press seam toward yoke.

5

Pin front and back yoke sections together at shoulders and upper sleeve edges, matching notches. Stitch seam.

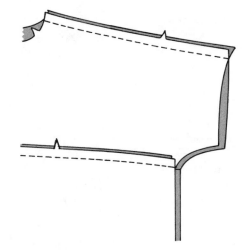

6

Press seam open.

7

Complete neck edges as directed by pattern instructions.

Kimono Sleeves

Cut-in-One with Yoke: Flat Construction, Continued

8

With right sides together, pin front and back together at sides and lower sleeve edges, matching notches. Stitch seam.

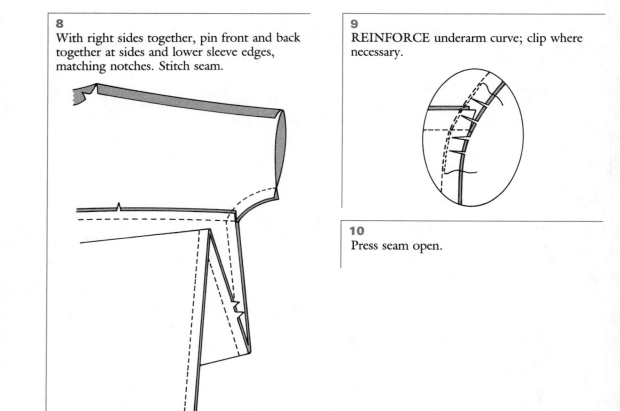

9

REINFORCE underarm curve; clip where necessary.

10

Press seam open.

Kimono Sleeves

PLAIN: REINFORCED AFTER STITCHING

1

With right sides together, pin garment front section(s) and back section(s) together at shoulders and upper sleeve edges, matching notches. Stitch seam.

2

With right sides together, pin front section(s) and back section(s) together at sides and lower sleeve edges, matching notches. Stitch seam.

3

REINFORCE underarm curve; clip seam. Press seams open.

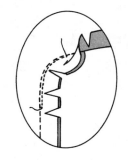

Kimono Sleeves

PLAIN: REINFORCED BEFORE STITCHING

1

Stay underarm curve of one section. Use bias tape that has been pressed flat and stretched to match curve of garment sections by steaming and pressing, or nylon stabilizing tape. On wrong side, place tape over seamline; baste.

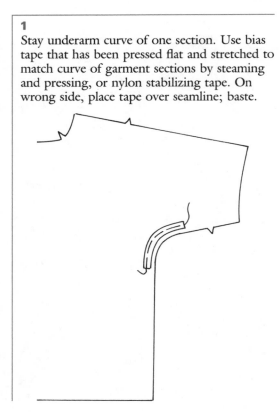

2

With right sides together, pin garment front section(s) and back section(s) together at shoulders and sides, matching notches. Stitch seam, REINFORCING underarm curve.

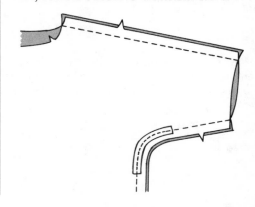

3

Clip curves, being careful not to clip tape. Press seam open.

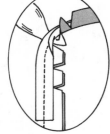

Raglan Sleeves

FLAT CONSTRUCTION

Preparing Sleeves

1

If armhole edges are very curved,
STAYSTITCH armhole edges of sleeve.

2

For one-piece sleeve with a dart, stitch dart
before applying sleeve.

For two-piece sleeve, with right sides
together, stitch sleeve front to back at overarm
seam.

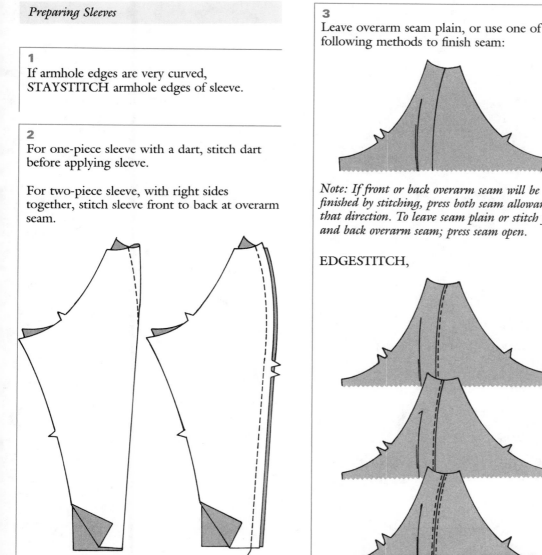

One-piece Sleeve   Two-piece Sleeve

3

Leave overarm seam plain, or use one of the
following methods to finish seam:

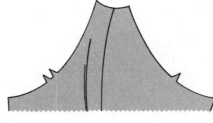

*Note: If front or back overarm seam will be
finished by stitching, press both seam allowances in
that direction. To leave seam plain or stitch front
and back overarm seam; press seam open.*

EDGESTITCH,

Raglan Sleeves

Flat Construction, Continued

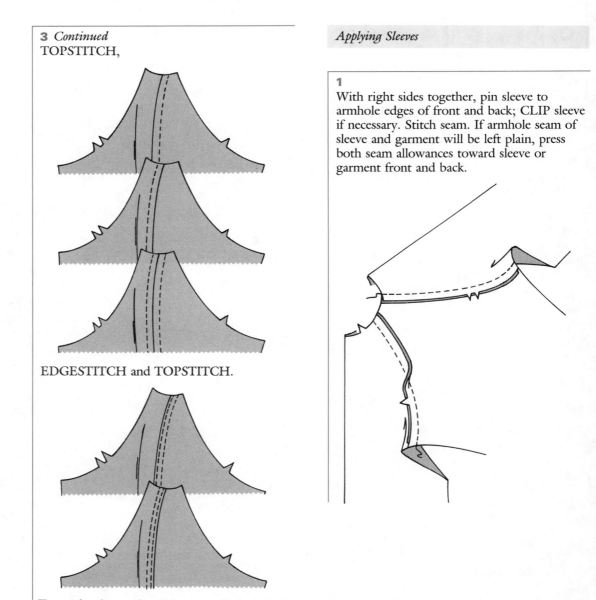

3 *Continued*
TOPSTITCH,

EDGESTITCH and TOPSTITCH.

To complete lower edge of sleeve, see Casings, Cuffs or Hems.

Applying Sleeves

1
With right sides together, pin sleeve to armhole edges of front and back; CLIP sleeve if necessary. Stitch seam. If armhole seam of sleeve and garment will be left plain, press both seam allowances toward sleeve or garment front and back.

Raglan Sleeves

Flat Construction, Continued

2

Leave armhole seam of sleeve or garment plain, or use one of the following methods to finish the seam:

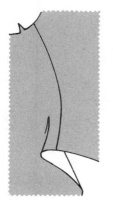

Note: If front or back armhole seam will be finished by stitching, press seam in that direction. To stitch front and back armhole seam, press seam open.

EDGESTITCH, TOPSTITCH

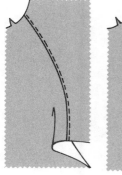 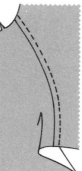

2 *Continued*
EDGESTITCH and TOPSTITCH.

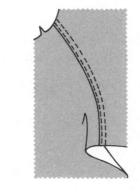

3

With right sides together, pin lower sleeve and side edges together; baste. Stitch seam.

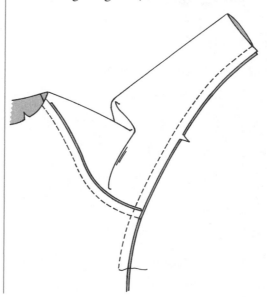

Raglan Sleeves

ROUND CONSTRUCTION

Preparing Sleeves

1

If armhole edges are very curved, STAYSTITCH armhole edges of sleeves.

2

For one-piece sleeve with a dart, stitch dart before applying sleeve.

For two-piece sleeve, with right sides together, stitch sleeve front to back at overarm seam.

3

Leave overarm seam plain or use one of the following methods to finish the seam: EDGESTITCHING, TOPSTITCHING or EDGESTITCHING and TOPSTITCHING (see Raglan Sleeves, Flat Construction, Preparing Sleeves).

4

Stitch sleeve seam.

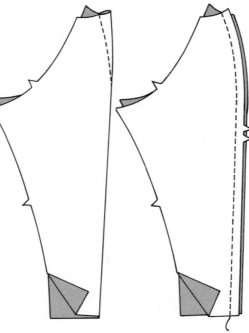

One Piece Sleeve   Two Piece Sleeve

To prepare and complete lower edge of sleeve, see Casings, Cuffs or Hems.

Raglan Sleeves

Round Construction, Continued

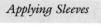

Applying Sleeves

1

With right sides together, pin sleeve to armhole edge. CLIP sleeve if necessary. Stitch seam.

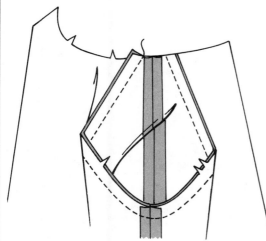

2

Press seam toward sleeve.

3

Leave armhole edge of sleeve plain or use one of the following methods to finish armhole seam:

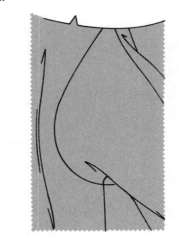

EDGESTITCH,

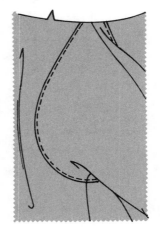

Raglan Sleeves

Round Construction, Continued

3 *Continued*
 TOPSTITCH,

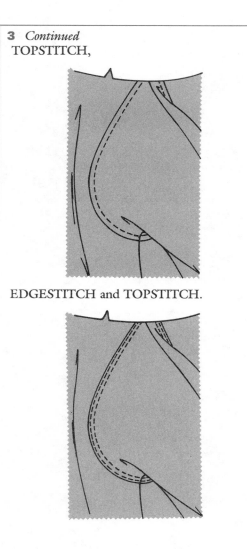

EDGESTITCH and TOPSTITCH.

Set-in Sleeves

FLAT CONSTRUCTION

To prepare sleeve opening or lower edge of sleeve, see Casings, Cuffs, or Hems.

1

If necessary, EASESTITCH or make two rows of GATHERING stitches on upper edge between small •'s.

2

With right sides together, pin sleeve to armhole edge, matching symbols and placing large ● at shoulder seam. If necessary, adjust ease or gathers; baste. Stitch seam.

3

Finish sleeve using one of two methods:

Seam Toward Sleeve

1

Stitch again ¼" (6mm) away in seam allowance.

2

Trim close to second stitching. Press both seam allowances flat.

3

Turn seam toward sleeve.

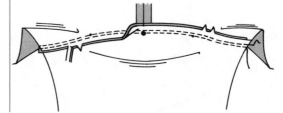

Seam Toward Garment

1

Press both seam allowances toward garment.

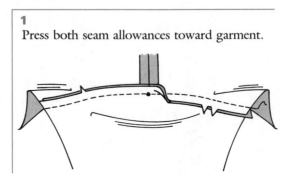

Set-in Sleeves

Flat Construction, Continued

2

Leave armhole edge plain or use one of the following methods to finish edge:

EDGESTITCH,

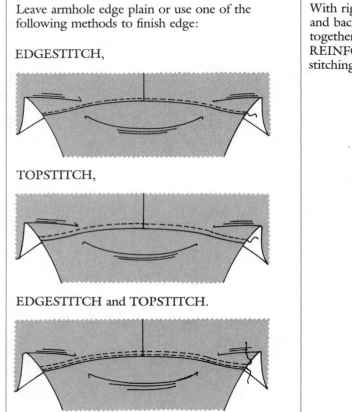

TOPSTITCH,

EDGESTITCH and TOPSTITCH.

3

With right sides together, pin garment front and back together at sides and sleeve edges together. Stitch in one continuous seam. REINFORCE underarm curve along previous stitching.

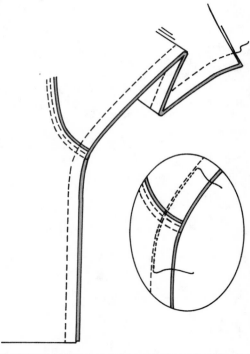

4

CLIP seam allowance, if necessary.

To complete lower edge of sleeve, see Casings, Cuffs, or Hems.

Set-in Sleeves

ROUND CONSTRUCTION: ONE-PIECE SLEEVE

1

EASESTITCH or make two rows of
GATHERING stitches on upper edge of
sleeve between small ●'s.

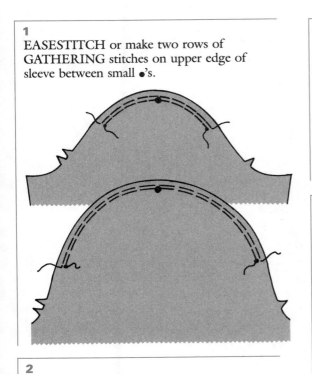

2

For plain seam, with right sides together, pin
sleeve seam. Stitch seam.

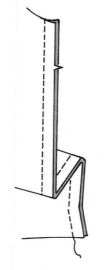

3

For sleeve with ease at elbow, EASESTITCH
back edge of sleeve between small ●'s or
notches.

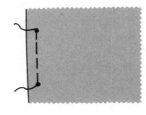

4

With right sides together, pin sleeve seam,
matching small ●'s. Adjust ease; baste. Stitch
seam.

For sleeve with elbow dart, stitch dart; press
down. With right sides together, pin sleeve
seam. Stitch seam.

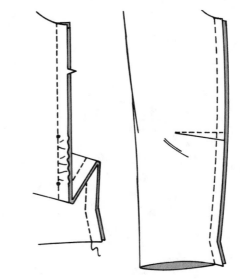

*To prepare sleeve opening or lower edge of sleeve,
see Casings, Cuffs or Hems.*

Set-in Sleeves

Round Construction: One-Piece Sleeve, Continued

5

With right sides together, pin sleeve into armhole, matching symbols and underarm seams and placing large ● at shoulder seam. Adjust ease or gathers; baste. Stitch seam.

6

Stitch again ¼" (6mm) away in seam allowance. Trim close to second stitching—entire armhole for eased cap, below notches for gathered cap.

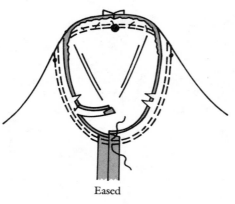

Eased

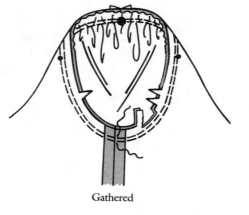

Gathered

7

Press seam allowances flat. Turn seam toward sleeve.

Set-in Sleeves

ROUND CONSTRUCTION: TWO-PIECE-EFFECT SLEEVE

1

For sleeve with ease at elbow, EASESTITCH
back edge of sleeve between small •'s or
notches.

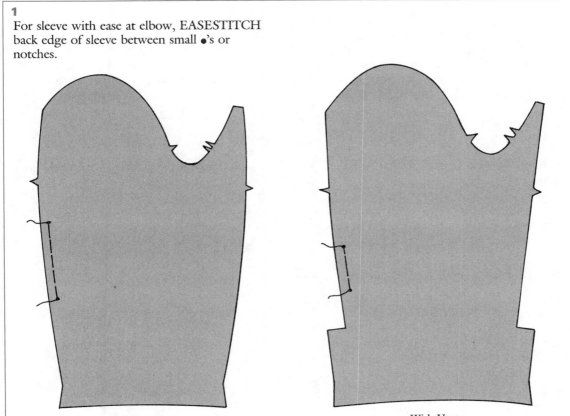

Without Vent   With Vent

Set-in Sleeves

Round Construction: Two-Piece-Effect Sleeve, Continued

2
With right sides together, pin sleeve seam, matching notches and small ●'s. Adjust ease; baste. Stitch seam. For sleeve with mock vent, stitch, pivoting at large ●. Clip front edge of sleeve above extension.

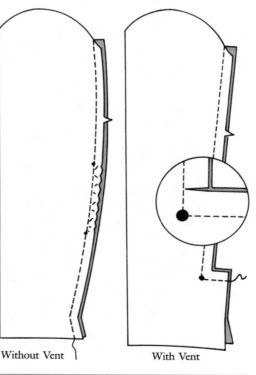

Without Vent   With Vent

3
EASESTITCH or make two rows of GATHERING stitches on upper edge of sleeve between notches.

3 *Continued*
To complete lower edge of sleeves without vents, see Hems.

To complete lower edge and vent of sleeves with mock vents, see Vents.

4
With right sides together, pin sleeve into armhole, matching symbols and placing large ● at shoulder seam and ■ at underarm seam. Adjust ease or gathers; baste. Stitch seam.

5
Stitch again ¼" (6mm) away in seam allowance. Trim close to second stitching.

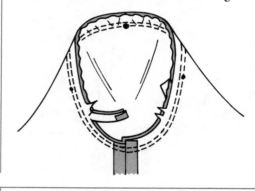

6
Press seam allowances flat. Turn seam toward sleeve.

Sleeves

336

Set-in Sleeves

ROUND CONSTRUCTION: TWO-PIECE SLEEVE

1

With right sides together, pin upper sleeve and under sleeve together at front edges. Match symbols, and if necessary, stretch upper sleeve to fit. Stitch seam.

2

For sleeve without vent, stitch remaining sleeve edges right sides together, matching notches.

2 *Continued*

For sleeve with mock vent or working vent, stitch remaining sleeve edges together, pivoting at large ●.

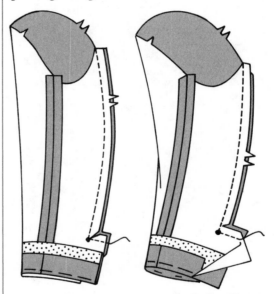

With Mock Vent   With Working Vent

To make vent and complete lower edge of sleeve, see Vents and Hems.

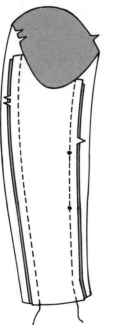

Without Vent

To complete lower edge of sleeve, see Hems, Interfacing.

3

EASESTITCH or make two rows of GATHERING stitches on upper edge of sleeve between small ●'s.

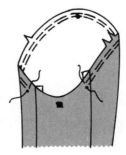

Set-in Sleeves

Round Construction: Two-Piece Sleeve, Continued

4

With right sides together, pin sleeve into armhole, matching symbols and placing large ● at shoulder seam and ■ at underarm seam. Adjust ease or gathers; baste. Stitch.

5

Stitch again ¼" (6mm) away in seam allowance. Trim entire armhole close to second stitching.

6

Press seam allowances flat. Turn seam toward sleeve.

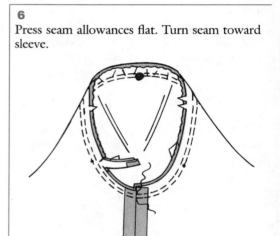

Smocking Preparation

ADDING A SMOCKED INSERT

Patterns with smocking details already include the fullness needed to create the pleats. However, to add a smocked insert to a garment that does not include it, allow 3" (7.5cm) of flat fabric for every 1" (25mm) of finished smocking.

1
Determine the length and width of the finished insert.

2
Cut fabric equal in depth to the finished insert plus two seam allowances, and equal in length to three times the finished insert plus two seam allowances. For example, to make a 10" (25.5cm) long and 5" (12.5cm) deep smocked section, cut fabric 30" + 1¼ " (76cm + 3.2cm) by 5" + 1¼" (12.5cm + 3.2cm).

FABRICS AND NOTIONS FOR SMOCKING

Select any fabric that is lightweight enough to gather easily—batiste, gingham, chambray, challis, broadcloth, crepe de Chine, dotted swiss, muslin or percale.

Use two or three strands of six-strand embroidery floss, depending on the fineness of the fabric. Embroider smocking stitches with a #7 or #8 crewel needle.

MARKING SMOCKING

Rows of evenly-spaced dots on the wrong side of fabric are the guidelines for smocking stitches and pleats. To achieve even-looking smocking with a professional appearance, space these dots evenly and in parallel rows. The easiest way to do this is by using a sheet of transfer dots. If the pattern includes smocking, transfer dots are provided. For a custom smocking detail, sheets of transfer dots may be purchased in many needlework and fabric stores.

1
When transferring dots to fabric, follow manufacturer's directions carefully and make a test sample first.

2
Transfer dots onto the wrong side of fabric so rows are parallel to the lengthwise and crosswise grain of the fabric. This guarantees that the finished smocking will fall into even, graceful folds.

Smocking Preparation

PREGATHERING

Use rows of RUNNING STITCHES to connect dots and draw fabric up into evenly-spaced pleats. Use two strands of contrasting thread, or one strand of heavy-duty thread, for each row of running stitches. Once pleats are completed, the sewing lines form a guide for the rows of embroidery stitches. When embroidery stitches are completed and the smocked section has been stitched to the rest of the garment, remove running stitches.

1

Because it cannot be joined in the middle, thread must be long enough to complete each row of stitches. Knot thread end before beginning.

2

Work on the wrong side of the fabric. Starting at the end of one horizontal row of dots, insert needle into fabric just before the first dot. Bring needle out of the fabric at the other side of the dot, picking up just a few threads of fabric. Work across the entire row, so that long running stitches form between dots. Repeat for the remaining horizontal rows of dots. Leave long thread ends.

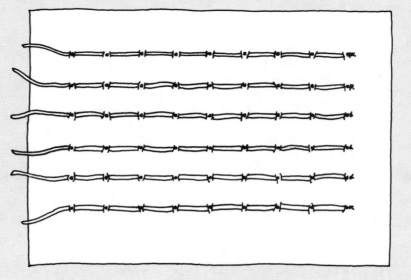

Smocking Preparation

Pregathering, Continued

3

Pull up on all threads at one time, forming straight, close, even pleats. Pull threads until fabric section is equal to the size indicated in pattern instructions or to the desired finished size plus seam allowances. Securely knot each thread end.

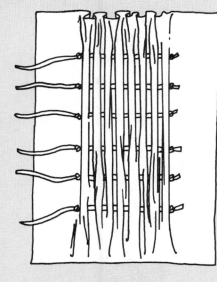

4

Place fabric on a flat surface and smooth the pleats so they are evenly spaced. Hold the iron slightly above fabric and steam the pleats, never resting the iron on the fabric.

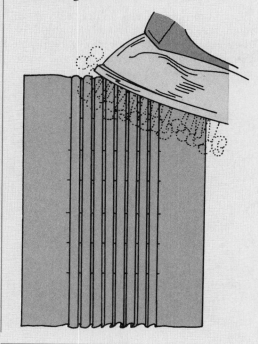

5

Let pleated fabric dry thoroughly before embroidering.

Accent Stitches

These stitches add the finished touch to a smocking design. Because they are sewn on the surface of the fabric, they can be applied before or after the running stitches are removed.

LAZY DAISY STITCH

To create a flower, use a series of lazy daisy stitches radiating from a center point. To create a leaf, use a single stitch.

1

Work from right to left. Bring needle out of fabric between pleats 1 and 2. Holding floss above and to the left of needle, insert needle a thread or two from first insertion and bring needle up between pleats 3 and 4.

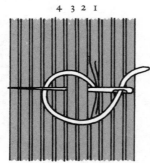

2

Draw up floss to form a loop.

3

To secure the loop, insert needle between pleats 3 and 4, to the left of the loop, and pull floss to wrong side of fabric.

4

To work loops in opposite direction or vertically on pleats, use the same spacing.

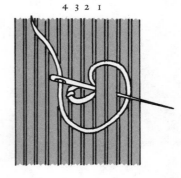

Accent Stitches

ROSEBUD STITCH

A French knot with several straight stitches around it creates a rosebud effect.

1
To form French knot, bring needle out of fabric where the knot will be. Hold floss taut in left hand and wind floss twice around needle while holding needle almost flat against the fabric.

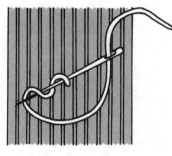

2
Still holding floss taut, insert needle back into fabric a thread or two away from first insertion.

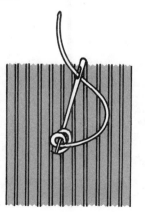

3
Gently pull needle through fabric, pulling thread taut to form knot.

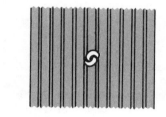

4
For the straight stitches around the French knot, bring needle out of fabric next to knot. Insert needle next to knot near first insertion and bring it out a few threads away.

5
Continue making straight stitches all around knot.

Regular Stitches

Use three strands of embroidery floss for all stitches. Thread the needle as for any embroidery. Be careful not to pull smocking stitches too tightly—the finished work should have some give. Catch only a few threads at the top of each pleat.

CABLE STITCH

Use three rows of RUNNING STITCHES for each row of cable stitches. A line of stitches alternating above and below the middle row of running stitches creates the cable design.

1

Work from left to right. Bring needle out of fabric on row A at left side of pleat 1, slightly above one row of running stitches. With floss above needle, take a stitch through pleat 2 so needle emerges slightly below the row of running stitches.

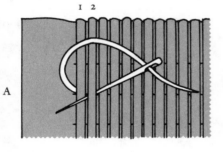

2

Pull needle down so floss forms a tight stitch. Hold floss below needle and take a stitch through pleat 3 so needle emerges slightly above the row of running stitches.

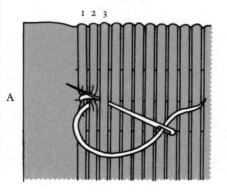

3

Pull needle up so floss forms a tight stitch.

4

Continue across fabric, alternating stitches in the same manner and spacing stitches evenly.

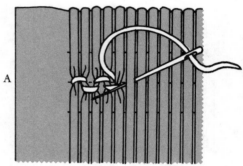

Regular Stitches

DIAMOND STITCH

Use three rows of RUNNING STITCHES as a guide for the embroidery stitches that create the diamond design.

1

Work from left to right. Bring needle out of fabric on row A at left side of pleat 1. With floss above needle, take a stitch through pleat 2.

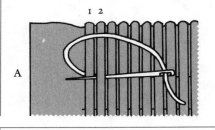

2

Draw up floss to form a tight stitch. Keep floss above needle, drop down to row B and take a stitch through pleat 3.

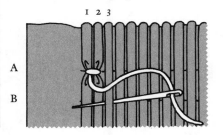

3

Work with floss below needle, continue on row B, and take a stitch through pleat 4.

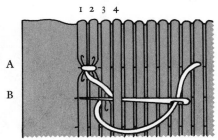

4

Draw up the floss.

5

Return to row A. Keep floss below needle and take a stitch through pleat 5.

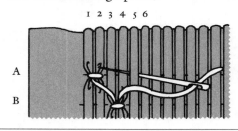

6

With floss above needle, take a stitch through pleat 6 and draw up floss. Continue across the two rows, alternating stitches in the same manner and spacing stitches evenly.

7

Beginning at pleat 1 on row C, repeat the stitches, working back and forth between row C and row B to complete the diamond pattern. While sewing, reverse position of floss in relation to needle so stitches above and below each other form a mirror image. Two sets of stitches will form along row B.

Regular Stitches

FEATHER STITCH

This stitch creates a gradual zigzag design between three rows of RUNNING STITCHES. To make each stitch, hold floss to the left and underneath needle, forming a loop.

1
Work from right to left. Bring needle out of fabric on row A at the right side of pleat 1. Insert needle through pleat 1.

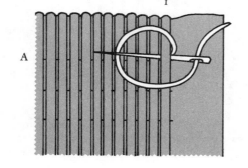

2
Draw up floss. Insert needle through pleat 2, slightly below first stitch.

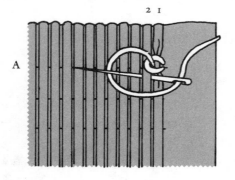

3
Draw up floss. Repeat, tapering stitches evenly down to pleat 6, row C. Repeat again, tapering stitches evenly up to pleat 11, row A. Continue across fabric in same manner, repeating previous steps and spacing stitches evenly.

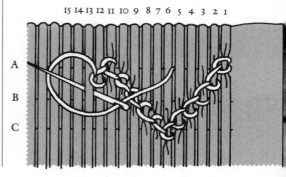

Regular Stitches

NARROW TRELLIS STITCH

This stitch creates a latticework design on three rows of RUNNING STITCHES. When tapering stitches up, keep floss below needle; when tapering stitches down, keep floss above needle.

1

Work from left to right. Bring needle out of fabric on row B at the left side of pleat 1. Keep floss below needle and insert needle diagonally from right to left through pleat 2 so needle emerges slightly above the row of running stitches.

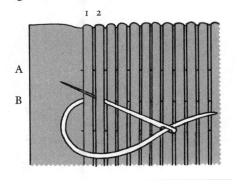

2

Draw up floss. Repeat, inserting needle diagonally into pleat 3, slightly above the first stitch so needle emerges slightly above where it was inserted.

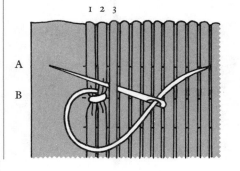

3

Repeat, tapering stitches up to pleat 5, row A.

4

Working with floss above needle and starting with pleat 6, repeat, tapering stitches down to pleat 9, row B and inserting needle diagonally.

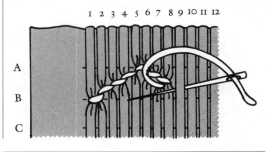

5

Continue across fabric in same manner, repeating previous steps and spacing stitches evenly.

6

Repeat trellis stitch again across fabric. This time, with floss above needle, begin at pleat 1, row B, and taper down to pleat 5, row C. Start with pleat 6 and with floss below needle, taper up to pleat 9, row B. Continue across fabric in the same manner.

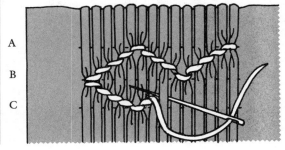

Regular Stitches

VAN DYKE STITCH

Use two rows of RUNNING STITCHES as guidelines to create this stitch that joins alternate pleats together in a tight zigzag pattern.

1

Work from right to left. Bring needle out of fabric on row A at the right side of pleat 1. Then insert it through the tops of pleats 1 and 2.

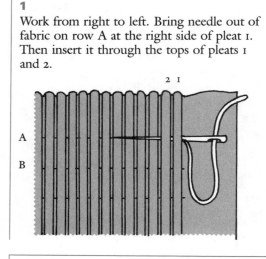

2

Draw up floss. With floss above needle, insert needle back through the same two pleats.

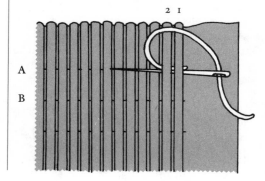

3

Draw up floss. Bring needle down to row B and insert it through pleats 2 and 3. Work with the floss below the needle and insert needle back through the same two pleats.

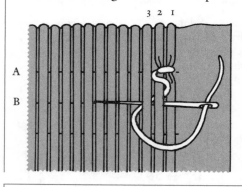

4

Draw up floss. Continue across the two rows in same manner, repeating previous steps and spacing stitches evenly. While sewing, reverse position of floss in relation to the needle so stitches above and below each other form a mirror image.

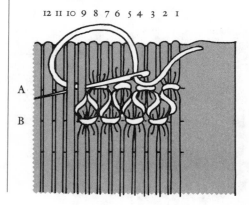

Regular Stitches

WIDE TRELLIS STITCH

This stitch is similar to the Narrow Trellis but is worked in a wider pattern across six rows of RUNNING STITCHES rather than three. When tapering stitches up, keep floss below needle; when tapering stitches down, keep floss above needle.

1

Bring needle out of fabric at the left side of pleat 1, between rows C and D. Keep floss below needle and insert needle diagonally from right to left through pleat 2 so needle emerges slightly above where floss came out.

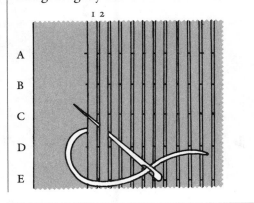

2

Draw up floss. Repeat, inserting needle diagonally through pleat 3, slightly above the first stitch so needle emerges slightly above where it was inserted.

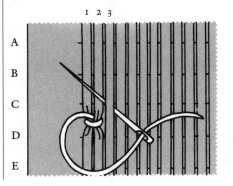

3

Draw up floss. Repeat, tapering stitches up to pleat 7, row A. Working with floss above needle and starting with pleat 8, repeat, tapering stitches down to pleat 13, between rows C and D.

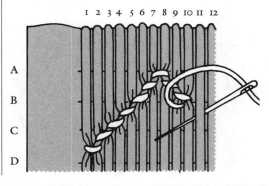

4

Continue across fabric in same manner, repeating previous steps and spacing stitches evenly.

Regular Stitches

Wide Trellis Stitch, Continued

5

Repeat trellis stitch again across fabric. This time, begin at pleat 1, between rows C and D, and, with floss above needle, taper down to pleat 7, row F, then, with floss below needle, start with pleat 8 and taper up to pleat 13, between rows C and D.

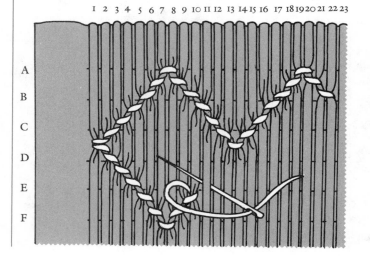

Gripper Snaps

To apply snaps, use one of the special tools which can be purchased where gripper snaps are sold—fabric or notions stores.

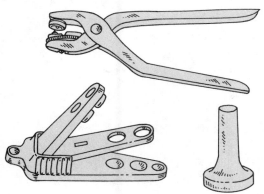

1
Apply ball section to overlap of garment at symbols or buttonhole markings, with prong section on right side and ball section on wrong side of fabric.

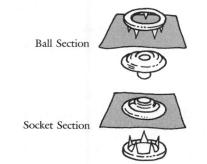

Ball Section

Socket Section

2
Use the tool to press the parts together through the fabric.

3
Repeat for the socket section, applying it to the underlap.

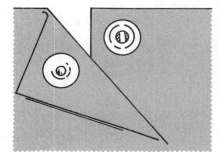

Overlap   Underlap

Sew-on Snaps

HANGING SNAPS

Use this method of applying snaps to fasten a collar or stand-up neckline with edges that meet.

1

Hand-sew ball section of snap to inside of collar or neckline. Take several stitches close together through each hole, picking up a thread of the garment with each stitch and being careful stitches do not show on right side. Do not break thread—carry it under snap from hole to hole.

2

Mark location of socket section by positioning garment as if fastened. Use a pin to mark position of socket section on underlap garment edge.

3

Hand-sew socket section to garment edge through one hole only.

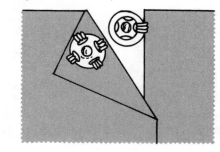

REGULAR SNAPS

Use regular snaps to fasten overlapping edges that will not be subjected to much strain.

1

Hand-sew ball section of snap to inside of overlap. Take several stitches through each hole, picking up a thread of the garment with each stitch and being careful stitches do not show on right side. Do not break thread— carry it under snap from hole to hole.

2

Mark location of socket section on outside of underlap by rubbing tailor's chalk on the ball section and positioning garment as if fastened. Or, push a pin through the ball section and mark underlap with chalk.

3

Sew socket section on as for ball section.

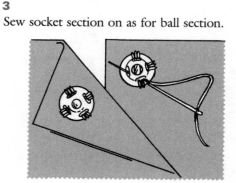

Sew-on Snaps

SNAP TAPE

Note: This method pertains specifically to inner leg closures on babies' and toddlers' clothing.

Stitch garment front and back together at sides and hem lower leg edges before applying snap tape. When applying snap tape, be sure to line up socket and ball strips so they will match when snapped.

1

Pin ball section of snap tape to *right* side of front inner leg seam allowance with one edge ¼" (6mm) away from seamline in seam allowance; turn in ends. Using a zipper foot, stitch tape in place.

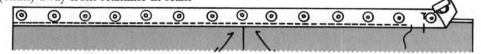

2

Turn snap tape to inside along stitching. Stitch close to remaining edge.

3

Pin socket section of snap tape to *wrong* side of back inner leg seam allowance with one edge ¼" (6mm) away from seamline in seam allowance; turn in ends. Using a zipper foot, stitch tape in place.

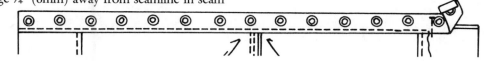

4

Turn snap tape to outside along stitching. Stitch close to remaining edge. SLIPSTITCH ends of tape in place.

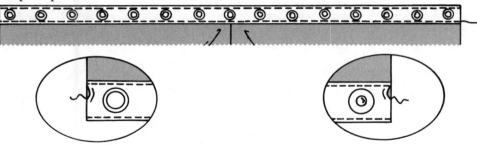

Tuck Guidelines

MARKING AND BASTING

Tucks are similar to pleats, but often not as wide; generally, if the fabric is not pressed below the stitching, the unpressed fold is called a tuck.

- Make tucks on the straight grain with the tuck fold parallel to the fabric threads.

- Mark symbols or stitching lines of each tuck on either the right side or wrong side of fabric, depending on which side tucks will be made. Remove pattern, fold tucks either to inside or outside of garment, as specified in the pattern directions, matching stitching lines. Baste in place, OR

- Mark tucks by making a cardboard measurement gauge, cutting one notch for the tuck depth and a second notch to indicate the

space from fold to fold. Place top of gauge along the fold of the first tuck. Using the first notch as a guide, make a row of basting stitches parallel to the fold, sliding the gauge. For the next tuck, move the gauge so that the second notch is even with the first fold; make the next fold at the top of the gauge. Repeat.

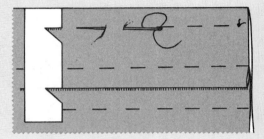

STITCHING

Stitch from the side of the tuck with visible markings. For narrow tucks, from ¼" to ¾" (6mm to 20mm) deep, use the needle plate on the machine as a guide for stitching.

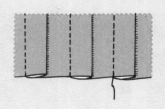

PRESSING

Press tucks after stitching each tuck, or immediately after stitching the series. First, press the tuck crease from the right side of fabric, on the underneath side of the fold.

Next, press the entire tucked area from the wrong side. Use very little steam to prevent puckering. To prevent tuck fold from making ridges on the fabric, use strips of brown paper under the tuck fold while pressing. Touch up the right side as necessary.

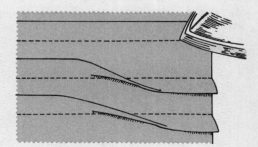

Released Tucks

STITCHED FROM INSIDE, PRESSED FLAT

1
On inside, bring lines of symbols together.
Stitch to lower symbol.

2
Press tuck(s) flat.

3
Baste across raw edges.

4
If desired, on outside, EDGESTITCH along
both sides of seam(s) through all thicknesses,
pivoting to symbol.

STITCHED FROM INSIDE, PRESSED TO ONE SIDE

1
On inside, bring lines of symbols together.
Stitch to lower symbol.

2
Press tuck(s) to one side.

3
Baste across raw edges.

4
If desired, on outside, EDGESTITCH along
seam(s) through all thicknesses, ending at
symbol.

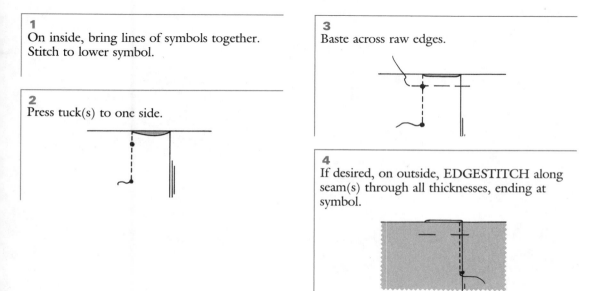

Released Tucks

STITCHED FROM OUTSIDE, PRESSED FLAT

1

On outside, bring lines of symbols together. Stitch to lower symbol.

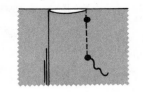

2

Press tuck(s) flat.

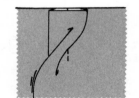

3

Baste across raw edges.

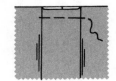

STITCHED FROM OUTSIDE, PRESSED TO ONE SIDE

1

On outside, bring lines of symbols together. Stitch to lower symbol.

2

Press tuck(s) to one side.

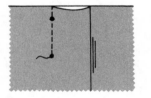

3

Baste across raw edges.

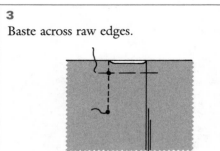

Stitched Tucks

1

On outside, bring lines of symbols together. Stitch.

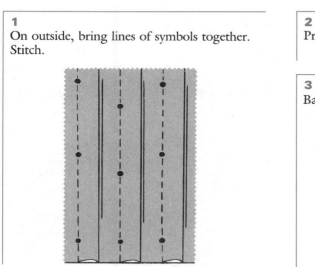

2

Press tuck(s) flat.

3

Baste across raw edges.

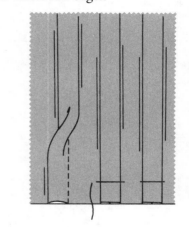

Stitched Tucks

STITCHED FROM OUTSIDE, PRESSED TO ONE SIDE

Pin Tucks

1
On outside, crease along tuck lines. Stitch ⅟₁₆″ (2mm) from creased edge.

2
Press tuck(s) in direction specified in pattern instructions.

3
Baste across raw edges.

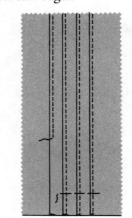

Regular Tucks

1
On outside, bring lines of symbols together. Stitch.

2
Press tuck(s) to one side, in direction specified in pattern instructions.

3
Baste across raw edges.

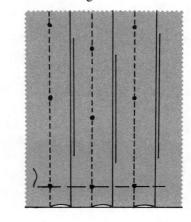

Underlining

CUTTING UNDERLINING

1
Always preshrink both fashion fabric and underlining before cutting out pattern.

2
Cut underlining from the same pattern pieces used to cut the fashion fabric.

MARKING AND BASTING UNDERLINING

1
Work on a large flat surface. Using dressmaker's carbon paper and tracing wheel, transfer all markings from pattern piece to underlining.

2
With wrong sides together, center the marked underlining over the unmarked fashion fabric. Pin together loosely along traced lines. Because the two layers were cut separately, cut edges will not always be exactly even.

3
From the underlining side, run a line of THREAD TRACING along the lengthwise center of each piece through both layers, following lengthwise grain.

4
Check whether the two fabric layers are working together by holding each pinned section over the body to see how the two layers react to the body's contours. If bubbles or ridges form in either fashion fabric or underlining, the two fabrics are not molding as one.

5
Remove all pins and, with the fashion fabric uppermost, fold both layers along the thread-traced center line. Insert a large magazine or cardboard between the folded fabric. Smooth the fashion fabric over the underlining; pin along all raw edges and construction lines.

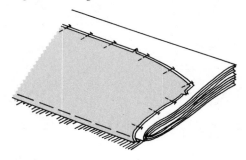

6
The underlining and fashion fabric are now relating to each other the way they will be when they are worn. The underlining will probably extend slightly beyond the edges of the fashion fabric. (The difference between the seam allowances will increase with the fashion fabric thickness. Try cutting seam allowances a little wider to compensate for this.)

Underlining

Marking and Basting Underlining, Continued

7

From the underlining side, run a line of
UNEVEN BASTING along all foldlines,
seamlines, and dart markings through both
layers. Baste next to, not on, the traced
seamline so basting threads will be easy to
remove later. Remove pins.

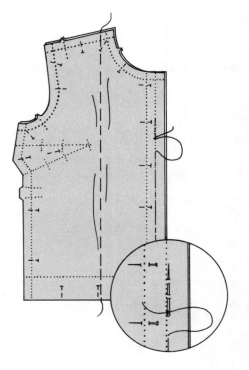

STITCHING UNDERLINING

Darts

1

Baste along the foldline of each dart through
both layers, beginning beyond each dart
point. Fold dart along center, matching
markings; pin and stitch.

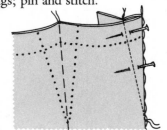

2

Remove basting that extends past dart point.

Seams

With right sides of fashion fabric together, pin
all four layers along seamlines. Stitch seams
through all layers, using seam allowances of
underlining as the guide for stitching seams.

Velcro® (Nylon Tape Fastener)

IRON-ON VELCRO®

1

If using Velcro purchased by the yard (meter), cut into sections to fit garment area.

2

Apply hook section on underlap part of garment and loop section on overlap, following manufacturer's directions for fusing.

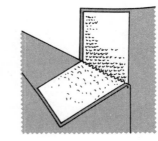

SEW-ON VELCRO®

1

If using Velcro purchased by the yard (meter), cut into sections to fit garment area.

2

If Velcro has adhesive, use it to position sections. If it doesn't have adhesive, pin sections in place.

3

Place hook section on underlap part of garment; place loop section on overlap.

4

For circles or squares, SLIPSTITCH Velcro in place.

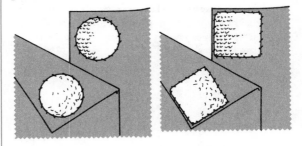

For strips, machine-stitch close to all edges.

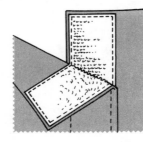

Jacket, Skirt or Dress Vents

FOR LINED GARMENTS

1

Turn in long edge of right back or left front extension along seamline.

2

Stitch center back or front seam and across upper edge of extensions, pivoting at large ●.

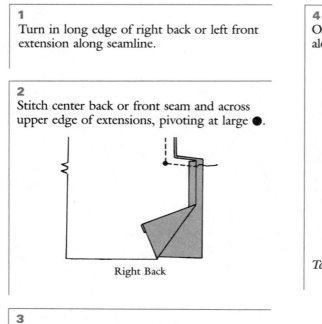

Right Back

3

Clip right back or left front seam allowance above extension. Turn extension toward left back or right front along foldline; press. Baste upper edges of vent in place through all thicknesses.

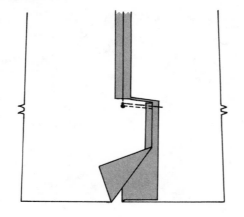

4

On outside, stitch left back or right front along stitching line between symbols.

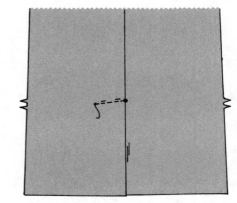

To complete vent, see Hems and Linings.

Jacket, Skirt or Dress Vents

FOR UNLINED GARMENTS

1

Make ⅝″ (15mm) NARROW HEM on right back or left front extension.

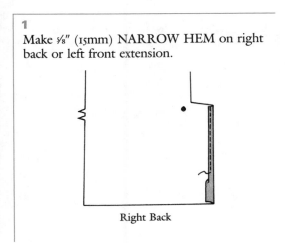

Right Back

2

FINISH outer edge of left back or right front self facing.

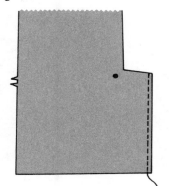

Left Back

3

Stitch center back or front seam and across upper edge of extensions, pivoting at large ●.

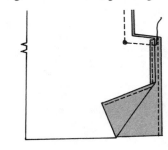

4

Clip right back or left front seam allowance above extension. Turn extension toward left back or right front along foldline; press. Baste upper edges of vent in place through all thicknesses.

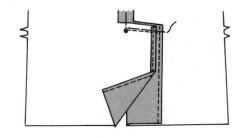

5

On outside, stitch left back or right front along stitching line between symbols.

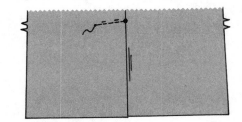

To complete vent, see Hems.

Sleeve Vents

MOCK VENT FOR TWO-PIECE-EFFECT SLEEVE

*Note: Prepare, stitch (see Set-in Sleeve, Round
Construction, Two-Piece Effect) and hem sleeve
before constructing vent.*

1

Clip self-facing seam allowance above
extension. On inside, turn self facing toward
sleeve front along foldline; press.

2

On outside, place front edge of sleeve along
placement line; baste.

3

On inside, CATCHSTITCH extension and
self facing in place.

Sleeve Vents

MOCK VENT FOR TWO-PIECE SLEEVE

Note: Stitch upper and under sleeves together at front edge (see Set-In Sleeve, Round Construction, Two-Piece) before constructing vent.

1

Pin sleeve interfacing to wrong side of sleeve. BLINDSTITCH in place along foldline, hemline and upper edge.

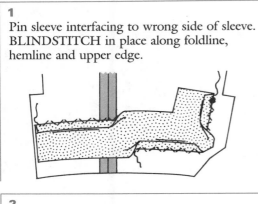

2

To miter lower edge of sleeve, fold lower edge, matching seamlines. Stitch. Trim.

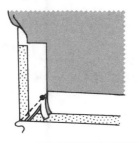

3

Press seam open with point of iron.

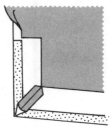

4

Turn miter and self facing to inside along foldlines, turning up hem. Baste close to lower edge.

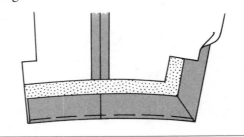

5

Open out self facing. Stitch remaining sleeve seam, pivoting at large ●. Clip under sleeve seam allowance diagonally to large ●.

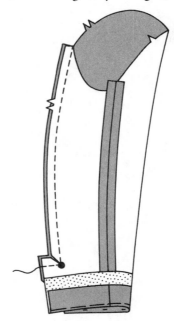

Sleeve Vents

Mock Vent for Two-piece Sleeve, Continued

6

Turn self facing toward sleeve front. Sew hem in place.

7

To press, hold iron over hem. Steam, never resting iron on fabric. Pat lightly with pounder or ruler.

8

Make buttonholes. Do not cut buttonholes open.

9

On outside, place front edge of sleeve along placement line; baste.

10

On inside, CATCHSTITCH extension and self facing in place.

11

Sew buttons at symbols through all thicknesses.

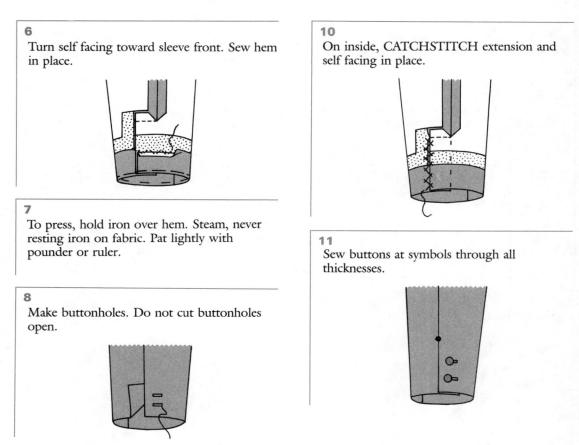
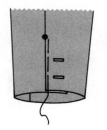

Sleeve Vents

WORKING VENT FOR TWO-PIECE SLEEVE

Note: Stitch upper and under sleeves together at front edge (see Set-In Sleeve, Round Construction, Two-Piece) before constructing vent.

1

Pin sleeve interfacing to wrong side of sleeve. BLINDSTITCH in place along foldline, hemline and upper edge.

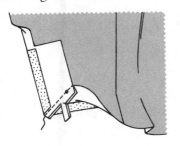

2

To miter lower edge of sleeve, fold lower edge, matching seamlines. Stitch. Trim.

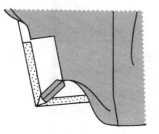

3

Press seam open with point of iron.

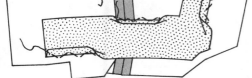

4

Turn sleeve self facing to outside along foldline. Stitch across facing. Trim.

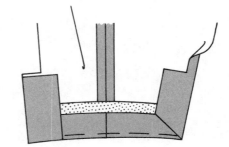

5

Turn miter and self facing to inside along foldlines, turning up hem. Baste close to lower edge.

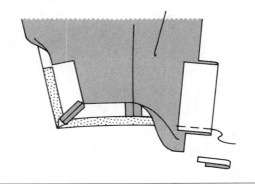

Sleeve Vents

Working Vent for Two-piece Sleeve, Continued

6
Open out self facing. Stitch remaining sleeve seam, pivoting at large ●. Clip under seam allowance above extension.

7
Turn self facing toward sleeve front. Sew hem and inner edges in place; CATCHSTITCH self facing to hem.

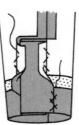

8
To press, hold iron over hem. Steam, never resting iron on fabric. Pat lightly with pounder or ruler.

9
Make buttonholes.

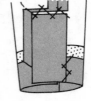

10
On outside, place front edge of sleeve along placement line; baste.

11
On inside, CATCHSTITCH extension and self facing in place.

12
Sew buttons to underlap at symbols.

Vents

Faced Waistband

STRAIGHT WITH CENTER BACK OPENING

Note: Apply zipper before constructing waistband.

1

INTERFACE wrong side of one waistband section.

2

With right sides together, pin interfaced waistband to upper edge of garment, matching centers, small ●'s to side seam(s) and large ●'s to opening edges. Adjust ease; baste. Stitch seam.

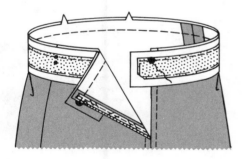

3

TRIM seam. Press seam toward waistband.

4

Turn in seam allowance on notched edge of waistband facing section. Press. Trim pressed seam allowance to ⅜″ (10mm).

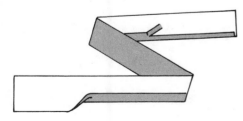

5

With right sides together, pin waistband and waistband facing sections together; stitch ends and upper edge.

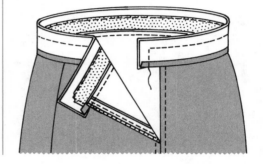

6

TRIM and CLIP seam.

7

Turn waistband; press. SLIPSTITCH pressed edge over seam and extension edges together.

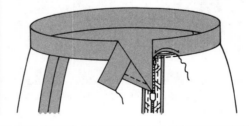

8

Leave waistband plain or use one of the following methods to finish waistband: EDGESTITCHING, TOPSTITCHING, EDGESTITCHING AND TOPSTITCHING (see Regular Waistband with Center Back or Side Slot Zipper Opening).

To make closures on waistband, see Buttonholes, Buttons or Hooks and Eyes.

Pull-on Waistbands

WITH ELASTIC CASING

Note: Stitch all seams in garment before applying casing. This method is for using one or more rows of elastic.

1

With right sides together, stitch ends of waistband, leaving open between small ●'s.

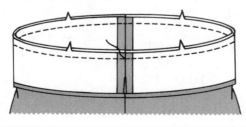

2

Turn in seam allowance on long unnotched edge of waistband. Press. Trim pressed seam allowance to ⅜" (10mm).

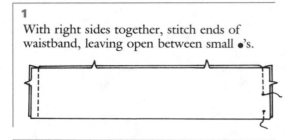

3

With right sides together, pin waistband to upper edge of garment, matching centers and notches. Stitch seam.

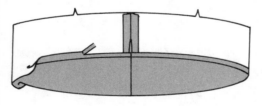

4

TRIM seam. Press seam toward waistband.

5

Turn waistband to inside along foldline, placing pressed edge over seam; baste close to edge.

6

For one row of elastic, EDGESTITCH basted and upper edges.

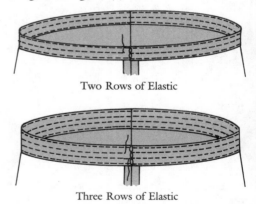

For two or more rows of elastic, EDGESTITCH basted edge, upper edge and along stitching line(s).

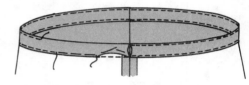

Two Rows of Elastic

Three Rows of Elastic

Pull-on Waistbands

With Elastic Casing, Continued

7
Cut elastic the measurement of waist plus 1″ (25mm). Insert elastic through opening(s), lapping ends; hold with safety pin. Try on and adjust, if necessary. Securely stitch ends of elastic.

8
SLIPSTITCH opening(s) in casing.

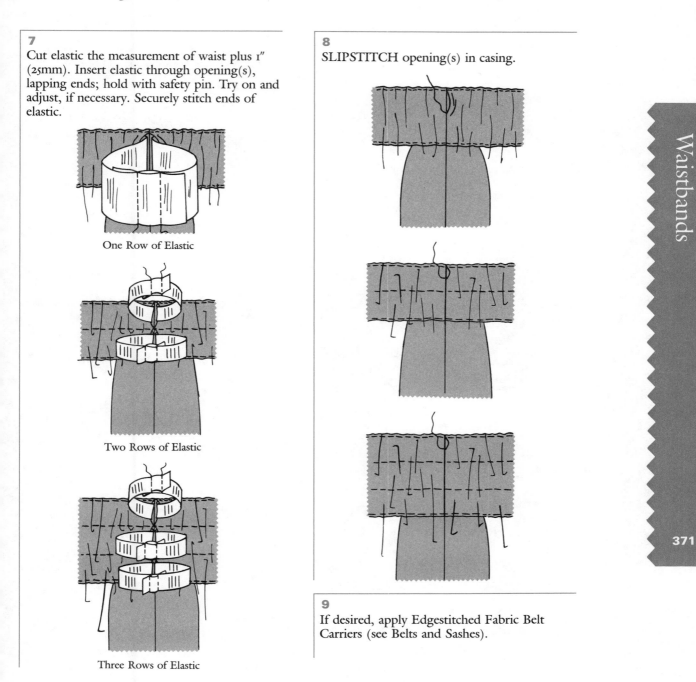

One Row of Elastic

Two Rows of Elastic

Three Rows of Elastic

9
If desired, apply Edgestitched Fabric Belt Carriers (see Belts and Sashes).

Pull-on Waistbands

WITH ELASTICIZED BACK

Note: Stitch all seams in garment front or back before applying waistband.

1
INTERFACE wrong side of front waistband.

2
Turn in seam allowance on long unnotched edge of front waistband. Press. Trim pressed seam allowance to ⅜" (10mm).

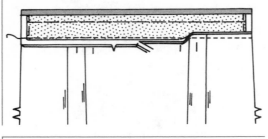

3
With right sides together, pin waistband to front upper edge, matching centers and notches. Stitch seam. TRIM seam. Press seam toward waistband.

4
To form casing for elastic, turn upper edge of back to inside along foldline, turning in ¼" (6mm) on raw edge. Press. EDGESTITCH upper and lower edges.

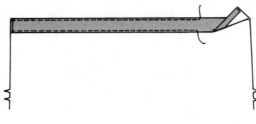

5
Insert elastic through casing, making ends even with raw edges. Baste along seamlines through all thicknesses.

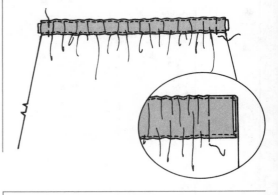

6
With right sides together, stitch back to front at sides.

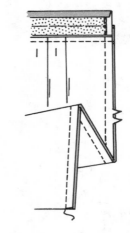

Pull-on Waistbands

7

Clip back seam allowances below casing. Press seams open below clips, pressing remainder of seam allowances toward front.

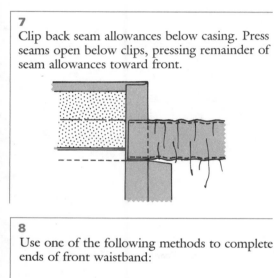

8

Use one of the following methods to complete ends of front waistband:

a) *If waistband will be left plain,* turn waistband to inside along foldline. Press. SLIPSTITCH pressed edges over seam, OR

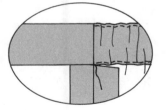

b) *If waistband will be stitched on the outside,* turn waistband to inside along foldline. Press. Baste.

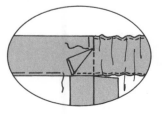

9

Leave front waistband plain or use one of the following methods to finish front waistband edges:

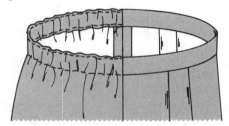

EDGESTITCH,

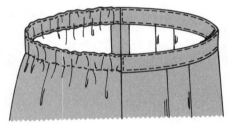

TOPSTITCH, or

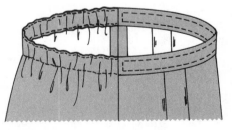

EDGESTITCH and TOPSTITCH.

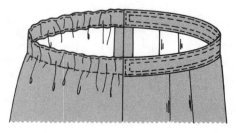

Pull-on Waistbands

WITH WIDE ELASTIC WAISTBANDING

Note: Stitch all seams in garment before applying waistband.

1

Cut a length of elastic waistbanding, using one of the following methods:

a) Use Guide for Waistband given in pattern, placing guide even with lower edge of elastic. Transfer markings, OR

b) Mark elastic the measurement of waist plus 1″ (2.5cm). Try on and adjust to fit comfortably; add 1¼″ (3.2cm) for seam allowances and cut.

2

With right sides together, stitch ends of waistbanding.

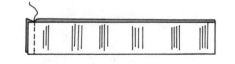

3

Open seam allowances; trim upper edges diagonally and stitch in place ¼″ (6mm) from seam. Trim seam allowances close to stitching.

4

STAYSTITCH garment ⅝″ (15mm) from upper edge. FINISH upper edge.

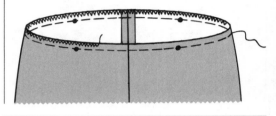

5

With garment right side out, lap waistband over upper garment edge to seamline, matching centers and symbols. EDGESTITCH lower edge of waistband and stitch again ¼″ (6mm) away, stretching waistband to fit.

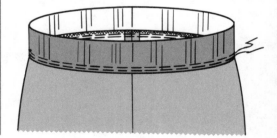

Regular Waistbands

Note: Apply zipper before constructing waistband.

1

INTERFACE wrong side of waistband.

2

Turn in seam allowance on long unnotched edge of waistband. Press. Trim pressed seam allowance to ⅜″ (10mm).

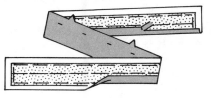

3

If desired, apply fabric belt carriers.

4

With right sides together, pin waistband to upper edge of garment, matching notches, small ●'s to side seams and large ●'s on waistband to opening edges; CLIP upper edge of garment if necessary. Stitch.

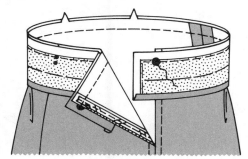

5

TRIM seam. Press seam toward waistband. With right sides together, fold waistband along foldline. Stitch ends.

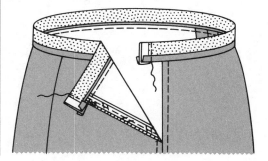

6

TRIM ends. Turn waistband. Press. SLIPSTITCH pressed edge over seam and extension edges together.

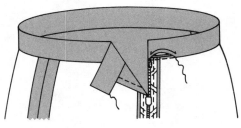

Waistbands

375

Regular Waistbands

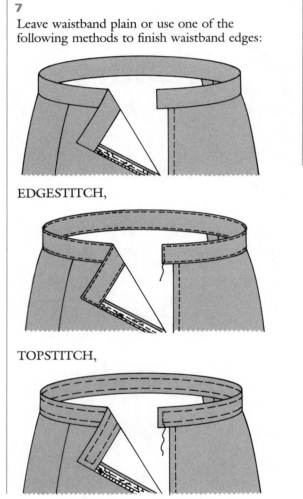

With Center Back or Side Slot Zipper Opening, Continued

7

Leave waistband plain or use one of the following methods to finish waistband edges:

EDGESTITCH,

TOPSTITCH,

7 *Continued*
EDGESTITCH and TOPSTITCH.

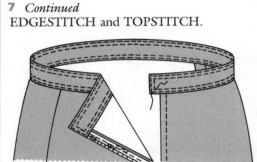

To make closures on waistband, see Buttonholes, Buttons, or Hooks and Eyes.

Regular Waistbands

WITH CENTER FRONT MOCK FLY ZIPPER OPENING

Note: Apply zipper before constructing waistband.

1

INTERFACE wrong side of waistband.

2

Turn in seam allowance on long unnotched edge of waistband. Press. Trim pressed seam allowance to ⅜" (10mm).

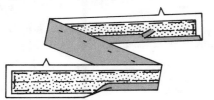

3

If desired, apply fabric belt carriers.

4

With right sides together, pin waistband to upper edge of garment, matching centers, small ●'s to side seams and large ●'s on waistband to opening edges. Stitch seam.

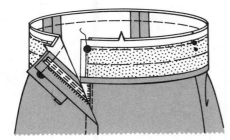

5

TRIM seam. Press seam toward waistband. With right sides together, fold waistband along foldline. Stitch ends.

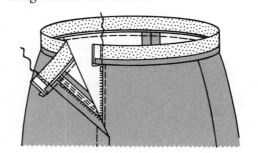

6

TRIM ends. Turn waistband. Press. SLIPSTITCH pressed edge over seam.

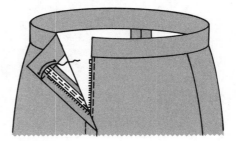

Regular Waistbands

With Center Front Mock Fly Zipper Opening, Continued

7
Leave waistband plain or use one of the following methods to finish waistband edges:

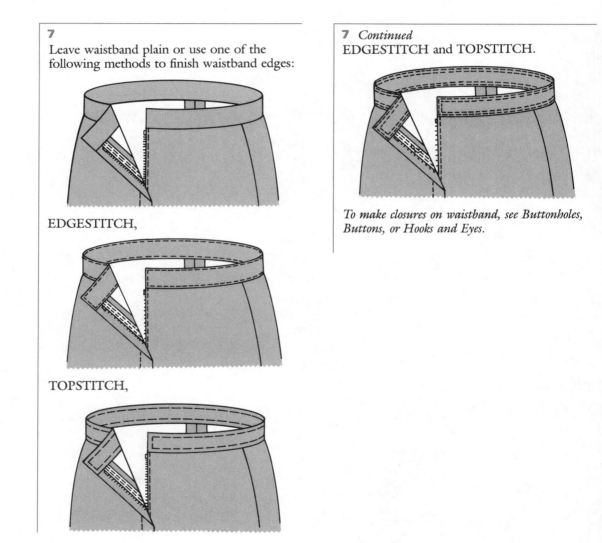

EDGESTITCH,

TOPSTITCH,

7 *Continued*
EDGESTITCH and TOPSTITCH.

To make closures on waistband, see Buttonholes, Buttons, or Hooks and Eyes.

Regular Waistbands

WITH LEFT AND RIGHT SIDE SLANT POCKET OPENING

*Note: Construct pockets and stitch them to
garment before applying waistband.*

1

INTERFACE wrong side of front waistband
and back waistband.

2

Turn in seam allowance on long unnotched
edge of each waistband section. Press. Trim
pressed seam allowances to ⅜" (10mm).

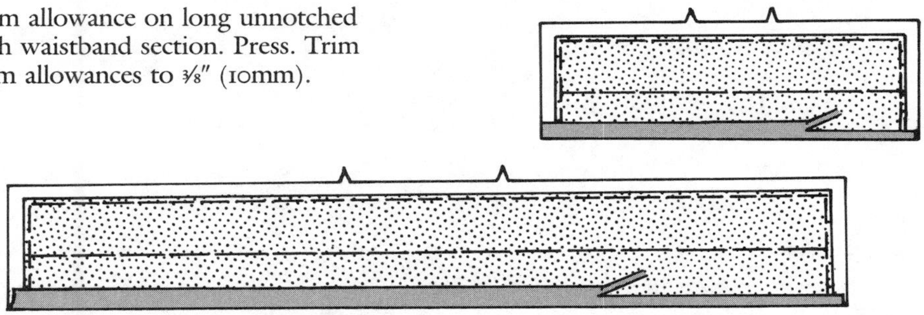

3

With right sides together, pin front waistband
to front upper edge, matching centers and
large ●'s on waistband to opening edges.
Stitch seam. Trim seam. Press seam toward
waistband.

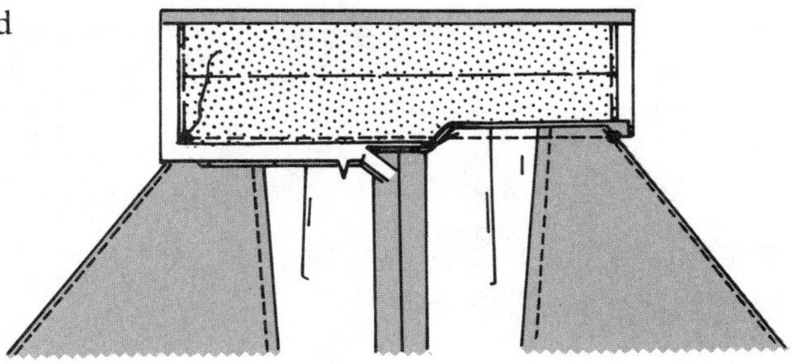

4

With right sides together, fold waistband
along foldline. Stitch ends.

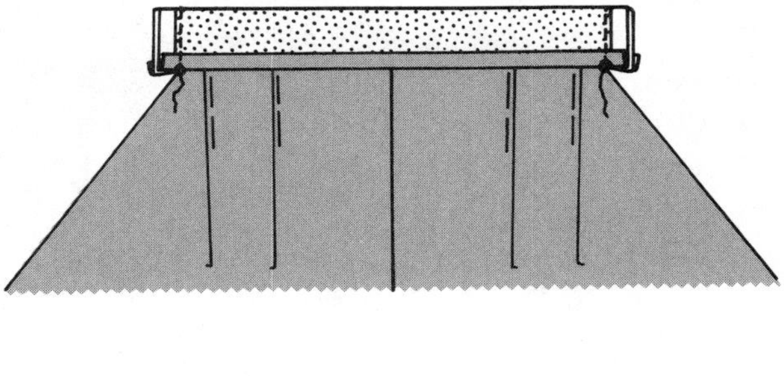

Regular Waistbands

With Left and Right Side Slant Pocket Opening, Continued

5

TRIM ends. Turn waistband. Press.
SLIPSTITCH pressed edge over seam.

6

Pin back waistband to back upper edge and
pockets, matching centers and placing small ●'s
at side seams and large ●'s on waistband to
finished edges of pockets. Stitch seam. Trim
seam. Press seam toward waistband.

7

With right sides together, fold waistband
along foldline. Stitch ends.

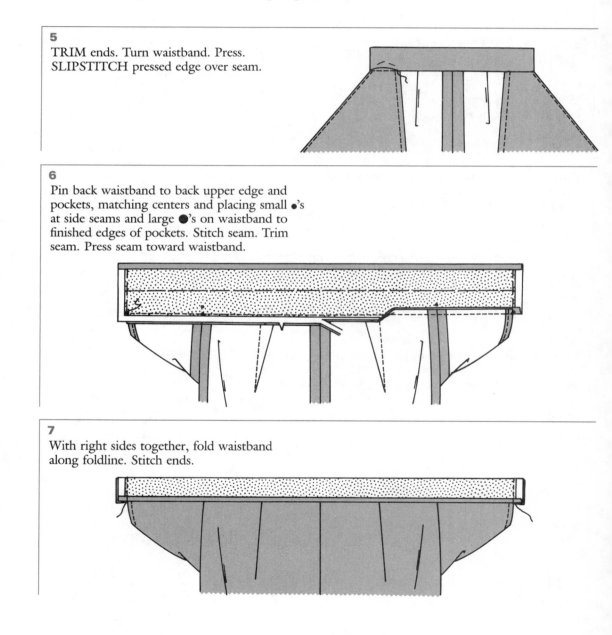

Regular Waistbands

8

TRIM ends. Turn waistband. Press.
SLIPSTITCH pressed edge over seam.

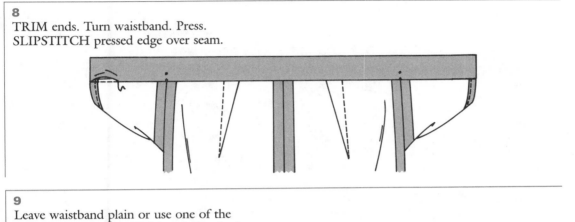

9

Leave waistband plain or use one of the
following methods to finish waistband edges:
EDGESTITCHING, TOPSTITCHING, or
EDGESTITCHING and TOPSTITCHING
(see Regular Waistband with Center Front
Mock Fly Zipper Opening).

*To make closures on waistband, see Buttonholes,
Buttons, or Hooks and Eyes.*

Regular Waistbands

WITH LEFT SIDE SEAM POCKET OPENING

Note: Construct pocket and stitch it to garment before applying waistband.

1

INTERFACE wrong side of waistband.

2

Turn in seam allowance on long unnotched edge of waistband. Press. Trim pressed seam allowances to ⅜″ (10mm).

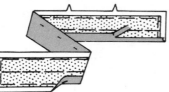

3

With right sides together, pin waistband to upper edge of garment, matching centers, symbols and large ●'s on waistband to finished edge of back pocket and to small ●'s on garment front. Stitch seam.

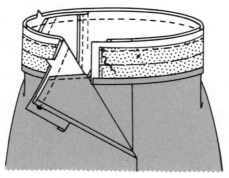

4

Trim seam. Press seam toward waistband. With right sides together, fold waistband along foldline. Stitch ends.

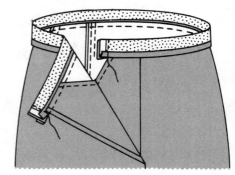

5

TRIM ends. Turn waistband. Press. SLIPSTITCH pressed edge over seam.

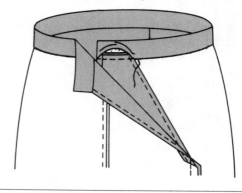

6

Leave waistband plain or use one of the following methods to finish waistband edges: EDGESTITCHING, TOPSTITCHING, or EDGESTITCHING and TOPSTITCHING (see Regular Waistband with Center Front Mock Fly Zipper Opening).

To make closures on waistband, see Buttonholes, Buttons, or Hooks and Eyes.

Regular Waistbands

WITH LEFT SIDE SLANT POCKET OPENING

Note: Construct pocket and stitch it to garment before applying waistband.

1

INTERFACE wrong side of waistband.

2

Turn in seam allowance on long unnotched edge of waistband. Press. Trim pressed seam allowances to ⅜″ (10mm).

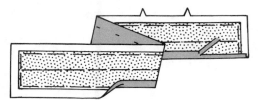

3

With right sides together, pin waistband to upper edge of garment, matching centers, small ●'s to side seams and large ●'s on waistband to front opening edge and finished edge of left back pocket; CLIP garment if necessary. Stitch seam.

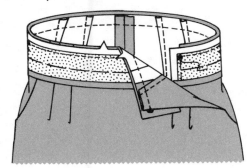

4

Trim seam. Press seam toward waistband. With right sides together, fold waistband along foldline. Stitch ends.

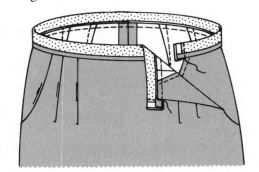

5

TRIM ends. Turn waistband. Press. SLIPSTITCH pressed edge over seam.

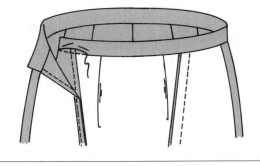

6

Leave waistband plain or use one of the following methods to finish waistband edges: EDGESTITCHING, TOPSTITCHING, or EDGESTITCHING and TOPSTITCHING (see Regular Waistband with Center Front Mock Fly Zipper Opening).

To make closures on waistband, see Buttonholes, Buttons, or Hooks and Eyes.

Back/Shoulder Yokes

1

With right sides together, pin one yoke section to upper edge of back, matching notches. Adjust any gathers; baste.

Note: Remaining yoke section will be used as a facing.

2

Turn in seam allowances on front edges of yoke facing; press. Trim pressed seam allowances to ⅜" (10mm).

3

Pin right side of yoke facing to wrong side of back, matching notches; baste. Stitch.

4

TRIM. Press seam toward yoke.

5

For garment with front self facings, open out facings. Pin front edges of yoke to upper edges of front, matching symbols. Adjust any gathers; baste.

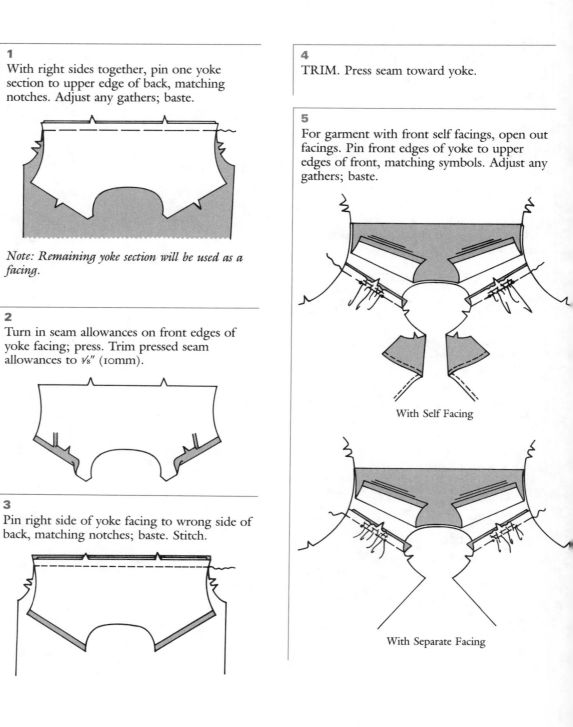

With Self Facing

With Separate Facing

Back/Shoulder Yokes

Continued

6

Turn front facings in; baste. Stitch front edges of yoke to upper edges of front, keeping pressed edges of yoke facing free.

8

SLIPSTITCH pressed edges of yoke facing over seams. Baste raw armhole edges and raw neckline edges together.

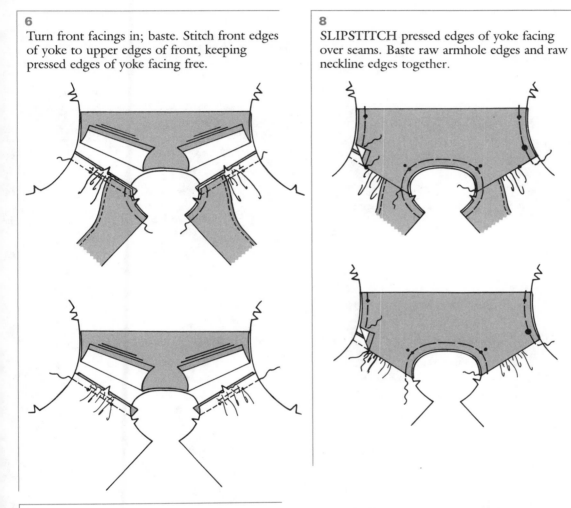

7

TRIM. Press seams toward yoke.

Back/Shoulder Yokes

Continued

9

Leave yoke seams plain, or use one of the following methods to finish yoke seams:

EDGESTITCH,

TOPSTITCH,

9 *Continued*

EDGESTITCH and TOPSTITCH.

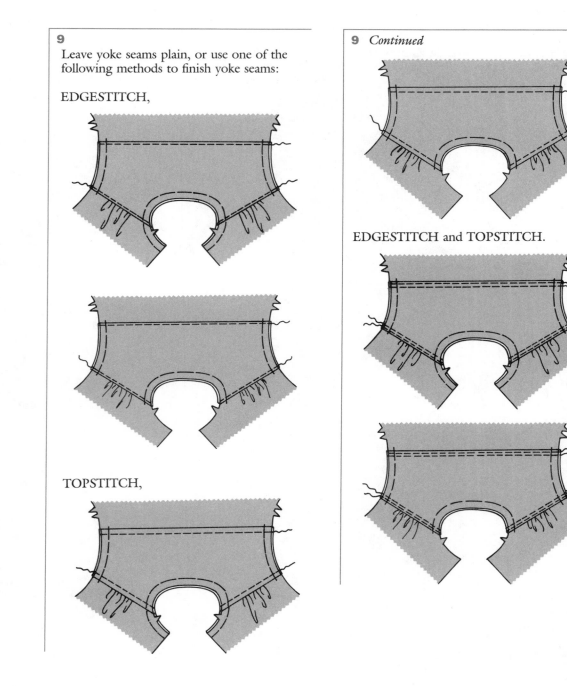

Zipper Guidelines

PREPARATION

• Choose weight and type of zipper based on weight of fabric.

• For washable garments, preshrink zippers that have cotton tape.

• Close zipper and press out creases before application. When pressing on right side of garment, use a press cloth to prevent any unsightly shine, puckers, or impression.

• STAYSTITCH seam allowances of zipper opening edges directionally.

• STAY bias seams or stretchy fabrics before applying zipper.

• Match design of plaids, stripes, etc. at zipper closing by SLIP-BASTING the seam edges together.

• Always pin zipper from the top downward.

• Use an adjustable zipper foot which permits machine stitching on either side of the zipper without turning the fabric.

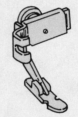

• Always close zipper before laundering or dry cleaning.

SHORTENING

To make a new zipper stop, place zipper along opening edge (with pull tab below seamline the distance indicated on pattern). On the zipper, mark placement of the new zipper stop. WHIPSTITCH across teeth at marking. Cut zipper ¾" (20mm) below new stop.

Zipper Guidelines

BASTING

Baste zipper to garment in the position specified by instructions for type of zipper application, using one of the following methods:

a) HAND-BASTE or MACHINE-BASTE to garment along center of zipper tape, OR

b) Place strips of basting or transparent cellophane tape on edges of zipper tape and finger-press zipper in position on seam allowances, OR

c) Use basting tape or glue stick to secure edges of zipper to seam allowances.

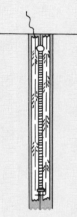
Hand-basting

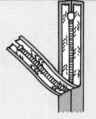
Tape

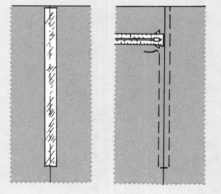
Basting Tape   Glue Stick

STITCHING

Use one of the following methods to provide a straight line to follow for final stitching on outside of garment:

a) Use transparent cellophane tape the width of the final stitching. Position tape over or along the basted seam, according to the specific zipper application. Follow edge of tape when stitching, OR

b) HAND-BASTE through all thicknesses, the distance specified in the zipper application. Stitch next to basting.

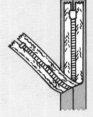

Zipper Guidelines

Stitching, Continued

By Hand

Apply centered or lapped zippers by hand on garments made of fine, delicate or hard-to-handle fabrics.

1

Use a fine needle and a double strand of regular sewing thread coated with beeswax; or use silk thread, topstitching thread or buttonhole twist for added strength.

2

BASTE zipper in position specified by instructions for type of application.

3

To secure zipper, use a PRICKSTITCH to sew from bottom to top of zipper, following basting or tape guideline.

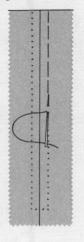

By Machine

1

BASTE zipper in position specified by instructions for type of application.

2

Using a zipper foot, machine-stitch from bottom to top of zipper, following basting or tape guideline.

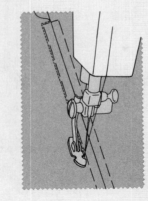

3

At bottom of zipper, pull thread ends to wrong side and knot.

389

Centered Zippers

1

For garment with facing, open out ends of facing. MACHINE-BASTE along seamline above large ●. Press open.

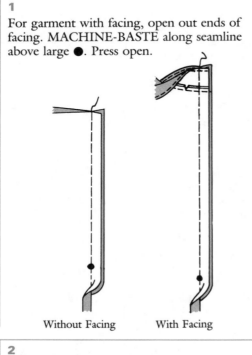

Without Facing   With Facing

2

Open zipper; place face down on extended seam allowance, placing zipper stop at large ● and zipper teeth along seamline. If necessary, shorten zipper (see Zipper Guidelines, Shortening). HAND-BASTE in center of zipper tape, keeping garment free.

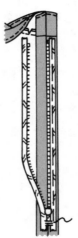

3

Close zipper; turn pull tab up. Spread garment flat. HAND-BASTE through all thicknesses, a scant ¼" (6mm) from zipper teeth and across lower edge, OR pin, then, on outside, center ½" (13mm) tape over seam.

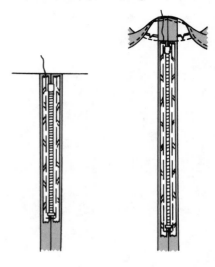

Centered Zippers

Continued

4

On outside, hand-sew or machine-stitch zipper in place along basting or tape (see Zipper Guidelines, Stitching).

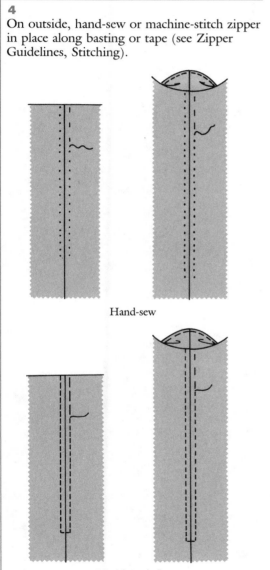

Hand-sew

Machine-stitch

5

For garment with facing, turn facing to inside, turning in ends to clear zipper teeth; press. SLIPSTITCH facing to zipper tape. TACK facing at seams. Sew hook and eye to facing edges above zipper.

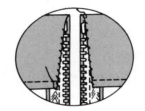

To complete garment without facing, see Waistbands.

Lapped Zippers

Zippers

1

MACHINE-BASTE along seamline above large ●. Press open.

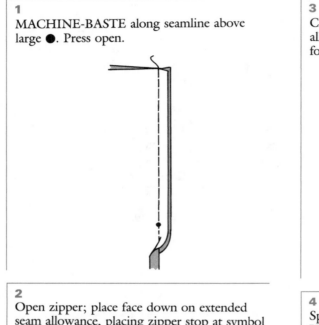

2

Open zipper; place face down on extended seam allowance, placing zipper stop at symbol and zipper teeth on seamline. If necessary, shorten zipper (see Zipper Guidelines, Shortening). HAND-BASTE in center of zipper tape, keeping garment free.

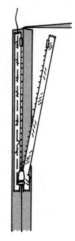

3

Close zipper; turn face up. Fold seam allowance along zipper teeth; stitch close to folded edge.

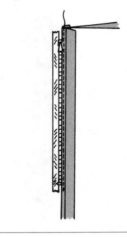

4

Spread garment flat. Turn pull tab up. HAND-BASTE, through all thicknesses, across bottom and up other side of zipper tape a scant ¼" (6mm) from center of teeth, OR pin; then, on outside, position tape ¼" (6mm) from seam.

Lapped Zippers

5

On outside, hand-sew or machine-stitch zipper in place along basting or tape (see Zipper Guidelines, Stitching).

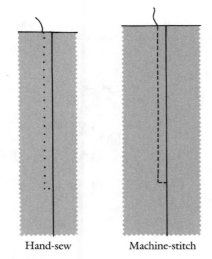

Hand-sew   Machine-stitch

To complete garment without facing, see Waistbands.

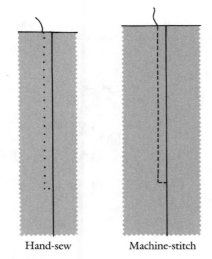

Zippers

393

Mock Fly Zippers

LEFT FLY LAPPED OVER RIGHT SIDE

Note: Zipper application below is shown on pants but will also work for a skirt. This is traditionally the way zipper openings lap on men's pants. Many designers also use this application on women's clothing.

1

Stitch center front seam between small ● and ■. MACHINE-BASTE along center front line above ■.

2

Turn right front extension to inside along foldline. Press.

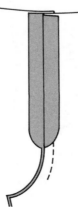

3

Place closed zipper (face up) under right front extension, placing zipper stop at large ● and zipper teeth close to pressed edge, pin or HAND-BASTE. If necessary, shorten zipper (see Zipper Guidelines, Shortening). Stitch close to folded edge.

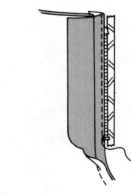

4

Pin remaining zipper tape to left front extension. Stitch in center of tape, keeping garment fronts free.

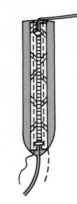

Mock Fly Zippers

5

Spread garment flat, turn left front extension toward front. HAND-BASTE in place.

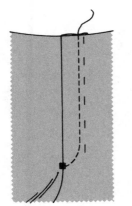

6

On outside, stitch left front along stitching line.

7

At bottom of zipper, pull thread ends to wrong side and knot.

8

If desired, make a bar tack at bottom of zipper (see Hand-worked Buttonholes).

To complete garment, see Waistbands.

Mock Fly Zippers

RIGHT FLY LAPPED OVER LEFT SIDE

Note: Zipper application below is shown on pants, but will also work for skirts. This is traditionally the way zipper openings lap on women's clothing.

1

Stitch center front seam between small ● and ■. MACHINE-BASTE along center front line above ■.

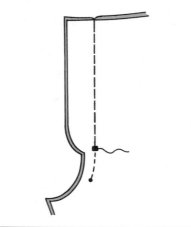

2

Turn left front extension to inside along foldline. Press.

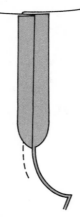

3

Place closed zipper (face up) under left front extension, placing zipper stop at large ● and zipper teeth close to pressed edge; pin or HAND-BASTE. If necessary, shorten zipper (see Zipper Guidelines, Shortening). Stitch close to folded edge.

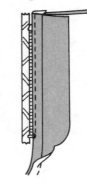

4

Pin remaining zipper tape to right front extension. Stitch in center of tape, keeping garment fronts free.

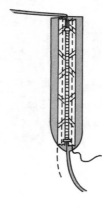

Mock Fly Zippers

5

Spread garment flat, turn right front extension toward front. HAND-BASTE in place.

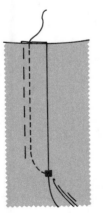

6

On outside, stitch right front along stitching line.

7

At bottom of zipper, pull thread ends to wrong side and knot.

8

If desired, make a bar tack at bottom of zipper (see Hand-worked Buttonholes).

To complete garment, see Waistbands.

Zippers

397

Separating Zippers

1

INTERFACE facings, if necessary.

2

FINISH unnotched edges. With raw edges even, pin facing to front opening edge. Stitch lower edge. Trim seam.

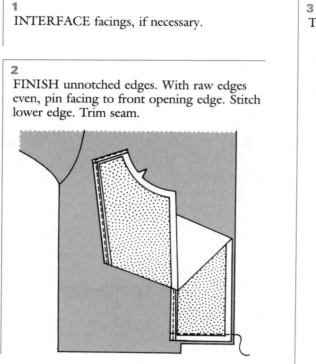

3

Turn facing to inside. Press.

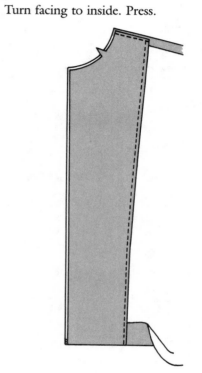

Separating Zippers

Continued

4

Open out facing. MACHINE-BASTE opening edges of fronts and facings together along seamline.

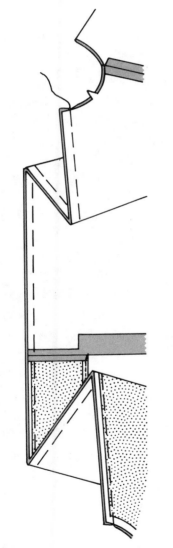

Press open.

5

Center closed zipper (face down) over front opening edges, turning pull tab up and placing zipper stop ¼" (6mm) above lower seam. HAND-BASTE through all thicknesses.

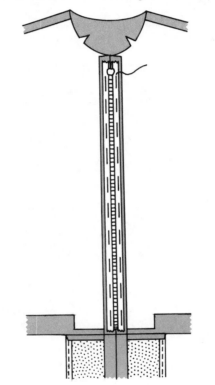

Separating Zippers

Continued

6
Turn facing up; with raw edges even, center basted seam over zipper teeth. HAND-BASTE raw neckline edges together. Hand-baste through all thicknesses a scant ¼" (6mm) from zipper teeth, OR pin, then on outside, center ½" (13mm) tape over seam. SLIPSTITCH finished edges along shoulder seams.

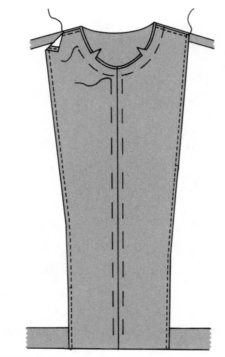

7
Remove basting at opening edges; open zipper.

8
Using a zipper foot, on outside, stitch zipper in place along basting or tape, from bottom to top (see Zipper Guidelines, Stitching).

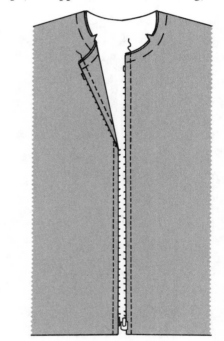

Index

Index

Index

Index

Index

Quick-Reference Sewing Vocabulary List

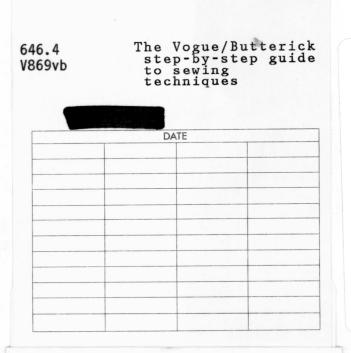